Advertising and the mind of the consumer

Max Sutherland should be congratulated for stimulating us to think about how and why advertising works.

Colin Wilson-Brown, Managing Director, Magnus Nankervis & Curl

Essential reading for all practitioners, mandatory for all students . . .

John Zeigler, Managing Director, DDB Needham Worldwide

A book on advertising that deals with substance rather than sensationalism—and one that is very readable.

Ray Newell, Regional Planning Director, Lintas Australia

Over the last five years Max Sutherland's research has forced us to question some deeply held beliefs and has had a fundamental impact on our understanding of the role of advertising . . .

Kerry Gleeson, Regional General Manager, Gillette (Australia) Pty Limited

The author has succeeded admirably. The book is a nice amalgam of psychology and sound practice. It strips away the mystery that often surrounds the black art of advertising in a sensible and readily comprehensible way without sacrificing scientific explanation. This is an excellent example of psychology in action. Intellectual integrity is not sacrificed for readability.

Stan Glaser, Professor of Management, Macquarie University Graduate School of Management

Dr Sutherland's book . . . adds to our understanding of advertising and its role in determining market attitudes, perceptions and images for brand success.

P.J. Dunstan, Chief Executive Officer, Australian Institute of Company Directors

THE ALLEN & UNWIN BUSINESS AND MANAGEMENT SERIES

General series editors:

Dr Bernard Carey
Director
Graduate School of Management
Macquarie University

Professor Elizabeth More
Deputy Director
Graduate School of Management
Macquarie University

Other titles in this series

Australian Public Sector Management
David Corbett

Managing People in Changing Times
Robert Burns

Advertising and the mind of the consumer

what works, what doesn't and why

Max Sutherland

ALLEN & UNWIN

First published in 1997 by
Allen & Unwin
9 Atchison Street,
St Leonards NSW 2065 Australia
Phone:(61 2) 9901 4088
Fax:(61 2) 9906 2218
E-mail:frontdesk@allen-unwin.com.au
Web:http://www.allen-unwin.com.au

National Library of Australia
Cataloguing-in-Publication entry:

Sutherland, Max.
    Advertising and the mind of the consumer.

    Includes index.
    ISBN 1 86373 358 2.

    1. Advertising – Psychological aspects. 2. Consumer behaviour.
    I. Title.

659.1019

Set in 10/11pt Times Roman by DOCUPRO, Sydney
printed by Griffin Press Pty Ltd, Australia

10 9 8 7 6 5

Contents

v

Tables

Figures

Acknowledgments

I realise now why acknowledgment pages of books are so lengthy. There are so many people that have contributed to this one that it is impossible to cite everyone by name.

The opportunity to work with the many valued clients of Sutherland Smith, to track their and their competitors' advertising over time, has provided much raw material from which to discover how advertising really does work as opposed to how folklore or pure theory says it works. I thank them sincerely and I especially thank my business partner, Bruce Smith, for his constant support and encouragement in the writing of this book.

It is through the communicating and sharing of ideas and case-study observations over many years that a body of knowledge such as this emerges. Therefore most of the Sutherland Smith staff have contributed either directly or indirectly to this book. It is a rewarding experience to work with these dedicated professionals.

On the production side of things, Effie Damaskopoulos, Tony Westerlo and Elick Teitelbaum assisted in the preparation of various case-study graphs. Kate Dundon, in her expert way, managed me at the same time as word-processing the book and collating the material. My wife Mel suffered through many iterations of the proof-reading in addition to a somewhat impoverished social and family life while this book was being written.

Many valued academic colleagues and friends have influenced my thinking over the years. In particular I want to mention Professor John Rossiter (Australian Graduate School of Management), Dr John Galloway (NetMap), Larry Percy, Professors Joe Danks and David Riccio (Kent State University), Dr Rob Donovan (University of Western Australia), Geoff Alford (Monash) and from the 'earlier years', Dr Bob March, Dr Stan Glaser and Dr Graham Pont. All of these and many others have influenced my thinking and hence indirectly influenced the content of this book. Of course that does not necessarily imply that they will all agree with everything that is written here. The ultimate responsibility for the content, together with any omissions or errors, must remain mine.

Lastly, I thank the three people who urged me to bring my writings together into a book for so long that it finally happened. These were Malcolm Cameron (Cameron, Moors, Watkins), Mike Hanlon (Niche Publishing) and Tom Valenta (Holt P.R.).

About the author

Max Sutherland is a Director of MarketMind Technologies, and a principal of Sutherland Smith Pty Ltd, one of the top ten market research companies in Australia. He simultaneously holds the position of Adjunct Professor of Marketing at Monash University's David Syme Faculty of Business.

Professor Sutherland is a registered psychologist with three degrees: a Ph.D in Psychology from Kent State University (U.S.A.), a Master of Arts degree in psychology from Sydney University and a Bachelor of Commerce (Marketing) from the University of New South Wales.

After failing and leaving secondary school he started a career in retail sales (major appliances and insurance) and resumed study later as a mature age student. He held positions in market research with the Coca-Cola Export Corporation and the Overseas Telecommunications Commission. He has held full time lectureships in market research and consumer behaviour at the University of NSW and the David Syme Business School (now Monash University) as well as Visiting Professorships at Kent State University and Santa Clara University in the U.S.A.

His company has specialised in tracking the effects of advertising for many of the leading advertisers in Australia and overseas including Gillette, Coles, Prudential, Kodak, Optus, McCain, A.W.C., H.I.A., Golden Casket, McEwans and various State Electricity Commissions.

He is a former editor of the *Australian Marketing Researcher*, a former Chairman of the Market Research Society of Australia (N.S.W.) and a Fellow of the Market Research Society of Australia.

Part A

Why advertising has remained a mystery for so long

Introduction

The subject of advertising seems to be riddled with mystique and apparent contradictions. This book resolves some of those contradictions. It had its beginnings in my regular column for the trade publication *Advertising News*; Part B brings together a selection of those columns. This book is aimed at advertisers but also at the people to whom they advertise. As one marketer commented (in the chauvinistic 1960s): 'The consumer is not an idiot. She is your wife!' Our wives, our husbands, our children are all consumers. The consumer is not an idiot. The consumer is you and me.

Many years ago Lord Lever-Hulme expressed the advertiser's dilemma in this way: 'I know that half my advertising is wasted—but I don't know which half!' Recent developments in market research are beginning to change that. This book draws on the experience of tracking week by week, the effects of hundreds of advertising campaigns over a period of nearly ten years.

Almost everybody is interested in advertising. Approximately $4.9 billion is spent on advertising in Australia each year. The average consumer is exposed to hundreds of ads every day.[1] By the time we die we will have spent an estimated one and a half years watching TV commercials.[2] Yet advertising continues to be something of a mystery. We as consumers generally believe it does not really work on us personally. Despite this, advertisers keep on advertising. So something must be working—but on whom, and exactly how?

This book de-mystifies the effects of advertising and describes some of the psychological mechanisms underlying them. It is written primarily for those who foot the bill for advertising, in other words those who work in the many organisations which advertise their products and services—the marketing directors, marketing managers, product managers and advertising managers. However, I hope

3

it will also be read by interested consumers who wonder how advertising works and why advertisers keep on advertising. I am sure it will come as a surprise to many consumers that those who foot the bill for advertising are often frustrated in knowing little more than the consumers themselves do about how, why or when their advertising works.

Advertising agencies, the makers of advertising, in fact know less about these things than they would like us to think. There are more ads that fail than there are ads that are outstandingly successful. The great majority of ads are at best mediocre in their effect. Alec Benn, an advertising agency principal in the United States, in his book *The 27 Most Common Mistakes in Advertising*, claimed: 'There is a great conspiracy participated in by advertising agencies, radio and television stations and networks, advertising consultants, newspapers, magazines and others to mislead corporate management about the effectiveness of advertising.'[3] Benn's experience is that advertising fails more often than it succeeds, usually because its effects are not measured objectively.

The hard facts are that many ads do fail. Until recently these failures stood a good chance of going unrecognised because the majority of campaigns were not tracked in a formal way.[4]

Advertising agencies are thought of as super-salesmen. However, their most important pitch is to organisations that want to advertise—companies that will engage the agencies' services to design and arrange placement of their advertising on an ongoing basis. To keep clients coming back, advertising agencies need to sell the effectiveness of their advertising to those clients. Too many agencies are much more accomplished at selling their clients on the great job the advertising is doing than they are at creating advertising that is truly effective.

Like those of tribal medicine men, ad agencies' powers and methods are seen to be all the greater because of the mystery that surrounds advertising. So in a way the mystique, the mystery and the aura of advertising works in favour of its makers—the advertising agencies—by inflating their image, status and profits. Books like Vance Packard's *The Hidden Persuaders*[5] enhance this image of advertising agencies because they portray them as having witch-doctor-like powers.

There are those who believe that the mechanism of advertising must be unconscious and subliminal and that this is why its effects do not seem to be apparent on introspection. Such views are associated with the 'dark and manipulative' view of advertising. This book reveals a much more benign interpretation of advertising's so-called 'unconscious' effects. In elaborating on some of the subtler mechanisms of advertising, it dispels many myths and exaggerated claims. At the same time it reveals just how subtle advertising's influences can be and how much impact it can have on the success or failure of one brand over another.

This book shows advertisers how to get better results from the advertising budget and their advertising agency. It shows consumers how advertising does influence which brands they choose—especially when the choice doesn't matter to them personally. Understanding the mechanisms and their limitations tends to lessen rather than heighten the anxieties people may have about wholesale, unconscious manipulation by advertising.

1 Influencing people: Myths and mechanisms

Why is it so difficult to introspect on advertising and how it influences us? Because we look for major effects, that's why! Too often, we look for the ability of an ad to *persuade* us. We look for a major effect rather than more subtle, minor effects.

Most effects of advertising fall well short of persuasion. These minor effects are not obvious but they are more characteristic of the way advertising works. To understand advertising we have to understand and measure these effects. When our kids are growing up we don't notice their physical growth each day but from time to time we become aware that they have grown. Determining how much a child has grown in the last 24 hours is like evaluating the effect of being exposed to a single commercial. In both cases, the changes are too small for us to notice. But even small effects of advertising can influence which brand we choose—especially when all other factors are equal and when alternative brands are much the same.

Weighing the alternatives: Evaluation

Think of this as low-involvement buying. It is like a 'beam-balance' situation in which each brand weighs the same. With one brand on each side, the beam is balanced. However, it takes only a feather added to one side of the balance to tip it in favour of the brand on that side. The brands consumers have to choose from are often very similar. Which one will the buying balance tip towards? When we look for advertising effects we are looking for feathers rather than heavy weights.

The buying of cars, appliances, vacations and other high-priced items is different. These are examples of high-involvement decision-making. This high level of involvement contrasts with the low level brought to bear on the purchase of products like shampoo or soft drink or margarine. For most of us, the buying of these smaller items is no big deal. We have better things to do with our time than agonise over which brand to buy every time we buy something.

The fact is that in many low-involvement product categories, the alternative brands are extremely similar and in some cases almost identical. It doesn't matter much to consumers which one they buy. It is in these low-involvement categories that the effects of advertising can be greatest and yet hardest to introspect upon.

Repetition

As with the amount by which our kids grow in a day, we are just not aware of the small differences advertising may make. Even though these imperceptibly small changes in time add up to significant ones, individual increments are too small for us to notice.

Similarly, the effects of advertising are often imperceptibly small, but because of the beam-balance effect, even small differences can tip the balance. Over time, through the process of repetition, these small increments can produce major perceived differences between brands. But we are rarely aware of the process taking place.

The cumulative effects of changes in brand image become starkly noticeable only in rare cases: for instance when we return to Australia after having been overseas for a long time and find that an old brand is now seen by people in a different light—that the brand has acquired a different image.

In summary, the reasons we are unable to introspect on advertising's effects in low-involvement situations are:

- the effect of each single ad exposure is small;
- it is no big deal to us which of the alternative brands we choose; and
- with repetition, even imperceptibly small effects can build into larger perceived differences between brands.

If you have ever wondered why advertisers seem to persist with repeating the same ad—if you have ever wondered why they think this could possibly influence sane people like us—then here is the answer. Much of advertising creates only marginal differences, but small differences can build into larger differences and even small differences can tip the balance in favour of the advertised brand. This is especially true of so-called 'image advertising'.

Image advertising

The effect of image advertising is easier to see in relation to high-involvement products, so let us start with a high-involvement example—Volvo cars.

Over the years, Volvo has focused its image advertising on safety. Through repetition, it has built up a strong image for the Volvo as a safe car. On a scale of 1 to 10 for safety, most people would rate Volvo higher than almost any other car. Safety is now an integral part of our perception of this brand. (The fact that the car actually delivers on this promise has of course been a very important ingredient in the success of the campaign—but that is another story.)

One effect of image advertising, then, is to produce gradual shifts in our perceptions of a brand with regard to a particular attribute—in Volvo's case, safety (in other words, to marginally change our mental rating of the brand on that attribute). This is often not perceptible after just one exposure because the change, if it occurs, is too small for us to notice.

Now let's take a low-involvement product category—hair spray—and examine the history of brand image advertising for it.

The first hair spray brands originally fought for market share on the basis of the attribute of 'hair holding'. That is, each of the brands claimed to hold hair. To the extent that they all claimed the same thing, they were what we called 'me-too' brands.

To break out of this, one brand began to claim that it 'holds hair longer'. Just as Volvo claimed that it was safer, and thereby moved Volvo up higher on the perceived safety scale than any other car, so this brand of hair spray made people aware that some brands of hair spray might hold hair longer than others. It then attempted to shift perceptions of itself on this attribute and marginally increase the mental rating consumers would give it on 'length of hold'.

The next brand of hair spray to enter the market, instead of tackling that brand head-on, cleverly avoided doing battle on 'length of hold'. This brand claimed that it was 'long holding', but also that it 'brushes out easier'—a dual benefit. In doing so it successfully capitalised on the fact that hair sprays that hold longer are harder to brush out—or were until then.

These examples of image advertising for hair spray and cars illustrate that one effect of advertising is to alter our perceptions of a brand. In other words, advertising can marginally change our image of a brand by leading us to associate it with a particular attribute (like 'longer holding' or 'brushes out easily'), and to associate the brands in our minds with that attribute more than we associate it with any other competitive brand.

Gauging the effects image advertising has on us is made even more complex because these effects may not operate directly on the image of the brand itself. Image advertising may produce small, incremental differences in the image of a brand, as in the case of Volvo—but sometimes it is aimed at changing not so much the image of the brand itself but who we see in our mind's eye as the typical user of that brand.

User image

In advertising for Levi's, Coca-Cola, Lux, Yves St Laurent and so on, focus is on people using the brand. What changes is not so much our perception or image of the product as our perception of the user-stereotype—the kind of person who typically uses the brand, or the situation in which the brand is typically used.

When these brands are advertised, the focus is very much on image but often with this important, subtle difference. The advertising aims to change not how we see the brand itself—the brand image—but how we see:

- the stereotypical user of the brand—the user image
- the stereotypical situation that the brand is used in.

In the advertising of these and many other brands the effect is to be found not so much in the brand image as in the user image or the situation image.

If the user image of a brand resembles us or the type of person we aspire to be, what happens when we come to buy that product category? The user image acts as a feather on one side of the beam balance. If everything else is equal it can tip the scale (but note, only if everything else is about equal).

User or situational image changes usually fall short of the kinds of rational, heavyweight reasons that make perfect sense of any choice. But they can nevertheless tilt the balance in favour of one brand. Minor effects such as these constitute much of the impact of advertising. Yet they are usually much more difficult for us as consumers to analyse introspectively and tend to be discounted precisely because they clearly fall well short of persuasion.

Persuasion is the exception

We have been told so often that the role of advertising is to persuade that we seem to have come to believe it.

How often have I heard the comment, 'It wouldn't make me run out and buy it.' This is common in group-discussion market research when participants are asked to analyse introspectively how they react to an ad—especially if it is an image ad. It demonstrates the myth of how advertising is supposed to have its influence.

I don't think anyone believes that any ad will make them run out and buy the advertised product. Nothing has that kind of persuasive or coercive power. So why do people say, 'It wouldn't make me run out and by it'? Because they can't think of any other way the ad could work. The effect of advertising is not to make us 'run out and buy'—especially with low-involvement products and especially with image advertising. It is beam-balance stuff.

High involvement

High-involvement purchases contrast with low-involvement, low-cost purchases. When people are parting with substantial sums of money to buy a TV, car or holiday, they do not take the decision lightly. These are high-involvement decisions for most consumers. Before making them, we actively hunt down information, talk with friends and generally find out all we can about our prospective purchase.

Furthermore, alternative brands at this level usually have many more differences. They are not likely to be virtually identical, as is the case with many low-involvement products.

Advertising is one influence in high-involvement buying decisions, but it is only one among many. Often it is a relatively weak one at that—especially by comparison with other influences like word of mouth, previous experience and recommendations by 'experts'. In the case of high-involvement products, much of advertising's effect is not so much on the final decision as on whether a brand gets considered—whether we include it in the set of alternatives that we are prepared to spend time weighing up. This is one of the ways that advertising influences our thinking indirectly.

For example, there are hundreds of brands and types of cars, far too many for us to consider all of them individually in the same detail. We seriously consider only those that make it onto our short list. But what determines which cars make it on to our short list? This is where advertising comes into play.

If we are unlikely to be in the market for a new car, refrigerator or whatever for several years, the advertising we see and hear for these products falls on low-involved ears. However, if our old car or appliance unexpectedly breaks down today, we may find ourselves propelled into the market for a new one. Suddenly, the ads we saw yesterday or last week or last month under low-involvement conditions become more relevant. One test of their effectiveness will be whether they have left enough impact to get their brand onto our short list.

A lot of advertising, even for high-priced items, thus has its effect in a low-involvement way. Again we see that in looking for the effects of advertising, we need to look for subtle effects. It is a case of 'feathers' rather than persuasion; things can influence which alternatives get weighed up, or things that add their little bit of weight to the weighing-up process.

Two mental processes in decision-making

There are two fundamentally different mental processes at work in choice decisions. We have already considered the most obvious ones, the weighing up of alternatives. But there is another process that consumers and advertisers tend to be less conscious of. *Weighing up the alternatives is one thing. Which alternatives get weighed up is another!*

Which alternatives get weighed up?

What determines the alternatives that are actually considered?

Think about a consumer decision that you probably make every day. It's getting on for noon, you are feeling hungry and you ask yourself, 'What am I going to have for lunch today?' Your mind starts to generate alternatives and to evaluate each alternative as you think of it. The process goes something like this:

'Will I have a pie?'
'No, I had a pie yesterday.'
'A sandwich?'
'No, the sandwich shop is too far away and besides, it's raining.'
'I could drive to McDonald's.'
'Yes . . . I'll do that.'

There are two things to note here. First, what the mind does is produce alternatives, one at a time. This 'mental agenda' of alternatives is ordered like this:

What's the choice for lunch?

1 Pie
2 Sandwich
3 McDonald's

4 Counter lunch at the pub
5 Pizza Hut

Second, the order in which the alternatives are arranged is the order in which they are elicited by the mind. This order can influence your final choice. You may enjoy Pizza Hut more than McDonald's. But in the example, you didn't go to Pizza Hut, you went to McDonald's.

Had you continued your thought process instead of stopping at the third alternative (McDonald's), you would probably have gone to Pizza Hut. But if Pizza Hut is only fifth on your mental agenda of lunch alternatives, it is unlikely to get much of your business. You didn't get to Pizza Hut because you didn't think of it before you hit on a satisfactory solution—McDonald's. You didn't get there physically because you never got there mentally. Even if we like or prefer something, if it is not reasonably high on our mental agenda it is likely to miss out.

How many times have you found yourself doing something and realised too late that there was something else you would rather have been doing but didn't think about in time? The most preferred alternatives are not necessarily the ones you think of first. (Anyone who has ever left an important person off an invitation list will appreciate this.) Next time you go out for dinner and are trying to decide which restaurant to go to, observe your thought pattern. There are two separate processes at work. One is generation of alternatives. The other is evaluation of the alternatives.

To affect the outcome of buying decisions, advertisers can try to influence:

• the order in which the alternatives are evoked
• the evaluation of a particular alternative; or
• both.

When we think of advertising's effects we almost invariably think of how advertising influences our evaluation of a brand. Yet much of advertising's influence is not on our evaluations of a brand but on the order in which alternative brands are evoked.

Agenda-setting effect

Influencing the order of alternatives has its basis in what is known as the agenda-setting theory of mass communications. This says: The mass media don't tell us what to think. But they *do* tell us what to think about! They set the mental agenda.

The agenda-setting theory was originally developed to explain the influence of the mass media in determining which political issues become important in elections. Adroit committee chairmen and politicians claim that if you can control the agenda you can control the meeting. It was not until 1981 that the relevance of this to advertising was recognised.[1]

We have mental agendas for lots of things. For example:

What's news?	*What's the choice for lunch?*
1 Gorbachev	1 Sandwich
2 State of the economy	2 Pie
3 Interest rates	3 McDonald's
4 A child abducted	4 Counter lunch at the pub
5 Wimbledon	5 Pizza Hut

We can discover our mental agenda by pulling out what is in our minds under a particular category and examining the order (in which it emerges). The category may be 'What's the choice for lunch?', 'What's news?', or what brand of soft drink to buy.

When we reach into our minds to generate any of these agendas, the items do not all come to mind at once. They are elicited one at a time and in an order. The items on top of the mental agenda are the most salient and the ones we are most likely to remember first.

It's the same with choosing which restaurant to go to or which department store to visit or which supermarket to shop at this week. It is the same with the decision about which cars or refrigerators to short-list and which dealers to visit. The order in which we retrieve the items from our memories seems almost inconsequential to us but may be critically important in determining the chances of our going to a McDonald's versus Pizza Hut.

This effect also occurs if we have a list of the alternatives or a display of them such as in the supermarket. Even here, where the brands are all set out in front of us, all of them do not get noticed simultaneously. In fact they do not *all* get noticed.

Think about the process. We stand there at the display. We notice first one brand, then another and then another. It happens rapidly—but in sequence. So despite the fact that the brands are all displayed, they are not necessarily all equal in terms of the probability that they will come to mind or get noticed. This raises a question. At supermarket displays, what makes a brand stand out? To use the marketing term, what makes it 'cut through the clutter' of all the alternative packs and get noticed? What makes one brand get noticed more quickly than others at the supermarket display?

This introduces the concept of salience, which is formally defined in the next section. In this context we ask how a brand can be moved up from fifth, to fourth to third, to second, to become the first one noticed. The higher up it is in this order, the better the chance it has of being considered, and consequently the better the chance of its being purchased.

The brand's physical prominence, the amount of shelf space it occupies and its position in the display are very important. But advertising can influence choice when other factors (like shelf space or position) are otherwise equal. Advertising can help tip the balance.

Asking what makes one brand more *salient*—more likely to come to mind or get noticed—than another is like asking what influences Pizza Hut's position on our mental lunch agenda. In the supermarket, instead of having to recall all the alternatives by ourselves, we are prompted by the display. However, which brands we notice and the order in which we notice them can be influenced by more than just the display.

Salience

We think much more often about people and things that are important to us than about those that are not. The psychological term for this prominence in our thoughts is salience. Advertisers would like us to think of their brands as 'more important' but they will settle for 'more often'. In other words, they would like their brands to be more salient for us.

My definition of salience is the probability that something will be in the conscious mind at any given moment. One way advertising can increase this probability is through repetition. We have all had the experience of being unable to get a song we have heard a lot out of our minds. The repetition of the song has increased its salience; it has increased its probability of being in the conscious mind at any moment. Repetition of an advertisement, especially a jingle, can have a similar effect. Through repetition of the ad, the salience of the brand—the star of the ad—is increased in our minds.

Another way advertising influences what we think about and notice is through 'cueing'. To explain this, let me ask you a few questions.

What's the first thing you think of when you see:
'Anyhow* . . . '?
What's the first thing you think of when someone asks:
'Which bank?'
What do you think of when I say 'How do you feel?'?
What do you think of when I say 'Uh, huh'?

Words or expressions such as these come up naturally in everyday conversation. When a brand is linked to them through repetition, they become cues that help increase the salience of the brand.

An actor in a play takes his cue from a line or some other happening or event. The human mind takes its cue from its intentions and its immediate environment. Such cues can influence what we think about next. That's how we go to sleep at night. We turn off the cues. We turn off the light, the radio and so on. We try to reduce distractions or cues so that things won't keep popping into our minds.

One way advertising can use cues is by tying a brand to something that frequently recurs in the ordinary environment. There are many common words, expressions, symbols or tunes that can be developed by means of repetition into mnemonic devices which trigger recollection of the brand. 'I feel like a Tooheys'. 'Anyhow* . . . Have a Winfield'.

If the cue frequently recurs in the particular circumstances under which the product is likely to be consumed, such as at lunch time, then all the better.

This cueing effect is so much a part of the way we respond to our environment that we are largely oblivious to it. As someone once said, fish are probably unaware of water because it is all around them.

However, most people are aware of cueing to some degree. Almost everybody has had the experience of a particular smell evoking a particular memory. Whenever a motorbike using Benzol fuel passes me in the street, the smell immediately evokes memories of racing go-karts as a kid. The memories not only pop into my mind but I am then prone to reminisce on those happy days.

If you have ever had trouble getting to sleep at night because your mind can't switch off, then you can relate to how involuntary this process usually is, in other words, that what pops into our minds at any point in time is not totally under voluntary control.

If you are over 30, chances are that 'Anyhow*' still makes you think of Winfield (Anyhow* . . . Have a Winfield)—even after all these years. When the campaign was running, Paul Hogan and the expression stood for the brand and triggered the brand name in people's minds. As did the classical theme music, which I still think of as 'the Winfield music'!

Our minds are in a sense a 'stream of consciousness'—an inexorable flow that is frequently diverted, sometimes paused but never stopped. Environmental cues can influence what enters the flow and what direction it takes. One type of advertising focuses on tying a brand to one or more such cues, so that whenever we hear, see or think of the cue there is a high probability that we will think of the brand or notice its presence.

The product category as a cue

Advertisers want us to think of their brand, but they particularly want us to think of their brand when we are making a decision involving the product category. One important cue is therefore the category itself. When I say 'soft drink' what do you think of? When I say 'lunch' what do you think of? When I say 'cars' what do you think of? If our conscious mind is in the process of being cued by a product category (e.g. it is noon and we are thinking 'lunch'), then what is likely to flit into it is not a brand of hair spray or a car—we are much more likely to see in our mind's eye the first item on the mental agenda we have for the category 'lunch'.

When our mind is cued in to a particular product category, we almost automatically begin to think of the 'top-of-mind' members of that category. In the case of the category 'lunch', we will think of Pizza Hut or McDonald's or some other food alternative rather than hair spray or cars or anything else.

The technical term for this is category-cued salience, or the probability that the brand will come to mind whenever its product category does.

It is possible to measure category-cued salience and assess the influence of advertising on it. This is done by asking people what is the first brand that comes to mind when they hear or see the product category name, and then the next brand and the next. In this way the agenda of brands can be elicited. The rank of a given brand in the product category agenda indicates its category-cued salience. It is a rough index of the probability that it will come to our mind when in the normal course of events we are prompted by the product category name.

If this questioning procedure is carried out with a different random sample of consumers every week, the agenda and the salience of each brand can be tracked, week by week, over time. Market research can detect any improvements resulting from advertising by the order in which the advertised brand is elicited. Advertising a brand generally improves its salience.

Point-of-sale advertising: How to upset the agenda

Many people wonder why Coca-Cola which is so well known, needs to advertise so much and why it needs to 'waste all that money' on signs in shops and milk bars. The answer is that if it did not have its signs in these places, Pepsi or some other competitor certainly would. These other brands would try to upset consumers' mental agendas by 'jumping the cue'—by inducing us, at the point of sale, to consider them as well as Coke.

Both point-of-sale, reminder advertising and our own mental agenda of brands can prompt us with alternatives to consider before we ask for what we want. Advertisers therefore try to influence a brand's salience at the point of sale by not leaving it to our mental agendas alone. They erect signs in an attempt to visually cue us into their brand.

When we walk into a milk bar to buy a soft drink, we are already in a category-cued state. We are already thinking about soft drink and which one we will have. If Coke is not already top of mind when we enter it almost inescapably will be once we have been inside for a moment, because Coke as a brand is likely to be prompted in our minds by a) the product category cue and b) the numerous Coca-Cola signs in the store.

Coke may be on top of most people's minds but if they are confronted with a Pepsi sign they may consider both brands. So Coke tries to dominate the clutter of mental alternatives as well as the clutter of point-of-sale advertising. This makes it difficult for other brands to cut through into people's minds at the point of sale. It protects Coke's category salience—something that it has invested a lot of money in building up through years of advertising.

Supermarket shopping: Mental agendas vs brand displays

In the supermarket, it may be thought that because the brands are all displayed, they are all equally likely to be noticed—and considered. If this were so, then our mental agenda of brands would be irrelevant to supermarket shopping. However, this is not the case.

In an observation study of supermarket shoppers that I conducted in Melbourne some years ago, 56 per cent of all buying episodes fell into the category of 'simple locating behaviour'.[2] That is, most people were simply locating the brand they bought last time or the one that they came in to buy and putting it routinely in their shopping basket with little or no attention to evaluating the alternatives.

For an alternative brand or pack to be noticed, let alone considered, it would have to cut through the display clutter and stand out in some way. In order to be considered it first has to cut through into conscious attention.

In low-involvement situations many people tend to do what they did last time unless there is something to interrupt the routine. Thus a brand or pack has to cut through the display clutter just as an ad has to cut through the clutter of other ads. And the two, the pack and the advertising, can work together.

The importance of being noticed was demonstrated in another study when we asked regular buyers of a product category if they had seen a particular new brand on the supermarket shelves. We showed them colour photographs of the new brand's packs so that it was a task of recognition rather than recall. Only 45 per cent said they had seen the brand, yet it had been in virtually every supermarket for over five weeks.[3]

Just because something is present in the environment it will not necessarily be noticed or considered. And the more cluttered the environment—the more alternatives in the product category—the greater the problem is for the advertiser. Advertising signs at the point of purchase can help considerably here, especially when they tie in with advertising that we have already seen. They are then more likely to 'connect' and orient us to notice the brand.

In the supermarket, it is not signs but usually the brands themselves that are displayed. Potentially we are able to be reminded of every brand in the display by its physical presence. So is our mental agenda of brands still relevant? Yes, though it is now one influence among several. In particular, it orients us by determining which brands we notice in the display.

To illustrate this, imagine you are in a supermarket doing the shopping. As you approach the detergent section, what is in your mind? The category 'detergents'. Why? Because the layout of the supermarket is familiar to you, or because when you approach that section the category is prompted by the display in front of you?

Even in the supermarket, then, the product category as a cue is likely to be triggered in our minds at a particular point and to trigger in turn expectations of the brands we are likely to see in that category. What we see first in the display is likely to be influenced not only by a brand's position and shelf space but also by our expectations of seeing the brand there. All other things being equal, we tend to notice first the brands we are familiar with. This is of course especially true when our mindset is that of looking to locate the one that we bought last time.

When something is heavily advertised, it is more likely to come to mind and, other things being equal, to be noticed faster in a display. We know from the psychological literature that people recognise the familiar more quickly, so it will come as no surprise that familiar brands will be very salient and be noticed more quickly. Advertising exposure of the brand and the pack helps to make the brand more familiar and increase its salience. Repeated exposure of the pack in TV advertising makes it more familiar and hence gives it a better chance of being noticed earlier or faster than its compet-itor.

The importance of this marginal effect is seen in the finding mentioned above—that 56 per cent of all purchases made in the supermarket are the result of simple locating behaviour in which shoppers hardly pause at the display but simply reach out and pick up the item they are after. So in the supermarket a brand or pack has to cut through the clutter—to stop people walking at 2 km/h— and get itself noticed.

Self displays, shelf 'talkers' and off-location displays are all ways to help a brand cut through clutter and get our attention. Advertising that we have been exposed to previously, however, also plays an important part in increasing the visual salience of a particular brand.

Measuring visual salience

Advertisers can quantify the visual salience of a pack or brand through market research in much the same way as they uncover the mental agenda. They give each brand in a supermarket display equal shelf space and then take a photograph of the display. Then they show the photo to a random sample of consumers and ask them to name the brands they see. The order and speed with which the brands are noticed provide a measure of their visual salience. (Actually researchers use several photographs and control for posi-tion in the display by randomly changing the position of each brand.)

Summary

One reason we find it difficult to analyse advertising's effects introspectively and why advertising has remained a mystery for so long is that these effects are often so simple and so small that they fall short of outright persuasion. Advertising influences the order in which we evoke or notice the alternatives we consider. This does not feel like persuasion and it is not. It is nevertheless effective. Instead of persuasion and other major effects we should look for 'feathers', or minor effects. These can tip the balance when the alternative brands are otherwise equal and, through repetition, can grow imperceptibly by small increments over time.

2 Image and reality: Seeing things in different ways

In Chapter 1 we considered the ways in which advertising can influence our decisions by influencing the order in which we evoke or notice the options. Now let us turn to advertising and its influence on our *evaluation* of brand alternatives.

Human beings have a remarkable capacity for seeing things in different ways. The same physical stimulus, the same product or service, if you will, can be seen in more than one way. Think of Figure 2.1 as a brand. You should be able to see it in two different ways.

When you see a vase in the figure your mind is seeing 'white figure on black background'. When you see two faces, your mind is seeing 'black figure on white background'. This white-on-black or black-on-white that you are using to make sense of what you see is called the frame of reference. You overlay a frame of reference on a stimulus to generate a perception.

A brand, company or service can also be perceived in different ways depending upon the frame of reference that people bring to it. Frame of reference is a psychological term that refers to a mind set or previous experience. It often includes images or attribute associations like 'comfort' or 'safety' or 'longer holding'. These form the attribute agenda—the chain of associations (visual or verbal) that a brand automatically triggers in our mind. They can be ranked in the order in which they are triggered, with the most salient ones at the top.

Evaluating a brand

When we evaluate brands we try to do so by evaluating their attributes or features. This is not always a straightforward task, for

Figure 2.1   We see the same thing in more than one way

two reasons. First, there is the problem of what attributes the brand has. Second, there is the problem of how to interpret these attributes.

For example, with the brand Volvo I think of heavy construction, safety, conservative styling and so on. Heavy construction is closely related to safety, which I rate positively. But I may also associate it with poorer fuel economy, a negative feature. Thus the same attribute, heavy construction, can be rated positively or negatively depending on how I look at it. Similarly, large size may suggest either comfort or poor fuel economy. And cloth seat coverings are more comfortable than vinyl and look better, but are harder to keep clean.

Our minds can interpret any attribute positively or negatively. For example, Levin and Gaeth have shown that our attitudes towards mincemeat vary markedly depending whether it is labelled '75 per cent lean' or '25 per cent fat'.[1] There are upsides and downsides to almost anything in life and a brand's features are no exception.

Positively or negatively charged features

Attribute associations can greatly influence the way we feel about something. 'Cars are imaged variously as shields against accidents, reliable companions, virile athletes or purveyors of fun.'[2] Similar variations occur in our images of product categories (pearls, refrigerators, fish paste), brands (Volvo, Pepsi, Close-Up), services (Australia Post, Better Brakes, Ansett), and organisations (BHP, Mayne Nickless, Coles Myer).

Consider the product category 'pearls'. Most people think of pearls as beautiful jewellery, whose salient associations are with gift-giving, attractive women, high fashion and expensiveness. But like any product, pearls also have non-salient features, aspects most people tend not to think of unless their attention is drawn to them for some reason.

A competitor (to pursue our example, perhaps DeBeers) may seek to remind us of these other attributes because it wants us to buy diamonds instead of pearls. It may point out that a pearl is an oyster tumour. Ugh! What unpleasant associations that statement triggers.

Under normal circumstances, however, we would never have cause to think about that aspect of pearls. Nevertheless, we would have to agree that it is true. The information that a pearl is an oyster tumour is there in our heads. But it usually occurs so far down on our mental attribute agenda that we would rarely, in the normal course of thinking about pearls, bring it to mind. It is not a salient feature.

Calling a pearl 'an oyster tumour' plays the focal beam of our attention on an unpleasant aspect of pearls. This is a 'feather' but if it were repeated often enough its salience would be likely to increase. (In a sense, this is what the conservationists have done with the product category of furs.) It may not make us stop buying pearls but it might take some of the shine off our perception of them.

Under normal circumstances the focal beam of our attention is only wide enough to encompass a few of the attributes of a brand or product. By shifting the spotlight and playing the focal beam of attention on other attributes, it is possible to marginally change our perceptions. This is what the graffiti artists are trying to do when they write 'Meat is murder' on walls and bridges. Most of us eat meat. We also know where it comes from. But we don't want to think about it too much. If we did, we would probably consider becoming vegetarians. The killing of animals in order to eat their flesh is hardly an association that we want to be reminded of.

Advertising influence on our brand attribute agenda

When I think of Volvo I think 'safety', 'reliable', 'heavy'. I could consider many other attributes, but my mind has only time to touch on a few. The advertiser wants safety to be high on the Volvo attribute agenda. So its advertising uses words and pictures to highlight the brand's association with that attribute.

With drinks, too, there are all sorts of attributes on which an advertiser can play the focal beam of attention. Some that will be familiar are:

Taste: 'Just for the taste of it—Diet Coke'
Non alcohol: 'Claytons, the drink you have when you're not having a drink'
Modern/up-to-date/with-it: 'Pepsi—The taste of a new generation'
Flavour: '7UP, the Uncola'
Quality: 'Is it as good as Bushells?'
Thirst quenching: 'Deep Spring breaks the drought'

One of the most important aspects of advertising, then, is to play the focal beam of attention on a particular attribute and make that attribute more salient for us when we think of the brand. In other words, advertising influences the attribute agenda for a brand by rearranging the order in which we think of its attributes.

Using positively charged features: Positioning

Words and images can be used to make the positive attributes of an advertiser's brand or product more salient; to increase the probability that when we think of that brand we will think of those positive attributes; to place them higher on the brand's attribute agenda.

What do you think of when I say 'Colgate'? Your agenda perhaps went something like this:

1 Toothpaste
2 Cleans teeth
3 Mrs Marsh
4 Prevents decay
5 The fluoride gets in.

Now, what do you think of when I say 'Close-up' toothpaste? Your agenda is likely to be heavily influenced by the advertising for Close-Up, which features scenes of couples kissing. It plays the focal beam of our attention on quite different attributes from those we associate with Colgate. It puts the brand's major selling point, the attributes associated with kissing, 'fresh breath' and 'sex appeal', high on our agenda of associations. This attribute agenda is quite different from Colgate's.

Using negatively charged features: Repositioning the opposition

Advertisers usually try to highlight the positive attributes of their own brand. An alternative strategy is to highlight the negative features of the opposition's product. We saw how this works with product categories when we discussed the examples of pearls and meat. Highlighting the negatives in the opposition brand is referred to as 'repositioning the opposition'—repositioning the opposition brand in people's minds.

The best-known example of this was the famous Avis rental car advertising campaign which used the line: 'Avis. We are number two, so why should you rent from us? We try harder!'

In this campaign Avis acknowledged that it was not the market leader and scored points and credibility for its honesty. At the same time it indirectly and subtly highlighted a negative attribute often associated with strong market leaders and monopolies—that they can be complacent and give poor service; that they don't try hard enough. The proposition that Avis as number two in the market would be trying harder to deliver better service was the positive flip-side of this. It was given more credibility by the company's apparent honesty in admitting it was not number one.

Thus, words and images can be used to make particular negative attributes of an opposition brand or product more salient: to increase the probability that when we think of the brand we will think of that negative attribute. It is a matter of advertising influencing which attributes our minds focus on when we think of the brand. When we think of pearls or brand leaders we don't usually think of the negative attributes, and this leaves them looking attractive. It is the fact that our minds are usually focused on the positive attributes (like 'jewellery', 'good-looking', 'valuable', 'great gift') that makes them attractive.

Just as there is a mental agenda of brands that we free-associate to the product category, so there is a mental agenda of attributes that we free-associate to entities like meat or pearls, or brands like Volvo or Pepsi. Advertising can make certain attributes more salient and therefore higher on a product's attribute agenda. As a consequence, when we think of the product we think of the advertised features before, and perhaps instead of, other negative but less salient attributes.

Point-of-sale advertising: Attribute cueing

Just as ads or signs at the point of sale can remind us of a brand, so too they can remind us of a particular attribute of the brand. Just for the taste of it!—Diet Coke. Benson & Hedges. When only the best will do.

The words and pictures used to label and describe a brand can direct our attention to quite different aspects of the same thing; they can help us to see it in different ways.

To illustrate: What do you think of when I say 'Dick Smith'? A biography of Dick Smith could conceivably carry any of the following subtitles: '. . . the man', '. . . the adventurer', '. . . the publisher', '. . . the philanthropist', '. . . the pilot'.

Dick Smith is one person but he has all of these attributes. Depending which subtitle was chosen, the book would attract a slightly different audience and have slightly different appeals. The same man is being described but what we expect to see in the book would be very much influenced by which title or description was used. Whether people bought it would be influenced by a combination of their own attribute agenda for Dick Smith and the attribute— i.e. how much they are interested in 'men' or 'adventurers' or 'publishers' or 'philanthropists' or 'pilots'—cued by the subtitle. Each description of Dick Smith plays the focal beam of our attention and our expectations on a different attribute of the same person. It consequently influences our perceptions and our expectations. It does not leave them solely to our own mental agenda.

Point-of-sale advertising does the same thing. It influences us by playing the focal beam of our attention on the brand and the featured attribute at the same time.

Influenced by the brand name

Advertisers frequently choose the name of a brand so the name itself can help direct attention, dictate people's expectations, and help determine the brand's most salient features. Names like Safe and Sound (baby seats), Instamatic (cameras), Posturepedic (beds), and Pure and Simple (cooking oil) not only name the product but also make an implicit statement about its salient attributes. So we expect baby seats with the name 'Safe and Sound' to have features like quality and safety. We expect beds called 'Posturepedic' not to damage our back, and so on.

This has a very long history. 'Erik the Red named the country he had discovered Greenland, for he said that people would be more tempted to go there if it had an attractive name.'[3] Erik the Red obviously had an intuitive feel for what influences people's expectations and a product's attribute agenda.

Another example from history: before the Civil War in areas of the US known as temperance regions, alcoholic beverages did not have a market. They were socially unacceptable. However, the marketers of patent medicines found these regions a big market for their products—especially those containing up to 44 per cent of the preservative alcohol.[4]

Summary

How we evaluate a brand, a service or a product depends on how we perceive it. This in turn, depends on the frame of reference we overlay on it. The frame of reference comes largely from our experience. Just as there is a mental agenda of brands that we associate with a given product category, so there is a mental agenda of attributes that we free-associate to a given brand.

Under normal circumstances the focal beam of our attention is only wide enough to focus on a limited number of the possible attributes of a brand or product. By shifting the spotlight and playing the focal beam of our attention on other attributes, it is possible to change our perceptions of the product. Words and images can be used to make its positive attributes more salient; to increase the probability that when we think of the brand we will think of those attributes.

Again, these may be 'feathers', but they may nevertheless be enough to tip the scales in favour of a particular brand—especially when all other factors are equal.

3 Subliminal advertising: The biggest myth of all

'Advertising is in an odd position. Its extreme protagonists claim it has extraordinary powers and its severest critics believe them.'[1]

The never-ending story

I hate the term 'subliminal'. There has been so much nonsense talked about so-called 'subliminal advertising' that there is always the risk that when I talk about it, I will fuel the uninformed hype.

The original scare on subliminal advertising came from a cinema owner in the US who flashed 'Drink Coca-Cola' and 'Eat popcorn' on the screen during a movie so fast that nobody was supposed to be aware it was happening. He reported that sales of Coca-Cola and popcorn increased dramatically. This caused such a scare that legislation was quickly prepared to ban subliminal advertising.

If subliminal advertising did indeed have that kind of effect on our behaviour, and without our knowledge, then we clearly would need protection from it. It is still widely believed that in the 1950s subliminal advertising was made illegal in the US. In fact, no such legislation was passed either federally or in any state. It was in Australia and the UK, however—though as we will see, this was unnecessary.

That was over a quarter of a century ago. Ever since, there have been numerous attempts—all unsuccessful—to replicate the effect claimed by the cinema-owner and more than 200 scientific papers have been published on the subject. Pratkanis and Aronson, after exhaustively researching that literature, concluded that 'no study has demonstrated motivational and behavioural effects similar to those claimed by the advocates of subliminal seduction'.[2] It is clear in this case, enthusiasm and myth outweighed fact.

In 1984, when confronted with the overwhelming evidence against subliminal advertising, the cinema owner, James Vicary, was reported in *Advertising Age* magazine as admitting that his original claim had been a fabrication.[3] So subliminal advertising was just a myth all along.

Self-help tapes

If that is so, you may ask, then what about those self-help tapes? The ones that are supposed to contain subliminal messages to help you give up smoking, improve your self-esteem and so on? Are they nonsense also?

In the same way that a sugar pill will relieve pain in about a third of sufferers if they think it is aspirin, so too will such tapes work on a proportion of the people who use them—because they expect them to. Pratkanis and Aronson convincingly demonstrated this several times by giving experimental subjects tapes of classical music marked 'subliminally improve your memory' or 'subliminally improve your self-esteem'. A significant proportion of the subjects reported improvements in their memory or self-esteem, depending how their tape was labelled, but the proportion was the same whether the tapes actually had subliminal messages embedded in them or not.[4]

The practical jokesters: Embedded words or images

What about the images and words like 'sex' that have been shown to be embedded in some advertisements? Don't they prove that subliminal advertising is being practised and that it must be working? They prove nothing of the kind! Despite the hoo-ha and the paranoia created by such books as *Subliminal Seduction* by Wilson Bryan Key,[5] I believe this is nothing but visual graffiti and practical-joke playing by those who design the advertising.

Most of the examples Key cites have been in print advertising. It is very easy for an art director to put something in an ad, a caricature of his boss for example, without his boss being aware that it is there. Ten years ago an art director friend pointed out to me a figure in one of the poster ads that he had drawn and which I must have seen a hundred times. There in caricature, right in the middle of the crowd scene in the poster, was the man who was at the time his and my boss. Like the Waldo character in the children's books, he was virtually invisible—until you looked. My friend and I had a hearty laugh and he swore me to silence. These things are rarely discovered. The infamous Robert Maxwell's own *London Daily*

Mirror once ran a cartoon in which the cartoonist inserted the words, 'Fuck Maxwell' in tiny letters among the squiggles.[6]

When the word 'sex' is found disguised in the shadows of ice cubes in a Gilbey's gin ad, I interpret it as an art director having a joke on his client or his boss or just seeing if he can get away with it without anybody noticing.

This kind of thing, however, gives ammunition to the conspiracy theorists who interpret words or images as proof that subliminal advertising is practised and must therefore be seducing us without our knowledge.

Why did the subliminal myth take hold?

For years, as I studied this subject through two psychology degrees and one marketing degree, I was plagued by this question: how, if subliminal advertising is just a myth, could the myth have been perpetuated for so long?

One reason is to be found in the fact that legislators moved so quickly to ban it. In doing so they lent a kind of legitimacy to unfounded beliefs about the power of subliminal advertising. The need to prepare legislation to ban it provided history with the prima facie evidence that subliminal advertising is a real threat. This helped enshrine and perpetuate the myth.

Another reason is that the myth fits the image of advertising that is perpetuated by the advertising industry. As we saw in Chapter 1, people believe that advertising has much greater powers to influence us than it really does. Once we started imputting witch-doctor-like powers to ad agencies, it was a small step to believing that they had the modern equivalent: power to persuade us subliminally.

The media have also done their bit to foster this belief. Mystique makes for good copy and greater reader interest. Subliminal advertising had the same mystique for audiences as TV programs like *Ripley's Believe It or Not* or *Strange Tales*.

But is that all there is to it? Just myth, hype and mistake? I believe there is another important reason why the belief in subliminal advertising has persisted for so long. A high-jumper can jump two metres, but this does not mean man can fly. There are limits to how high we can go, unassisted. Similarly, as the earlier chapters of this book have shown, we are able to learn without full conscious awareness—but only to a point.

Claims about subconscious learning had a kernel of truth. Claims about subliminal advertising were wildly exaggerated and they distorted this truth. Advertising often works without our being able to keep track of the process. There is no need for subliminal exposures on TV and cinema screens. The process happens naturally. It is what low-involvement communication is all about.

There is no doubt that we can be influenced without awareness, but as the earlier chapters show, there is nothing necessarily unique or evil or manipulative about this. It is a quantum leap from here to believing in wholesale manipulation of people's minds through subliminal advertising. Just because we can learn without full awareness does not mean that advertising practises mass manipulation on us. People can jump two metres—but flying is something else.

Thirty years of research later

So let's look at the claims—more than 30 years later—in light of the substantial body of scientific research that has accumulated in cognitive psychology since then.

The notion of subliminal advertising was based on the belief that awareness was an all-or-nothing thing. That is, we are either aware of something or we are not. This is demonstrably untrue. Research in cognitive psychology over the past 30 years has shown that *conscious awareness is a dimension and not a dichotomy. It is a matter of degree.*

By way of illustration, let me draw your attention to the sounds around you right now. What can you hear? Were you aware of the sounds before I drew your attention to them? Probably not. The reason is a matter of degree of consciousness. You were not paying attention to the sounds but that does not mean they were 'subliminal' in the sense that they were unable to be heard.

A more useful way of thinking about this issue is in terms of depth of mental processing. Instead of subliminal we could use the term 'shallow processing'.

The logic and illogic of subliminal advertising

The concept of subliminal advertising was based on the notion of a threshold. Subliminal meant 'below the *limen*, or threshold'. This was thought to be a fixed point below which awareness does not extend. This 'limen' was just another name for the threshold.

We know that for some sounds, dogs have a much lower threshold than humans. They can hear sounds that we can't. This is the principle of the dog-whistle.

When we have a hearing test, the loudness of a tone is gradually increased until we indicate to the doctor that we can hear it. This is the threshold at which sound enters our consciousness.

The same applies to sight. If a word is flashed on a screen for 50 milliseconds we will not be aware of it. If the time of the exposure is increased, at a certain point the word crosses the threshold and enters our conscious awareness.

Subliminal advertising was supposed to be pitched just barely below the threshold of awareness. If it was too far below it would not work. The theory was that the exposure should be sufficiently long for people to register the message unconsciously but not long enough for them to become aware of it.

Research has since shown that there is no absolute threshold below which we are always unconscious of something and above which we are always conscious of it. For example, when we are hungry we recognise food words at much shorter exposures than non-food words. The threshold is lower for these words when we are hungry and higher if we have just eaten.

Thresholds therefore turn out to vary in the same person from day to day and even from hour to hour. This is partly because sometimes we are more alert than at other times.

They also vary as a result of tiredness, lack of sleep or drugs like alcohol or caffeine. And they vary from person to person.

For an advertiser always to pitch his message precisely at or just under the threshold would therefore seem impossible. Psychologists have now redefined the threshold of awareness in probabilistic rather than absolute terms—as the exposure level that enables a subject in repeated trials to detect a word 50 per cent of the time. To reach everyone, a message would have to be exposed for a relatively long period. But since this would put it above many people's threshold, the message could no longer be termed subliminal. Subliminal advertising as originally defined is therefore a myth.

Awareness and attention: Limits to our capacity

Attention is not an all-or-nothing thing. Even though some people seem to be able to attend to more than one thing at a time, there are limits. Psychological studies show that the more things we allocate our attention to, the shallower the mental processing of any one of them.

Psychology experiments on shared attention show that there are real limits to our attention capacity when other things in the environment are competing for our attention. We only have a limited amount of mental processing capacity at any one time. Therefore some things are given shallow mental processing. Others are given deep attentional processing. There are just too many things around to process them all in the same depth.

Interestingly, the more attention that is paid to something, the easier it is for us to recall it later.[7]

So what happens when some of our attention is directed away from the ad on the radio or TV? What happens when we are barely aware of the advertising around us? To answer, let me take you into the fascinating world of the experimental psychologist and introduce you to what is known as the split-span attention experiment.

Split-span attention

Split-span listening experiments at first glance seem akin to a slow form of torture. Psychologists get subjects to listen through head-phones to two different stories (or ads) simultaneously—one in the left ear and one in the right ear. (Experimental psychologists use stories as the stimulus while marketing psychologists might use radio ads.)

The subjects are tested immediately afterwards for what they remember. Not surprisingly, they recall only part of what they have heard and there is often a lot of confusion between what they heard in the right ear and what they heard in the left ear. Compared to subjects who are exposed to only one ad at a time, these people recall substantially less and their recollections are more confused. That is, the competition between simultaneous stimuli reduces the degree of recall.

This is not surprising. It is why many of us didn't do as well as we could have at school. And it's why television ads also have to be intrusive and interesting—to cut through and hold our attention, especially for low-involvement product categories.

Choosing what we attend to: Selective processing

We can choose what to attend to and process deeply. The more interesting the stimulus the more we are likely to pay attention to it and the more of it we recall—in other words, the more impact it has.

What happens if the experimenter asks subjects to listen to the messages in both ears while 'shadowing' (repeating aloud) what they hear in one ear? In this way the experimenter can get the subject to direct even more attention to (process more deeply) the message coming into one ear. What happens when the experimenter tests for recall? It is no surprise that for the shadowed ear the degree of recall is very high. This illustrates that the greater the attention and the deeper the processing, the greater the recall will be.

But when the experimenter tests for recall of the message heard in the unshadowed ear, the result is zero. The subjects remember nothing—indeed, it is almost as if they have not been exposed to the other ad at all. (Poor recall of radio advertising is reflective of this phenomenon.) But if the subjects can't recall this message, does it mean it had no effect on them? Not necessarily.

The fact that some, albeit minimal, processing can occur at a very low level of consciousness is revealed by a further refinement of the split-span experiment. In this version, the experimenter interrupts the subject while he is shadowing the ad in one ear and asks what he heard in the last second or two in the unattended ear? Lo and behold, the subject recalls the previous 1–2 seconds of the unshadowed message. Perfectly! This is amazing, is it not? Especially since we know from the previous experiment that 30 seconds after the experiment the subject will remember nothing of that ad.

Thus the ad, even though it may not be recalled after the event, may nevertheless be processed, albeit at some very low level of attention.

Choosing what not to attend to: Shallow processing

The problem is that the unattended message is not processed deeply enough. Its content is not retrievable after more than a few seconds unless we are induced to process it further by having our attention directed to it or by repetition.

It seems that a minimum level of attention is necessary for conscious awareness and recall to be retained. The more stimuli one is exposed to the less attention is left for processing other stimuli. Advertising which receives only shallow processing, far from being frighteningly powerful, is actually likely to be very inefficient, and almost certainly has less impact than advertising which is processed at a more conscious level.

This is not to say that such advertising has no effect—just that its effects seem to be marginal, and the shallower our processing of the ad, the weaker these effects are likely to be. What are these effects?

There is some evidence that shallowly processed or so-called subliminal advertising can cue a primary drive (e.g. remind us that we are hungry or thirsty). This is no different to ordinary advertising. Even at a low level of conscious processing we can be reminded that we are hungry or thirsty. The implication of it is that a theatre owner may be able to increase drink or food sales, but cannot direct the extra demand toward specific items such as Coke or popcorn—unless these items are the only things immediately available.

A well-known producer of freshly baked biscuits is said to harness this phenomenon by pumping out baking smells from its stores in shopping centres.[8] Anyone who has ever walked past a hot-bread shop knows that an aroma can tweak our senses. There is nothing subliminal about it. It would thus seem much more sensible for a theatre owner to use popcorn smells, or regular advertising, to remind people that they are hungry than to rely on less efficient stimuli such as so called subliminal messages flashed on the screen.

Shallow processing: Effects on behaviour and brand image

What about the impact of shallowly processed advertising on brand image, brand salience and brand choice? Can it produce small brand image shifts, or increase brand salience and thereby affect choice when everything else is equal?

The scientific evidence is mixed at this stage. One experiment seemed to show it could,[9] but another which attempted to replicate this result, failed to find the same effect.[10] The problem seems to be that in the experiments, subjects are exposed to only one or two repetitions of an ad. In the real world, the effect of one or two exposures may be too small to observe or even measure.

Tracking many advertising campaigns continuously over weeks, months and sometimes years gives a better picture. The influence of low-involvement messages on the image and salience of particular brands seems to me to be much the same as, but less efficient than, advertising that is attended to more closely and processed more deeply. Over time, advertising appears to be able to produce small but cumulative image shifts and salience increments. Often, the advertising needs to be continued to maintain these effects. When it stops, the gains are eroded.

These small changes are like the 'feathers' we talked about in Chapter 1. With repetition, they can eventually tip the balance—assuming everything else is equal.

When everything else is equal is when advertising is most effective

There is no evidence that low-involvement messages can directly influence or manipulate our conscious choices by overriding consciously received input or reasoning.

Whether it is processed at a shallow or a deep level, however, advertising of a particular product or brand is likely to have greatest impact when the alternatives weigh in equally and we don't care too much about the outcome. So its influence is in situations where we don't care much anyway. Or, in situations where we do care and it helps remind us of a favourable alternative or a nice thing to do that we might not have thought about otherwise when it puts a favourable alternative on the agenda.

As the story of subliminal advertising shows, we need to be very careful that we don't jump to the wrong conclusion in evaluating advertising's effects.

Summary

Subliminal advertising, which began as a hoax in the 1950s became enshrined in myth. Legislators, in reacting so quickly to ban it, lent a kind of legitimacy to beliefs about its power.

Human beings can learn without full conscious awareness, but there are real limitations to this. We only have a certain amount of mental processing capacity at any one time. Therefore some stimuli receive only shallow mental processing. Others receive deep processing. So conscious awareness is a dimension, not a dichotomy. It is a matter of degree.

The more attention we pay to a message, and the more consciously we process it, the more aware we are of it and the easier it is for us to recall it later. Advertising which receives shallow processing, far from being frighteningly powerful, is likely to be very inefficient and is almost certainly weaker than advertising which engages us at a more conscious level.

4 Conformity: The popular thing to do

'In our society a celebrity is a person who is famous for being well known.'[1] The same is true of brands. And companies!

Seeing things as others see them

As we have discussed, there are a number of different ways of seeing the same thing. What we perceive as 'reality' is very much influenced by how other people see it—the popular consensus. In making choices people are influenced by two things:

• what they think, and
• what they think other people think.

Let me illustrate this with an experiment (see Figures 4.1 and 4.2). Look at Card 1. Imagine that the line on it is a brand. Call it Brand A. Brands have images and this one is no exception. I am going to ask you to compare this brand with others. The 'image characteristic' I want you to judge it on is its length.

Its competitors are on Card 2. Which is most similar to Brand A? Brand B? Brand C? Or Brand D? Before reading any further, look at the card. Which one is closest in length to Brand A? Brand B is the correct answer—of course. It's so obvious that nobody is likely to give any other answer, right? Wrong!

What happens if I get several people together in the same room. Unbeknown to my subject, all of them except him are stooges who are going to say what I have told them to say—that Brand C is the same length as Brand A. Imagine yourself as the subject. Everyone who answers before you has given what you believe is the wrong answer. Now comes your turn. Imagine your dilemma. You break out in a sweat. Your senses are telling you that B is the right answer but all these other people seem so certain that C is correct.

Figure 4.1   Card 1

A

Figure 4.2   Card 2

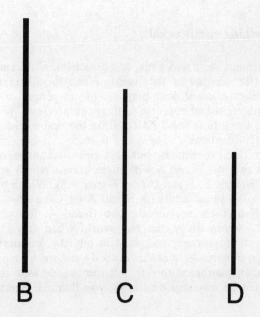

B   C   D

How can this be? you ask yourself. What is wrong with me? Or them? What do you say? Can you resist conforming to the consensus?

This is a classic psychological experiment first performed by Solomon Asch many years ago. He showed that 75 per cent of people in this situation go against their own perception and give the popular response.

The thought process behind this will be familiar to anyone who has ever attended a business meeting. When we see things differently from others, do we always back our own perception and go public? Or do we play safe and go along with the popular opinion? Very often we play safe. We conform. But how does the conformity so vividly illustrated in Asch's experiment operate outside the laboratory? Advertisers can't organise stooges or enforce conformity in everyday situations. So what relevance does this have for advertising?

To answer this, let's vary the experiment. We have demonstrated that when people make choice decisions, they do so on the basis of two types of information:

• objective evidence, and
• what they think other people think.

Popular opinion can influence not only compliance and conformity but indeed how we perceive reality.

When everything else is equal

In our experiment there was a real and noticeable difference between the brands (the lengths of the lines). When the difference is this obvious it takes a lot of peer pressure to get people to go against their own judgment and conform to the popular view. What happens if we reduce the differences? After all, in the real world, brands are often virtually identical.

We repeat the experiment, but this time, we have our subject compare the original Brand A with three brands which are closer to it in length: Brands E, F and G (see Figure 4.3). Which brand (line) on Card 3 is the same length as Brand A on Card 1?

In fact, all of them are identical to Brand A. But you have to choose, just as you do in the real world when faced with three identical brands (assuming you want to buy the product).

Imagine your surprise when everybody before you picks E (as they have been instructed to do). All the brands *look* the same to you. You must be missing something, you think. E looks about the

Figure 4.3   Card 3

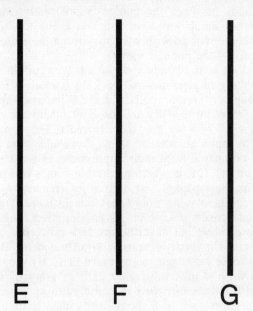

same length as A—but so do the other lines. How is everybody else
so sure the answer is E and not F or G or all of them?

In this situation people tend not only to conform by giving E as
the answer but also to doubt the evidence of their own senses. This
is the beginning of the belief in differences between brands.

It makes sense that in this situation the person will naturally have
less conviction about the conclusion coming from his/her own
senses. When there is less evidence to go on, or the evidence is
ambiguous, people are less sure of their perceptions. The less sure
they are, the more readily they will go along with other people's
'perceptions'. As the real differences between brands diminish,
people rely more and more on outside cues to help them make
judgments and decisions. This is when advertising seems to be most
effective. When everything else is equal, it takes only a 'feather' to
tip the balance and influence the choice.

The bandwagon effect: Indicators of the norm

Conformity—being with the in group, not being out of step—is a
powerful human motivator. It can make the crucial difference in

many brand choice decisions. When there is no real difference between brands or when the choice is not really important to a person, it takes much less than full consensus to influence their judgment. People will go with what they think the *majority* of other people perceive—the popular view.

This is known as the bandwagon effect. It occurs in situations as diverse as voting in elections and backing favourites in horseraces.

Canned laughter, opinion polls and the *Billboard* Top 100 are all indicators of the norm. They tell us how others are reacting and thereby influence how we are likely to react. They provide signals about what to laugh at, what to think about and what to listen to.

How else do people form their impressions of what is popular or what is the norm? This is where marketing comes into play. TV and radio stations, newspapers and magazines frequently claim to be Number One. There is no doubt that this influences where media buyers and advertisers place their advertising. Some other indicators are even more subtle but nevertheless very powerful.

Arizona State University researchers infiltrated the Billy Graham organisation some years ago and revealed that: 'By the time Graham arrives in town and makes his altar call, an army of six thousand wait with instructions on when to come forth at varying intervals to create the impression of a spontaneous mass outpouring.'[2]

In the US, bartenders often 'salt' their tip jars with a few dollar bills at the beginning of the evening. This gives customers the impression that tipping with paper money is the norm.[3]

On telethons, inordinate amounts of time are spent reading out names of people who have donated money. The message is clear: everybody else has donated—what are you doing?

As real differences between choices diminish, people rely more and more on outside cues to help them make decisions. One such cue is what other people are thought to be choosing. The beam balance effect, therefore, is another reason why product positioning works. When everything else is equal, conformity may be the feather that tips the balance.

Insecurity: A motivator for conformity

People seem to have a natural aversion to being seen to be out of step with others, or different from the norm. This often leads us to take the safe course. We try to anticipate what others would do and then do the same. This can spare us embarrassment and it can sometimes save us from thinking too hard.

Management in bureaucratic organisation is notoriously motivated by this. If a decision-maker does what everybody else would do, then if it turns out wrong, he or she won't be blamed. The personal risk is minimised. As the saying goes: 'Nobody ever got fired for buying an IBM.'

People conform most when they are insecure. Adolescence is a time of great insecurity and uncertainty. It is no surprise, then, that teenagers are highly conformist. While rebelling against the outmoded values of their parents, they are at the same time the ultimate slaves to conformity—within their own peer group. This characteristic determines and maintains success in the advertising of products such as jeans, soft drinks, T-shirts, sporting footwear, records and radio stations.

Perceived popularity

How popular a brand is thought to be, or how familiar a company is thought to be, is an important dimension of image.

Popularity is a magnet. It attracts. And advertising can enhance its power to attract. Try to think of a single product of which the most popular brand is not advertised. I can't. Does this mean, though, that advertising causes popularity? Not exactly. Advertising makes the brand *appear* popular. It influences its *perceived* popularity. The more a brand is advertised, the more popular and familiar it is perceived to be.

Advertising usually delivers specific messages that associate the company or brand with an image dimension or target attribute, such as 'reliability', 'environment-consciousness', 'value for money', 'good taste', 'ease of use'. Sometimes the attribute is 'popularity'. The advertiser may explicitly tell us that the brand in question is popular (e.g. 'Australia's number one margarine—Meadow Lea').

The interesting thing about communicating popularity, however, is that the advertiser doesn't necessarily have to do so in so many words. We as consumers somehow infer that a product is popular simply because it is advertised.

A supportive study

Some years ago I conducted a study in which people were asked which brand in various product categories they thought was the most popular.[4] Irrespective of which brand they named, they were then asked why they thought it was the most popular. Thirty-six per cent of the responses took the form 'It must be popular . . . because it is advertised so much.' (Others included . . . because it has so much shelf space in the supermarket'.) This was compelling evidence that presence, and especially a sustained advertising presence, translates into an image of popularity. It leaves a perception of popularity in our minds.

Advertising 'side-effect'

Unlike other image dimensions (such as reliability, taste, price etc) this perception of popularity is largely independent of the specific advertising message. In other words, it is a 'side-effect'.

The graph shows a brand which positioned itself largely on the attributes of taste and suitability. Note, however, the effect of advertising on people's perceptions of its popularity. The mere fact of its being advertised significantly increased the proportion of people who associated it with the attribute 'everybody seems to be drinking it'.

So, whether advertising is designed to communicate the image of taste, style, reliability or whatever, it is also likely to increase the perceived popularity of the product advertised. This is a 'side-effect' of the advertisement.

Agenda-setting

The mechanism behind this side-effect is one we have already met. It is 'agenda-setting'. The amount of media weight that an issue gets in newspapers, on TV, etc indicates to people the degree of importance that the issue should have in their thinking. It sets their mental agenda. In marketing, the agenda that is set is not made up of political issues, but of the brands that are thought to be popular. For 'popular', read 'important'. Our agenda-setting mechanism is not necessarily logical or rational. After all, is a brand advertised because it is important? Or is it important because it is advertised? There is a circularity here which is difficult for logic and rationality to come to grips with. But logic and rationality do not reign here.

Is perceived popularity a plus?

If a brand *seems* to be popular, are people more likely to buy it? Yes.

Advertising and media weight affect the perceived popularity image of a brand. They affect people's feelings of familiarity with the brand as well as their perceptions of the popularity of the brand. And that, in turn can affect their buying of the brand.

Figure 4.4 Image of increasing popularity—everybody seems to be drinking it

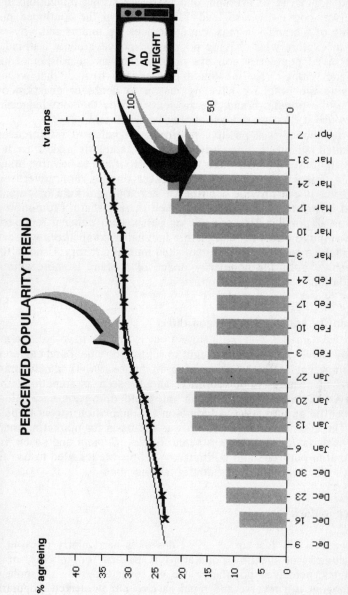

PERCEIVED POPULARITY TREND

TV AD WEIGHT

tv tarps

% agreeing

Note: The mere fact of something being advertised can increase its perceived popularity.
Source: MarketMind® Continuous Tracking. Sutherland Smith Research.

There is clear evidence that advertising can impact on the perceived popularity of a brand, and there are strong indications that perceived popularity also lends 'legitimacy' to the continued purchasing of a brand—in most circumstances. To understand why, we need to explore what 'having popularity' conveys about a brand.

Perceived popularity conveys notions such as 'a million people can't be wrong'; that the brand is tried and trusted; that we are choosing the best. We have no reason to doubt or question our choice of a popular brand. We are reassured by the knowledge that others use it, that we are swimming with the tide.

So popularity is a positive reinforcer. It helps to reinforce our continued, unquestioning, buying of the brand. It makes us less likely to question ourselves as to why we continue to buy that brand. It is a feather on the scales of repeat buying. For advertisers, therefore, it can provide a basis for developing a kind of defence shield, to try to protect the established market share. Promotion of a brand as popular does not rely on persuasion; rather it represents a pre-emptive effort to fend off the inevitable competitors who will try to take over the brand's established mental territory. Used in this 'defensive' role, the popularity image of a brand is more akin to inoculation than to persuasion.

Popularity and the bandwagon effect

As we have seen, people tend to climb on the bandwagon of anything that seems to be gaining in popularity. If a new brand begins to acquire 'high visibility' and be seen as something that 'everyone is talking about' or that 'more and more people are using', this can be an attraction, a 'come-on', a temptation for us to try it too. The creation of high visibility is the basis for marketing many fads such as *Teenage Mutant Ninja Turtles*, *Batman* and so on, not to mention pop stars and politicians.[5] People are tempted to try 'the latest'—the one that everybody is talking about.

Overpopularity

The expression 'fast up . . . fast down' is particularly relevant in this context of creating popularity. If pushed too quickly, or to extremes, perceived popularity can go 'over the top'. The pole of the magnet can reverse and repel us rather than attract us. Advertisers have to guard against creating overpopularity, which can suddenly become a liability for their brand.

This is more often a danger when perceived popularity is used in an offensive role, to get us to try a brand initially, than when it is used defensively, as simply a reinforcer reminding us to buy the brand again. It is no accident that this type of marketing is often associated with products with short lifespans such as movies, children's toys . . . and, perhaps, politicians. As the saying goes, 'One day a rooster, the next a feather duster.'

Using high visibility to persuade us to try a brand is very different from using it to maintain the brand's position. High visibility can help persuade us to try a brand but the success of this strategy risks being very short-lived. For the brand, it may well be a case of 'fast up, fast down'.

Why popularity can become a turn-off

Perceived popularity is not always positive. When too many people use a brand, it risks becoming perceived as common. It is not just a case of familiarity breeds contempt. Overpopularity can degrade the currency.

Peter De Vries, an American novelist, once said in another context: 'Everyone hates me because I am so universally liked'. Astute advertisers have learnt to guard against this type of reversal. They know that simply giving a brand as much 'hype' as possible in as short a time as possible is not necessarily a good idea. Instead, they try to manage the perceived popularity of the brand as part of a long-term process of image development and ensure that they consolidate a lasting market share.

The case of Ben Ean

In the early 1970s Ben Ean became the most popular brand of wine in Australia. At the same time it became less and less acceptable for taking to other people's places or serving to guests. Why? Since everybody was drinking it, it was seen as commonplace. Ben Ean was *too* successful.

For me, to take a bottle of Ben Ean to a dinner party today would be unthinkable. It would signal that I am a cheapskate, that I have no taste. But these are not the main reasons. More important is what Ben Ean would signal about how I regard my host and the occasion.

Gifts and special occasions

We mark special occasions by the use of things out of the ordinary:

a very old bottle of red, hiring a limousine, eating out at a restaurant. Such symbols mark the specialness of the occasion. Similarly, when we want to express our care and esteem for others, we give or do something special.

Positioning a brand or product as suitable for gift-giving or special occasions can be a very successful strategy. If it gets too successful however, its success has within it the seeds of its own destruction. Overpopularity can 'devalue the currency'.

Price, exclusivity and popularity

Unless a brand's image is kept up through high price or other image-lifting devices (as with Mercedes-Benz, Pierre Cardin, Reebok), it risks degradation from too much popularity.

Grange Hermitage wine also became 'popular' but in a very different sense from Ben Ean. Grange remains most acceptable, but not very affordable—and this is the point. Grange, like Mercedes and to a lesser extent Pierre Cardin, uses price to try to protect it from the commonness that would otherwise go with great popularity. Its high price confers a degree of exclusivity, which in effect makes the well-known brand an aspirational symbol. Exclusivity offsets the turn-off risk—the risk of the brand's being seen as common.

Advertising examples

Many advertising themes have tapped into the desire to conform. These include:

- 'Meadow Lea—Australia's No. 1.'
- 'Nashua—number one in photocopiers.'
- 'Fosters. Famous in Australia. Famous around the world.'
- 'Why go with the number two when you can go with the number one in rental cars?'

These are some of the more obvious examples. Others are more subtle. For example:

- 'Everybody's jiggling. Lipton's jiggling.'
- Peters ice-cream, 'The health food of a nation.'
- 'Going Ford is the going thing.'
- 'I'm as Australian as Ampol.'

Summary

As some wit once said, 'Conformity is something you can practise without making a spectacle of yourself.' In making choices we are influenced by two things:

• what we think, and
• what we think other people think.

Conformity is a powerful human motivator. Especially when everything else is equal, it can tip the balance in many brand choice decisions. We are more likely to go against our judgment and conform to the popular view if there are few real differences between brands. As the real differences become negligible, we rely more and more on outside cues to help us make our decisions. The more insecure we feel, the more likely we are to be influenced by others.

The more a brand is advertised the more popular and familiar it is perceived to be. Popularity is like a magnet. Advertising can enhance its power to attract. We as consumers somehow infer that something is popular simply because it is advertised. If pushed too quickly or to extremes, perceived popularity can go 'over the top'. The pole of the magnet can reverse and repel rather than attract us. Overpopularity tends to 'devalue the currency'.

5 The advertising message: 'You ain't got the message, Sol. Oils ain't oils and ads ain't ads'

Heard in a typical boardroom: Are we getting our message across? What message are buyers taking out of our ad? These are questions which advertisers traditionally ask of advertising agencies. They are based on the assumption that advertising is meant to be informational. But advertising has moved a long way from simply imparting information.

Advertisers frequently rely heavily on 'message take-out'. Usually consumers are asked something like: 'What was the ad trying to say to you?' or 'What was the message that the advertiser intended?' This process can provide valuable feedback to advertisers and quickly tell them if their commercial is communicating what they want it to communicate; if the commercial is an informational one, that is. But entertainment commercials, including image, musical or drama commercials, are very different from lecture-style commercials.

As TV viewers, we mentally process 'image' ads such as those for Pepsi, Reebok, beer or perfume quite differently from informational ads, such as those announcing this week's special at Coles or Joe Bloggs's 50th birthday sale. Indeed, it is difficult with many ads (image ads especially) to work out what message they intend to convey.

Advertisers themselves find these ads the most difficult to evaluate, largely because there is little point in asking people what message they get from them. The message in image commercials is often a 'Clayton's type' message—the message you get when you're not getting a message. Or, more accurately, when you're not aware of getting a message.

If you think of the current advertising for various image-advertised brands, you may find that the ad or the message, or both, is difficult to recall. What is missing from some of these ads is the sense that someone is trying to tell you something. This does not mean that they are ineffective—just that they do not work by way of clearly elaborated messages.

There is a very real difference between advertising that has a clear, spoken, unambiguous message and advertising that is more akin to drama or entertainment. We mentally process different types of ads in very different ways.

What is a message?

In the latter type of advertising, we are not being lectured to. We are experiencing life or being entertained—but in the process, information gets in. If someone tells me: 'Mike Tyson is tough,' that is a message. But what if, instead of telling me that Mike Tyson is tough, you show me a video clip of Mike Tyson beating the hell out of someone? Answer: I get the same message! Yet if you asked me 'What was that clip trying to communicate to you?', I would probably think the question odd. It is not obvious that the film clip is trying to communicate anything to me. Even so, after seeing it I would definitely be inclined to agree with the statement, 'Mike Tyson is tough.'

In other words I get the same message. But it doesn't seem like a message: it's a Claytons message (the message you're getting when you're not getting a message). The impression, that Mike Tyson is tough, is communicated just the same.

While advertisers frequently use 'message take-out' or message playback as a measure of an ad's success, it is not necessary that viewers be able to parrot back the message for an ad to be working. Communication of impressions can be just as effective as communication of facts.

Window on the mind

Let me ask you a question: How many windows are there in your home? Answer before you read on.

Now think about the mental process you went through to retrieve this information. Did you visualise each room in turn and add up all the windows? If so, you are now more aware of a way in which our minds arrive at information other than by simple memory retrieval: by re-processing other information that we have mentally filed away.

The stored information may be verbal or visual. We put these previously unconnected bits and pieces together in our minds and arrive at something new. Sometimes the 'something new' is another piece of information (like the number of windows there are in your home). At other times however, it may be a new attitude or a new feeling about something.

We as consumers often construct our attitudes to brands out of stored information in this way. The attributes or images that have become associated with the brand may have lodged in memory without ever having been part of a verbal message. They may have originated in visual images from advertising or experiential learning or input from other people. It is therefore a mistake to think about advertising communication solely in terms of conscious message take-out.

Ask yourself who you think is the typical user of Pepsi, of St Laurent products or of Volvo cars? While you don't have a complete answer, you are not without impressions either. For example, do you think the typical owner of a Volvo would be more or less conservative than the owner of a Holden? More or less affluent? Most people would agree that the Volvo owner is likely to be more conservative and more affluent than the Holden owner. Yet they have not acquired those pieces of information through any direct message.

Advertising for many product categories, such as soft drink, beer, confectionery, perfume, is dominated by ads that appear to have very little message. Image ads convey associations and are totally different from informational ads that communicate 'news' (such as one that communicates the existence of a new product or one that announces what's on special this week at Coles supermarkets). Images are like the number of windows. Associations are like individual windows. The number of windows in your home is not a piece of information that someone has communicated to you in a message. It is not directly stored in your memory. But you have the bits and pieces to generate it, nevertheless. In this way we can learn things or know things without being much aware of the process or the result. There is nothing necessarily manipulative or devious about this. It happens all the time. It is part of life.

Learning without awareness

What is missing from some communications is the sense of someone trying to tell us something or trying to communicate a message. As we saw earlier this does not mean that they are ineffective—it is just that the learning is not by way of someone clearly elaborating messages.

Some psychologists have labelled this type of indirect learning

'learning without involvement'.[1] Others have called it incidental learning or 'learning without awareness'.[2] Strictly speaking this latter is inaccurate. It is not that people are unaware but rather that the 'focus of processing' is on something else in the communication. Our attention is focused on something other than the message *per se*.

In the TV series *Sesame Street*, messages were embedded in entertainment. Messages such as 'cooperation' and 'sharing' were communicated by drama and song. Learning the alphabet or learning to count is not a chore for *Sesame Street* viewers, but an experience. These skills are effectively conveyed in an entertaining kaleidoscope of sounds and visuals.

We can learn skills, information, image associations or almost anything by this incidental learning—provided it is not inconsistent with what we already know or believe. (Just as a person under hypnosis will not accept a directive that conflicts with their own values, so too do our minds reject things which are inconsistent with our existing belief structures.[3] Communications that violate this principle risk being ineffective because they tend to invite rejection.)

We have thus discovered yet another reason why people find it hard to analyse introspectively effects advertising has on them. Sometimes advertisements do not obviously impart information to us. (While this can be true of any type of commercial, it is more especially true of ads based on image, emotion or drama.) The important point is that there is a lessened sense of someone trans-mitting information—indeed if there is any sense of it at all. Such ads may communicate mood more than message; feelings rather than words.

When psychologists study the effects of this type of incidental learning, they compare people's learning of the same material or skills in two situations: with and without intent to recall. They have concluded that incidental learning does not differ qualitatively from intentional learning. The difference is quantitative, i.e. in the amount that is retained under different conditions.[4]

Memory and association

As we saw earlier in the chapter, the number of windows in your home was not a message or a piece of information that someone has communicated to you. It was not directly stored as a piece of information in your memory. But you had the bits and pieces to generate it, nevertheless. Once again: how many windows are there in your home? That was quick! You didn't have to think about it this time: you already had the answer, because it is now stored in its own 'slot' in your memory in a more readily accessible form. Having put the component bits and pieces together, you can now access that piece of information much more quickly and efficiently at any time you want it by accessing it directly. You don't have to go through the process.

Just like a commercial, this chapter firstly helped evoke in you the necessary images or pieces of information to let you go through the process of arriving at that summary piece of information. Having arrived at it, you stored it yourself as a new piece of information in a memory slot of its own.

In the consumer world, what gets stored in memory slots like this is not just information. It may be an attitude, a judgment, a position or a conclusion. But once formed and stored, these things are more readily accessible and hence more available to influence future buying decisions—especially those types of decisions that tend to be made 'on the fly'.[5]

The all-important effect of a relatively subtle ad may rest on its ability to build the right visual or mood associations for a brand and lock them into memory; to put those associations on the brand's attribute agenda. Rather than communicating directly by a specific verbal message, the ad may be communicating indirectly, by associational imagery.

It is worth repeating that strictly speaking, this is not learning without awareness. It is not that people are unaware but rather that the 'focus of processing' is on something else in the communication rather than the 'message'.

Learning by association

I visit a city for the first time and go to a scenic lookout. What an experience! What a view! What is the view trying to tell me? What sort of a silly question is that? It is not *trying* to communicate anything. Views, just like some commercials, come across as an experience rather than an articulated message.

Nevertheless, after several visits to the lookout I may come to permanently associate the city with this wonderful visual experience. This splendid view is now higher up on the agenda of attributes that I associate with the city. The process is not necessarily logical but it is real and natural, nevertheless. An image can be built without any specific message.

In a sense it could be said that I have learnt much the same information as if I had simply been told 'x is a beautiful city'. In that case I would have received a clear verbal message. However, two things are different:

- I have learnt the information experientially instead of verbally. And this means that I probably have a much richer or deeper sense of it.
- I have learnt the information 'without awareness' i.e. without awareness of being taught something. There is no sense of any intended message.

This is not new. Years ago, the psychologist Charles Osgood demonstrated that when a given adjective is repeatedly paired with a given noun, the 'meaning' of the noun, as measured by a scale called 'the semantic differential', undergoes change—in the direction of the adjective.[6] For example, when the noun 'snake' is repetitively paired with the adjective 'slimy', we begin to think of snakes as slimy creatures (even though they aren't). Little is made of such findings today but the phenomenon seems to underlie much of the process by which image advertising works.

Image advertising's effects

To 'play back' the message from an ad we need to be able to articulate our experience—to describe what we see as the message. As an index of an ad's effectiveness, this playback (or 'message take-out') is more appropriate for ads that are designed to communicate 'news' about a brand.

For the more subtle types of ads our inability to play back much in the way of a message does not in itself, mean that the ad is not working. How then, you may ask, does anyone detect these more subtle effects? How do advertisers know that any such effects are happening? How can the invisible be made visible?

The answer is, by inference—by looking at how the ad has influenced our image of, attitude to or behaviour regarding the brand. We would be unable to see an invisible man but if he put on visible clothes we would know he was there. In the same way we cannot observe these invisible advertising effects directly but we can infer their existence by observing other things, such as:

- Changes in brand image dimensions, as measured by questions such as 'Which brand do you most associate with . . .? (safety/best taste/most popular, etc)'
- Changes in brand attitudes, as measured by questions such as 'How do you feel about brand x overall?' 'How much do you like it?'
- Changes in behaviour, as measured by changes in sales and market share.

With image commercials, the invisible can be made visible by measuring the degree of association with image attributes; the degree to which the image feature appears in the brand's attribute agenda and how high up it is on that agenda. These measurements are often taken indirectly and calibrated in the form of belief statements about the brand (e.g. 'liked by everyone', 'best quality' etc).

A fairly typical image-building strategy is to make an ad (like those for Coke, Fosters etc) that features the brand in a range of enjoyable situations. Blend in a musical sound track with appropriate lyrics and then serve with generous quantities of exposure. Again the important point to note about this type of advertising is that there is a lessened sense of someone transmitting information—indeed if there is any sense of it at all.

Communication by association

In 1990 a new brand was launched into a frequently purchased snack-food category. The TV ad was musically based with a very catchy jingle. The words made musical reference to the glowing attributes of the new brand. Message take-out was measured by asking a random sample of people what the message was. They responded with the attributes that were verbalised in the jingle. These were: 'better/best brand' and 'this brand is good for you'.

A subsidiary objective of the ad was to have the brand seen as 'modern and up-to-date' and 'a brand of today'. This was not expressed in words but was to be inferred from other pieces of information as well as the ad's tone, pace and fast-cut visuals. There was very little playback of this attribute. While some people said the ad was trying to communicate newness, almost no one mentioned 'modern', 'up-to-date' or 'a brand of today'.

However, as Figure 5.1 shows, a growing number of people were positioning the brand in their minds in association with this attribute. When they were asked: 'Which brand or brands do you most associate with the description "a modern, up-to-date brand"?', the associative linkages created by the ad became visible. The effect was more evident the longer the ad continued to be aired.[7]

The increased association of the brand with this attribute was also linked with a significant improvement in overall attitude towards the brand and, to a lesser extent, increases in market share.

Any advertiser who relied only on conscious message take-out as a measure of this ad's effectiveness would be severely misled. People could articulate that the ad was trying to communicate 'better/best brand' and 'good for you'—the message of the jingle—

Figure 5.1 Image effects revealed—snack food product

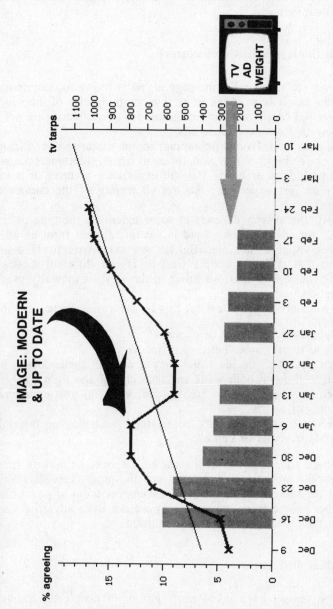

IMAGE: MODERN
& UP TO DATE

TV
AD
WEIGHT

Note: Even though 'modern and up-to-date' was not part of the audio message that people 'took out', the association with this attribute is clearly affected by the advertising.

Source: MarketMind® Continuous Tracking. Sutherland Smith Research.

but the 'modern and up-to-date' message was a Clayton's message. Yet it was in no way hidden. It was simply communicated visually rather than verbally.

Do you think in words or pictures?

When we are asked what message an ad is trying to communicate to us, the result is an index more than anything else of the success of the verbal communication in the ad. However, words are not the only way that we experience ads.

What does a television commercial communicate to you? Pictures, words or feelings? When you listen to a radio commercial, what goes on inside your head? Do you experience pictures or words? Or do you just experience the overall *feeling* of the commercial message?

Clearly, the answer depends to some extent on the type of commercial. An ad for Dunk Island is vastly different from an ad for this week's specials at Coles. But we now know from psychological research that different people tend to favour different modes of thinking. In other words, we differ in the way we mentally process information.[8]

You can start to get a feel for this by answering these questions:

- Do you think in words or pictures?
- Do you recall names better than faces?
- When you can't decide which way a word is spelt, does it help to write it down both ways and then choose the right one?
- When you hear a radio commercial, what do you experience? Pictures or words?
- When you remember a TV commercial, what do you remember first? Is it visual or verbal?

Compare your answers with those of a spouse or a close friend. Most people are surprised to learn that the other person's answers are not the same as their own. We assume, without any real basis, that other people think the same way we do. Even advertisers tend to base their strategies on this assumption.

Individual differences

Over the years I have asked many groups of people the question: 'Do you think in pictures or words?' About a third say unequivocally that they think in pictures. Usually somewhat less than a third say unhesitatingly that they think in words. And the rest say either that they think both ways, or that they can't answer the question.

The proportions vary from group to group but the really interesting thing is the reaction of the 'word thinkers' to the 'picture thinkers' and vice versa. The strict 'picture thinkers' becomes positively astounded with those who say they think in words and not pictures. 'How can you think in words?' they ask disbelievingly. 'How can you possibly think in pictures?' some of the 'word thinkers' throw back at them, not so much as a retort but in equal puzzlement and disbelief.

So even in an informal research exercise like this, it becomes readily apparent that people are not in agreement on the way in which their basic mental processes work. There are very definitely those who believe they are primarily visualisers (picture thinkers) and those who believe they are primarily verbalisers (word thinkers).

The significance of whether we think in words or in pictures comes when we retrieve the commercial or its message from memory—say at the point of sale when we recall that we have seen a commercial for the brand. Do we hear the ad in our mind? Do we see in words what it said? Or do we retrieve the visual images or impressions that are associated with it?

The cues that advertisers use at the point of sale, such as pack design, shelf talkers, slogans and so on, are designed to remind us of the verbal messages or to retrigger the visual associations that have been communicated by the ad.[9]

Summary

What is missing from some ads is the sense of someone trying to tell you something or communicate a message. This does not mean that such ads are ineffective—just that they do not work by way of clearly elaborated messages.

We mentally process image ads and visual experiences quite differently from informational ads or messages. We can learn or know things without being much aware of the process or the result. There is nothing necessarily manipulative or devious about this. It happens all the time. It is not that we are unaware of this in any subliminal sense but rather that our 'focus of processing' is often on something else in the communication rather than a verbal 'message' *per se*. We can learn skills, information, image associations or almost anything by this incidental learning—provided it is not inconsistent with what we already know or believe.

This is yet another reason why we find it hard to analyse the effects advertising has on us. As consumers we use the many bits and pieces which we receive from advertising, experiential learning or other people. They are put together as information, attitudes, judgments, positions or conclusions. Once stored in their own memory slots, these are more readily accessible to us and more available to influence other related decision-making. They have the potential to influence our future buying decisions—especially those that tend to be made 'on the fly'.

Think you've got the message now, Sol?

6 Silent symbols and badges of identity

The logo of the South Sydney or Carlton football team is a brand symbol, the wearing of which makes a statement about one's association and identification with that team. In the same way, the act of consuming a soft drink such as Pepsi can be transformed from the simple quenching of thirst to an expression of self identity. Football supporters don't wear scarves just to keep them warm. And teenagers don't drink Pepsi just to quench their thirst.

We have become accustomed to teenage idols such as Prince, Michael Jackson, Michael J. Fox, Kylie Minogue and John Farnham being used to endorse Pepsi and Coke. When a brand is seen being consumed by these people, it becomes more than a brand—it becomes a symbol of association with an 'in group'.

By consuming and displaying brand symbols which are associated with these entities or otherwise showing that we value them we:

- reinforce in our minds our identification and closeness with the person or group they stand for
- make an expression of our own identity—a subtle statement or symbol to the outside world about ourselves.

So the act of consuming a brand can become a way for us to express our identity—who we are, what we are like, what are our concerns, what we enjoy doing, what we value, who our friends are and so on. Above all it becomes a way of sharing, of participating, of representing or identifying with something greater than oneself.

There is something about being part of a club. 'Join the club . . . join the club . . . join the Escort club,' the ad used to go.

Expression and self-presentation

One can identify privately with someone or something without needing to tell anybody else. In this sense identification can be a very private thing.

The other side of it however is that very often we want to signal our feeling of identification—who we are and what we stand for—to the outside world. We do this non verbally in our self-presentation and self-expression. We use symbols, mannerisms, gestures, idioms, flags etc to communicate non verbally, messages to the outside world. We can do this by displaying symbols (wearing Reeboks or blue jeans and no shoes, or driving a Mercedes or a four-wheel drive), or using products that are symbolically associated with our favourite entities.

In the US, more students wear their college T shirts on the Monday following a football game when the college team wins (especially after a big victory) than when it loses.[1] The motivation is not simply the desire to bask in reflected glory. It is related to the reasons people wear branded jeans (e.g. Lee, Levi's, Fabergé), designer clothes (Pierre Cardin, St Laurent, Lacoste) and branded sportswear (Esprit, Nike). The broader, underlying motivation is one of personal identity and participation in (or association with) a larger, symbolic group.

Identification and conformity

As a motivator, identification is to be distinguished from conformity. Conformity is the need to avoid standing out from the crowd. It is partly based on the fear of being different; the need to go along with the ideas or choices of others for fear of the consequences that might happen otherwise.

Identification is a very different flip side to this. It is very similar to, but at the same time very different from conformity. Most humans enjoy feeling part of something greater than themselves; their family, their school, their nation, their church, their football team etc. This is more than just trying to avoid being different. It is a positive desire to be like something; to be part of it; to find identification with it. It is a desire for the secure feeling of knowing we are not isolated—that we are not alone. There is a warm feeling in sharing common values, common symbols, common ideas with others.

In valuing with others the same things others do, we reinforce to ourselves and make a statement to others about the degree to which we value our identity as part of 'the group'. Teenagers, for example, find a great deal of camaraderie in worshipping the same pop idols and movie stars as their friends.

Such identification and bonding becomes even stronger when we share the same emotions or experiences with others. The more powerful the common emotions or experiences, the greater the feeling of mutual closeness. As teenagers most of us share feelings of insecurity, of not knowing where we are going, and this brings us closer to those of our own age.

Pratkanis and Aronson adopted the term 'granfalloons', originally coined by American novelist Kurt Vonnegut, to refer to the entities we identify with.[2]

Granfalloons

Some granfalloons we are born into. The most important of these is our family. Most of us identify with our family and express this in our buying behaviour at Christmas, Mother's Day and so on.

Other granfalloons we choose to identify with. Our choice here, however, is frequently influenced, if not determined, by the groups we already identify with. Many of us passionately support what we call 'our football team', but this often turns out to be the same team our family supported. Thus, identifying with one granfalloon such as our family can lead us to identify with other related granfalloons such as a particular football team. The reason we consume certain products or display certain brand symbols (such as sweaters in the team's colours) can often be traced back through a chain of associations to the people and entities we identify with.

The stronger this feeling of identification, the more we defend the group and display its symbols. The more the granfalloon is attacked by outsiders, the stronger the feeling of comradeship within it. (This is why the promotion of nationalism and even war, is sometimes used by politicians. It functions as a very powerful, cohesive mechanism.)

Even when our assignment to a group is random, such as in schools which have inter-house sporting competitions, identification takes place. When complete strangers are formed into groups on the basis of something as trivial as the toss of a coin, this same thing happens.[3] Though our reasons for belonging are unclear or meaningless, we nevertheless identify with the group. Any brand or product that associates itself symbolically with our 'house'—our family, team, peer group or values—taps into this motivation.

This even happens with groups such as Amnesty International, in which most members never meet, and it also happens with individuals. We can be influenced in our own behaviour by observing what another person does or imagining what they would do in the same situation. We identify with them and model ourselves after them. The closer our identification, the more likely it is that our behaviour will be affected. In other words, the more similar we see the other person is to us the more likely this modelling or copying influence is to take place.

Children who are terrified of dogs can be greatly affected by watching another child play happily with a dog for twenty minutes a day. In one experiment, after only four days of observation, 67 per cent of previously phobic children were willing to climb into a playpen with a dog and stay there alone petting the dog.[4]

The for and against position

Football team supporters wear badges that say 'I support Hawthorn' or whichever team they identify with. They also wear badges that say 'I hate Collingwood'. This illustrates that one can find identity not only in being for something but in being against something else. Our identification with something can be expressed either way.

Teenagers show their identification with their peer group by looking and acting like them but also by denigrating the tastes and preferences of the 'out group'—their parents.

At its extremes this 'anti' motivation manifests itself in the form of jingoism and religious zealotry. In the super-strength, concentrated form it is a motivation sufficiently powerful for people to fight and die to preserve the integrity of the group and its values and symbols. Some people will even die in defence of the symbols alone (such as a country's flag).

At the opposite end of the scale the influence of this motivation is much more subtle and more difficult, though not impossible, to measure.

Reaction to symbols

We react to symbols. At a red light we react by stopping. At a green light we react by going. When we see a swastika we feel revulsion. The 'man' symbol on a public toilet affects half the population one way and the other half the other way.

Whether our reaction to a symbol is external (stop, go) or internal (revulsion) it is a learnt reaction. It is learnt by association of the symbol with other things. In this way a symbol gradually develops an ability to influence us in its own right and to evoke common reactions.

Meaning is an attachment

It is through a process that psychologists call 'discrimination learning' that a symbol or a brand acquires meaning. An odd thing about this is that once we have learned via this process we become relatively unconscious of it. It is like our ability to drive to work without ever being conscious of having braked or being conscious of the process of changing gears. It takes place without much conscious awareness.

For example, when you see the letter

q

you are hardly likely to say to yourself 'Hey, that's romantic'. Nor do you say to yourself: 'This is a symbol that I am meant to decode as representing the letter q.' Instead you simply experience the letter q. You have become unconscious of the mental process whereby meaning is attached to the symbol. The meaning is experienced not as something that *we* attach to the symbol. It is not experienced as us attaching meaning to it. The meaning is just there—in it.

A lesson in the origin of a kiss

Look at these symbols:

> <

What do they mean? Certainly there is nothing romantic about them. To us they mean 'greater than' and 'less than'. In primitive society, however, either one could be used to represent a bird's beak and, by extension, a mouth.[5]

If you bring these two symbols together what do you get? An 'X'. If the symbols are read as mouths, you also get two mouths together—a kiss. Hence the shorthand symbol for a kiss that we often use on greeting cards and letters is an X.

We all use this symbol and understand that it means a kiss. Yet most of us don't know why it does. (This is a vivid illustration of how the meaning of a word or symbol, once established, can become divorced from its origins and operate independently of any knowledge of them.)

Our ancestors, looking at this symbol, decoded it as signifying two beaks in contact and deduced that this was meant to convey a kiss. As time passed, however, the intermediate associations gradually disappeared and the symbol came to elicit its meaning more directly.

The origins of such symbols and their meaning are often buried under layers of antiquity. But once a symbol's meaning is learnt, it is no longer necessary for us to know its origin or how our reactions to it came about. Even though we are no longer conscious of how it was learnt, we all use it and we all react to it just the same.

So symbols are like adults. We usually react to them as they are. But in order to understand them more fully we need to know something about their childhood and how they developed into and became what they are today. This is important because once learned, we regard meaning as being in the symbol itself rather than an attachment process that takes place below the level of consciousness. Any sense of the mental process of attachment disappears.

To learn how brands are built into symbols we need to understand the way symbols acquire meaning and how we interpret that meaning. The real differences between brands such as Coke and Pepsi, or Kodak and Agfa, or Colgate and Cussons may be quite small, but when the focal beam of attention is played on these symbolic aspects of the brand the differences may be significant.

Discrimination learning

Let me illustrate how crucial small differences can be. What do the following symbols mean?

qp6bd9

To us they mean 'the letter q', the letter p', 'the number six' and so on.

When my daughter was about six years old she was learning numbers. She counted up eight toys. I gave her another one and asked her how many she had now. I asked her to write it down. She said 'nine' and wrote it like this:

p

This is not so uncommon when kids are learning to write. They sometimes get the symbol correct but write it back to front.

What happened next taught me a first-hand lesson about discrimination learning. I told her she was right but that the number nine was written this way:

9

She looked at it, puzzled. Her reply stunned me. She said: 'But Daddy, that's a q.'

After recovering my composure I explained: 'No darling, this is a q,' drawing a tail on her symbol and realising how small a difference it really was.

q

How subtle our learning of symbols and labels is! We take for granted the same basic symbol is a nine when its tail is bent to the left but when it is bent to the right we are expected to have an entirely different reaction—it transforms it into an entirely different symbol.

It was not until many years later that I discovered that this is the origin of the phrase 'mind your p's and q's'. Apprentice typesetters were urged to mind their p's and q's because of the similarity in the shape of the letters.[6] As adults we are so accomplished at making the distinction that we are too close to it. We are no longer conscious of how we come to instantly recognise:

qpbdq

as five quite different symbols.

Making brands into symbols

Brands are like letters. They can be transformed into symbols. They can become shorthand ways of communicating. They can be made to summon up or stand in for associations. In this way small differences can have big implications. They can become triggers for different mental associations.

Just as 'Anyhow*' cues us to think of Winfield and 'uh huh' cues us to think of Pepsi, so brand names can cue us to think of people and images that are closely associated with them. (Coke and Kylie Minogue, Carpet-call and Dennis Lillee, Garuda Airlines and Elle Macpherson, Samboy and Jeff Fenech, Pepsi and Ray Charles.)

Just as drinking beer can be to a teenager a powerful sign that he or she is now no longer a kid, so the consumption or wearing of other products can make powerful statements about us. The importance of the communication is as much to the user or wearer as it is to the outside world.

A brand can become a badge of identity in several different ways:

- By being a symbol of the group (e.g. Carlton or South Sydney badge)
- By being seen to be valued by members of the group (e.g. Coke is valued by pop idols)
- By being seen as supportive of the group (e.g. a sponsor such as Tooheys and the Sydney Swans, or CUB and the Carlton football team)
- By being seen as characteristically used or displayed by members of the group.

Summary

We react to symbols. Whether our reaction is external or internal it is a learnt reaction. It is learnt via association of the symbol with other things. In this way a symbol can influence us in its own right by evoking certain reactions. Symbols come to stand for other things in our mind and the act of consuming a brand can become a symbolic way for us to express our identification with the entities associated with it.

Our internal reaction to a symbol may be emotional or unemotional. Brands are initially unemotional marks; advertisers use advertising to try to transform these (trade) marks into symbols that summon up certain mental associations. When a symbol elicits a cognitive or emotional response in us, we in turn can use it to express that idea or emotion to others.

We can identify privately with another person or a group without needing to tell anybody else. But often we want to signal this feeling of identification to the world. We do this by displaying and consuming symbols (such as football team badges, old school ties, Levis, Reeboks, Mercedes etc), or using products that are symbolically associated with our favourite entities. Identification is the flip side of conformity. It is not just the avoidance of seeming to be different. It is a positive desire to be like something; to be part of it; to find identification with it.

The difference between brands in the same product category may be quite small, but when the focal beam of attention is played on these symbolic aspects, the difference can tip the balance. Consuming or displaying certain products can make powerful statements about us. The importance of the communication is as much to the user or wearer as it is to the outside world.

7   Vicarious experience and virtual reality

> The theatre is a form of hypnosis. So are movies and TV. When you
> enter a movie theatre you know that all you are going to see is
> twenty-four shadows per second flashed on a screen to give an
> illusion of moving people and objects. Yet despite this knowledge
> you laugh when the twenty-four shadows per second tell jokes, and
> cry when the shadows show actors faking death. You know that they
> are an illusion yet you enter the illusion and become a part of it
> and while the illusion is taking place you are not aware that it is an
> illusion. This is hypnosis. It is a trance.[1]

The latest computer technology, which has been developed partly
from video games, partly from cinema and partly from flight sim-
ulators, is 'virtual reality'. It is based on the concepts of illusion
and immersion. It creates the illusion of being immersed in an
artificial world.

Years ago Morton Heilig (the inventor of Sensorama), after he
had seen Cinerama and 3D, said: 'When you watch TV or a movie
in a theatre, you are sitting in one reality, and at the same time you
are looking at another reality through an imaginary transparent wall.
However when you enlarge that window enough you get a visceral
sense of personal involvement. You *feel* the experience and don't
just *see* it.'[2]

Anyone who has been in an Imax big-screen theatre will relate
to this. As Heilig put it: 'I felt as if I had stepped through that
window and was riding the roller-coaster myself instead of watching
somebody else. I felt vertigo.'

What has this got to do with advertising? Sometimes studying the
extremes of a phenomenon can provide insights into its milder forms
that would not otherwise be intuitively obvious. Ads that are mini-
dramas work by mildly immersing us in a story rather than talking
to us as viewers sitting out in front of the TV set.

Just as there are technological ways (like 3D, Cinerama and virtual reality) to increase the feeling of immersion or involvement in movies and games, so too are there ways that advertising can be designed creatively and structurally to increase the immersion of the viewer in a commercial—and thereby enhance its effect.

Ads as mini-dramas

By mini-drama ads I mean those that depict a story or vignette. Mini-drama ads usually invite viewers to mentally migrate out of their lounge-room reality and step into the fantasy world of the ad. Take for example the Coca-Cola ad in which the young pizza delivery man, infatuated with Kylie Minogue, delivers her order himself. When he arrives at her hotel room exhausted from running up the stairs, she shares one of her Cokes with him. Or the much older ads in which Michael J. Fox, the hero, overcomes various problems in order to fulfil the attractive heroine's need for a Pepsi. These ads invite us to step into the role of the character in the same way as we would in a movie.

Part of the reason for the popularity of movies is that they offer us a kind of out-of-body experience—a chance for a little while to be someone else—to experience life as someone else. TV offers a less complete out-of-body experience, but an out-of-body experience nevertheless. A chance to experience life, if not as someone else, then at least experience someone else's experiences.

Role-play

Children's games are full of role-playing. Kids pretend to be firemen, truck-drivers, doctors and nurses. They also imagine themselves in the role of their favourite TV or movie characters: Superman, Robin Hood, Cinderella or the Teenage Mutant Ninja Turtles.

Television allows us to role-play in the same way. When we watch TV, we have the opportunity to 'try on' other people's identities. We do this with TV serials and soapies, our favourite movies, and even advertisements. Ads which use this process to get a message across are sometimes dubbed 'slice-of-life' ads. They often portray stereotypical situations in which an individual experiences a problem and finds a solution. The solution is linked to the advertised product. In this way, we indirectly experience the self-relevant consequences associated with using or consuming the brand. We learn how the brand or product is (purported to be) instrumental in attaining the desired goal.

Identifying with a character

Our feeling of immersion in a TV program or an ad seems to be greatly enhanced if we find ourselves identifying with one or more of the on-screen characters. This not only increases the feeling of involvement but also increases the likelihood that we will adopt the trappings of that character. These trappings may be the character's:

- brand solution
- behaviour style (e.g. using Meadow Lea)
- badges of identity (e.g. Coke, Reeboks, Levi's, Pierre Cardin, Mercedes).

Because identification with a character in an ad is much more fleeting than with a movie character, it tends to be less conscious. It takes place quickly and evaporates. But it is fleetingly resurrected at the next exposure of the ad, and in this way, permanent associations or links can develop between the feeling of identification and the brand itself.

'During identification with an ad character, empathising consumers begin to feel as if they are participating in the character's experiences. That is, consumers imaginatively experience the story's events from the perspective of the character with whom they identify: consumers begin to perceive similarities between aspects of their own self-identity and that depicted by the character.'[3]

Immersion and empathy

Identification with a character is not the only way immersion can take place, although it is probably the most powerful way. So what else might make these ads work? If you can't have identification, empathy is probably the next best thing. Some ads invite us to observe the character and take in what the character is experiencing without any expectation that we will necessarily identify with, or want to 'be like', that character.

Take the famous Castrol commercial 'Oils ain't oils, Sol.' With whom are we supposed to identify? The crime boss? The rather pathetic and intimidated motor mechanic? It is hard to personally identify with any of the characters, although we might empathise with the mechanic to some extent.

Empathy means that we understand at a deep level what the character is experiencing and feeling. It means that we have the impression we are experiencing some of the same feelings as the character. But we don't necessarily identify with the character. Identification goes one final step further in the process. It is a more complete projection. A viewer who identifies with a character desires to be like that character or feels that he or she is like that character.

Vantage point and immersion

The ad 'Oils ain't oils, Sol' was entertaining. It was not necessarily addressing us as the audience 'out there', but nor was it inviting conscious identification with the characters. We did not so much identify with Sol or the crime boss characters as we were simply entertained by observing the interactions between them. Our 'vantage point' seems to be not out front as audience and not inside the character but somewhere in between. From this in-between vantage point we were nevertheless able to immerse ourselves in the characters' experiences and take in the claims that were made about Castrol oil.

Just as we 'experience' windows in our home and then, when called on, can generate an answer to the question 'How many windows are there in your home?', so too did we observe Sol and the crime boss and then, if called on, we can clearly remember the main proposition—that 'Oils ain't oils'.

Registering the claim in our minds does not necessarily mean we will believe it. But we become aware and recall that there are claimed differences between oils and that Castrol is purported to be the best. This is a proposition, a 'feather' if you will, that when everything else is equal may tip the balance of brand selection at some point—even if only to prompt us to find out if it is true.

In some product categories it is very difficult for advertisers to claim specific differences between brands. Soft drinks are a case in point. Ads for soft drink are often particularly vague on claims (e.g. 'the real thing', 'the taste of a new generation', 'time for a change'). The focal beam of attention is therefore not on a claim as such but on the character's experiencing the brand and its attribute(s).

Emotions

Just as we experience life by observing our neighbourhood out of our window so too can we vicariously experience life through our television window. Advertisements frequently show characters experiencing life and experiencing emotions. In the midst of these situations the advertised brand is cast either in a feature role or as a central prop.

Such ads utilise qualitatively different channels of communicating which may be visual, musical or associational. They tap into our existing associations with things such as:

- personal desires (for fun, social recognition, achievement, dominance, power)
- belonging (acceptance)
- caring, human values (feeling good about and valuing others)

In other words emotions and desires that we already experience.

A US study which analysed the content of American TV commercials found that 'happiness' or 'having fun' was the value most commonly depicted—in 57 per cent of all TV ads and in more than 80 per cent of ads for soft drinks, children's toys and restaurants. Social recognition was the second most frequently depicted value (in 26 per cent of commercials). These values were depicted as being achieved through a viewer or character becoming 'capable' (27 per cent of all commercials), 'helpful' (26 per cent) and 'smart' (24 per cent).[4]

Just as advertising can associate a piece of information with a brand (e.g. safety and Volvos) so too can it associate an emotion with a brand (excitement and the Ford Capri). If we are concerned about safety then Volvo is a symbol of it. If we are interested in fun and good times a Ford Capri has a better symbolic fit.

The connection of a brand with an emotion by means of characters experiencing life and that emotion, increases the brand's relevance for us. It connects the brand with an emotion that is already there inside us. It may be something that was previously inactive in our mind or active but unassociated with the brand. The brand takes on associations and the more the brand takes on these associations, the more it can function as a symbol—a symbol that expresses or stands in for that emotion and a symbol that tends to elicit that emotional response. Instead of being connected to a piece of information, a brand may thus be connected in our minds to:

- generalised positive emotion (e.g. 'You can't beat the feeling'— Coke; 'Oh, what a feeling'—Toyota.).
- a specific emotion like fun ('When you're having fun you're having Fanta'), excitement ('Life's pretty straight without Twisties') or achievement ('Benson and Hedges—when only the best will do'; 'Inter-Continental Hotels—the place to stay when you know that you've arrived').

The viewer's vantage point

Ads can work without generating identification or even without much empathy with the characters, but if so they usually rely on our remembering or at least registering the explicit or implicit propositions or claims they convey about the product. The more entertaining commercials invite us to immerse ourselves in their mini-dramas and experience events from the vantage point of a participant or a bystander in the commercial.

Vantage point influences processing

Commercials vary in the degree to which they invite the viewer into a 'participant' or 'bystander' role. The role in which we are cast influences the way we are likely to mentally process the ad and what details of it we recall.

This suggests that the role or 'vantage point' we as viewers are invited to take in a commercial will influence how we mentally process the commercial and what specific details of it we are likely to recall. The implication of this is that in analysing any commercial we should ask: What role are viewers being cast in? What character are they expected to identify with? Or empathise with? Are there structural aspects of the ad that enhance or inhibit identification? (Voice-over, for example, can be an inhibitor. Many narrative ads use voice-over to tell us what the character is thinking and feeling. This tends to interfere with the development of empathy by distancing us from the characters, in much the same way as using the third person in a story rather than the first person.)

Immersion as attentional inertia

Observational studies of children watching TV indicate that for much of the time they do not actually watch the screen. In one study 54 per cent of all looks at the screen were for less than three seconds.[5] However, if a look lasts longer than about fifteen seconds, a child is very likely to become progressively 'locked in' to the program. After about ten seconds, the researchers often noted that the child's body relaxed, the head tended to slouch forward and the mouth to drop open.

This phenomenon is called 'attentional inertia', but at least one writer has directly related it to the 'hypnotic or trance-like quality of television watching'.[6] This 'attentional inertia' is not confined to children. It has been documented in samples of college-aged adults as well.[7]

TV, hypnosis and reality

The quotation by Robert Pirsig at the beginning of this chapter likens TV-watching to a mild form of hypnosis. TV and hypnosis do have some striking similarities.

A popular belief about hypnosis is that a person has no knowledge of what he is doing while hypnotised; that he is compelled to do what is suggested to him; and that afterwards he can remember nothing of the experience. The truth is very different.

First, people do remember what happens to them under hypnosis and they feel completely conscious of it at the time. Only if the hypnotist gives them a posthypnotic suggestion to forget everything will they be unable to remember.

If they know what is going on, why, you may ask, do they follow the hypnotist's suggestion? This is an intriguing question. Most people who have been hypnotised will tell you that they felt as though at any time they could have ignored the hypnotist's instructions but went along with them anyway. In other words, they did not feel compelled to act as suggested.

However this begs the question. Why *do* they go along? Most subjects say they just felt like it—that they could have acted differently if they wanted to, but they didn't want to. This is not unlike our own response when we ask ourselves why we have just spent several hours in front of the TV set. It is because we wanted to. We could have turned the set off and got back into reality at any time. We watched because we wanted to; because we felt like it. Just like the person under hypnosis.

The more an ad can immerse viewers (i.e. make the mediated experience momentarily more interesting, more involving, more immersing than what is otherwise going on around them), the more successful it will be. The best advertising does not remind viewers that they are viewers.

Tactics for increasing immersion

Immersion and identification are a matter of degree. The difference between reading a story written in the first person and reading a story written in the third person is that the former is like listening to somebody tell you directly about their own experiences whereas the latter is like listening to somebody tell you about somebody else's experiences. The action is more easily experienced in the first person because we project ourselves into the identity. The difference is in the degree to which we are reminded of our own identity or the external reality.

This is related to virtual reality. By decreasing the awareness of stimuli other than those coming from the cinema screen, TV or book, we increase the 'reality' of the mediated experience and lessen the sense of it as mediated. It is like the difference between listening to music on your stereo through headphones and through loudspeakers. With headphones one feels more immersed in the musical experience. The new technology of virtual reality is headphones for the eyes.

The more complete the experience of virtual reality becomes, the more we can let go temporarily of one reality and become immersed in another. This represents the ultimate in 'switching off'. So anything that lessens the salience of our own current 'reality' and instead helps immerse us, the viewers, in the world of the ad makes the ad that much more powerful.

Summary

When we watch TV or sit in a cinema we are sitting in one reality, and at the same time looking at another reality through an imaginary transparent wall. Just as we experience life by observing our neighbourhood out of our window so too can we vicariously experience life through our television window. Advertisements frequently show characters in 'real-life' and emotional situations. In these situations the advertised brand is cast either in a feature role or as a central prop.

Ads that are mini-dramas work by mildly immersing us in a story rather than addressing us as viewers who are sitting out in front of the TV set. We have the opportunity to 'try on' other people's identities. Identification with an ad character can build permanent associations or links between the experience and the brand itself. Some ads invite us to observe the character and take in what he is experiencing without any expectation that we will necessarily identify with, or want to 'be like', that character. Fantasy may not be true, but we can learn from it nevertheless, as *Sesame Street* showed.

Commercials vary in the degree to which the viewer is invited into a 'participant' or a 'bystander' role. The role in which we are 'cast' influences the way we are likely to mentally process the ad and what details of it we recall. What we often recall is the association of a piece of information or an emotion with a brand. The more the ad immerses us—the more the mediated experience is momentarily more interesting, more involving, more absorbing than what is going on around us—the more we can *feel* the experience and not just *see* it.

Registering a claim or an association in our minds in this way does not imply anything necessarily about believing it. We will, however, recall differences being depicted between the brands—that 'oils ain't oils'—and will recall the name of the brand that was cast as the best or safest or most exciting. These are 'feathers' that, when everything else is equal, may be enough to tip the balance of brand selection—even if only to prompt us to see if the association or claim is true.

8   What's this I'm watching? The elements that make up an ad

In an earlier chapter we saw that 'ads ain't ads'—that ads vary enormously. There are many types of ads but their basic elements are much the same: sound, voice, music and pictures.

The term 'advertising execution' refers to the way that these elements are put together to make up a particular ad. A brand like Coke will often have several different ads on air in the same week. The message is usually the same but the ads may all be executed in different ways.

The way the executional elements of an ad are blended can help determine which of the consumer's mental processes become engaged and which do not. In short they can help modify how a person will opt to mentally process the ad. The way in which we as consumers mentally process ads is naturally influenced by our individual interests, but it is also heavily influenced by those executional elements of the ad itself.

What executional elements? And how do they work to modify the way in which we process an ad? We have now entered the mystical realm of the advertising agency creative department, whose art has traditionally been intuitive rather than encoded in any set of well-formulated principles. The creative team's job is to design and make ads. Good creative teams are paid a lot of money for their so-called intuitive sense of what will be effective advertising. Their task is to make ads that are not only interesting or attention-getting but will also influence our brand choice.

Articulating what makes for creative success in advertising is an underdeveloped science. Researchers and psychologists intrude on the creative team's domain at their peril. They risk finding themselves under hostile attack in enemy territory. Increasingly, however, principles of psychological processing are gradually coming to light that further our understanding of how the executional elements of an ad work, or don't work, as the case may be. In this chapter we bring these to bear on analysing the executional elements of an ad.

Music

Today, music is common in advertising. With Barbra Streisand's help, the 'memories' commercials for OTC (the old Overseas Tele-communication Commission) persuaded us to 'mentally migrate' to music—and 'phone home' to the old country. Hungry Jack's, Yellow Pages and Winfield are just a few more of the many advertisers which have used hit tunes and other music to support their advertising.

The inclusion in an ad of a tune that is already well known can help get attention as well as set the appropriate mood. Association of the brand with a popular piece of music also increases the salience of the brand in our minds and makes it more likely that we will think of that brand whenever we hear the music. This principle is reflected in the saying: 'Sophistication is being able to hear the William Tell overture without thinking of the Lone Ranger.'

Words to music: The jingle

Many ads set their own words to established or specially written tunes. When the words of an ad are set to music they tend to wash over us rather than invite us to intellectualise. The jingle is said to have been invented in Australia and we have come a long way since the days of 'I like Aeroplane Jelly'.

Consider these:

'Oh, what a feeling . . . Toyota.'
'You know what we like most? Headin' for the West Coast.'

Or this for Sorbent from many years ago:

What's the gentlest tissue
in the bathroom you can issue
why it's Sorbent, Sorbent, Sorbent for sure.
Sorbent's economical,
Its sales are astronomical.
Buy Sorbent at your favourite store.

These and many other jingles can easily be dredged out of our past memories. A host of extraordinarily memorable campaigns owe much of their longevity in memory to the fact that the words were set to music. Music is a cutting edge that helps etch a commercial into long-term memory.

There is another effect that music seems to have. Why is it that when the words of an ad are set to music we do not have the same sense of somebody trying to convince us or sell us on something? By setting the words to music, somehow the edge is taken off what might otherwise be a strident message.

This is because we seem to process lyrics differently from spoken messages. As teenagers particularly, we seem to learn to process lyrics and music in a different way to other communications. And we do this in terms of 'enjoy/don't enjoy' rather than in terms of truth or falsity. We learn to process the experience as an experience rather than as a proposition which is supposed to faithfully represent real world reality. Indeed much of the content of MTV (Music Television), for example, when it is processed in a rational way is clearly unrepresentative of reality. It is designed to let fantasy and feelings *in* rather than shut them out.

Harpic invited us to be seated to its 'rhapsody in blue'. When flies disturbed us, the solution to our brand choice was in our musical memory: 'Hit em with the old Pea-Beu.' Musical commercials have become so much a part of our advertising environment that we almost forget they are there. We seem to respond to them as we respond to traffic lights: without thinking much about them. Putting words to music is a well-established creative technique—the rhythm method of advertising. In putting words to music it lessens the chance of conception that anyone is trying to tell us or sell us something and it reduces our tendency to counter-argue with what is being said.

'News' or 'entertainment'

As we saw in Chapter 7, we tend to process ads differently depending whether we feel we are being talked to as prospective customers or whether we see ourselves as merely bystanders looking on. A related way of conceptualising this is by asking, 'Am I being informed or entertained?' We can process an ad as 'news'—or as 'entertainment'.

Some advertising creative teams are heavily into making 'news' commercials. Others are more 'entertainment' focused and may find having to make straight 'news' commercials rather boring. One US ad man, Larry Bisno, presented evidence at an Advertising Research Foundation workshop in 1991 that ads seem to work best when they have something new to say. Bisno said: 'Ads are essentially about creating or broadcasting news about a brand' and 'News is the

oxygen that lets brands live and breath and grow.'[1] 'News' advertising is closely related to, but not quite the same as, 'informational'
advertising. The latter term is used in advertising in a very specific
way.[2] 'News' advertising provides news or information about the
brand. It may be:

- a new formulation (new, improved Omo)
- a new benefit about the brand (lemon-charged, longer holding,
  brushes out easier, sugar free)
- a new variant (Diet Pepsi, anti-dandruff formula), or
- a price comparison (now half the price of the leading brand).

How we mentally process 'News' advertising is significant. Our
minds are invited to process it in the same way that we process the
evening news on television or when we are reading the contents of
the morning newspaper. The focus of processing is on what the
news is telling us that we don't know; what it is adding to our store
of knowledge; how interesting the news is; how surprising it is; and
how important it is to us or to people we know.

With news programs we don't necessarily have to enjoy what is
being communicated. We watch news and current affairs programs
for the information and not just for the entertainment. Evidence is
emerging that the same applies to 'news' ads. Likeability may be
critical to the effectiveness of entertainment commercials. With
'news' ads it is not necessary that we like the experience of watching
provided the ad is imparting valuable news and information to us.
This explains why some ads which are disliked (such as Mrs Marsh
for Colgate) can still seem to work. The experience and enjoyability
is secondary—especially if it is a category where we are highly
involved in making sure that we make the right brand decision. In
other words for the ad to be effective it is not crucial that we like
the ad if it gives us some news about the brand that is relevant to
removing some irritation or problem we have with the product that
we are currently using. This contrasts with ads that rely on entertainment for which liking of the ad assumes much more importance.[3]

Entertainment commercials

The opposite of 'news' is 'entertainment'. When we watch entertainment programs like *The Cosby Show, Neighbours*, movies and
so on, our interest is not in any information they may be communicating but in the entertainment they provide for us. It is important
that we like the experience—otherwise, why would we continue to
watch?

'News' ads like the news bulletin clearly cast the viewer as the recipient of information. Entertainment commercials are different. We are not being addressed but simply experiencing. With entertainment commercials we react like an audience rather than as a sales prospect.

Even brand managers and ad agencies can run out of new things to say about humdrum, old products. They then look for ways to 'create news' rather than reporting it. Trivial and often irrelevant differences are created in order to have something to say (e.g. caffeine-free cornflakes). Or there is increasing reliance on 'beat-ups', as with 'new and improved' (yet again) Omo! These pieces of 'news' are mostly harmless creations which ultimately risk boring us. There is a limit to how many times we can accept without questioning the idea that an old brand (like Omo) can be yet again 'new and improved' in any meaningful way.

When nothing new can be said about the brand, there is always the entertainment commercial. Entertainment ads may be 'drama' (Oils ain't oils) or 'musical variety' (the commercials launching Diet Coke) or 'animation' (Mr Sheen). While they may not communicate news about the brand in the sense of delivering a message, they can nevertheless create 'feathers'. They can increase the salience of the brand and influence, at least marginally, the image or feeling that we have about the brand (or its users) relative to other brands.

One of the crucial ways entertainment commercials vary is in how integral the brand is to the execution and what role it plays. The brand can take various parts, including:

• a prop (e.g. the Michael Fox Pepsi ads)
• a setting (e.g. various McDonald's drama ads), or
• the hero (e.g. Mortein in the Louie the fly ads).

Some ads relegate the brand to a bit part while in others it is the star. The more integral the brand is to the ad the more effective it tends to be. It is true that there are times some of these commercials become so entertainment focused that they lose the plot. They lose sight of their identity as commercials and become simply clever pieces of cinema posing as advertising.

Entertainment commercials are particularly important when the differences between brands are marginal or non-existent. On the beam balance of choice all brands weigh equal and it only takes a feather to swing the balance. In this context it is important to note that the advertising for a brand is in fact one attribute of a brand's personality. If we like something about someone's personality, then the chances are greater that we will like that person. If we like a brand's advertising, the chances are greater that we will like that brand—however marginal this difference may be. It may be marginal but when everything else is equal, it can tip the scales.

Drama

Earlier we saw that people seem to process lyrics and music quite differently from spoken messages. Such processing, far from shutting fantasy and feeling out, deliberately lets it in.

'Drama' commercials are similar to music in this respect. Drama, like music, is supposed to be experienced and enjoyed. Experience and enjoyment are the focus of our mental processing. Our mental processing is not usually set to engage in the analysis of drama in terms of truth or falsity. Nor is it set to analyse what information goes in to our heads in the process.

Classic drama commercials include the Big M car chase ads, the Smiths Gobbledocks ads and the Shell Ultra 'What's the difference?' ads. The 'Oils ain't oils' ad for Castrol was so successful that it enjoyed several carry-over seasons. Another classic was the Pepsi production starring Michael J. Fox, who had to overcome various obstacles in order to get the girl a Pepsi. And still playing after a record run of two years was the Telecom ad starring the cute kid telephoning his grandfather about bunyips and Tasmanian tigers.

These ads appeal to us emotionally. We can relate to them and they entertain us at the same time as educating us. They are like plays or dramas as distinct from lectures. They not only have people and faces but also characters and plots. All of these elements help the ads stick in people's minds.

They are mini-movies rather than ads that reason with us. There is a world of difference between listening to a lecture or a debate and attending a concert or a movie. The former are an invitation to reason. The latter are an invitation to experience.

With drama commercials, this is the difference. We tend to record the incidental information or message that happens to get conveyed while the focus of our attention is on being entertained. Sometimes by putting both music and drama together we get musical drama (e.g. Smiths Lites). Throw in a touch of animation and you get favourites like Mr Sheen and Louie The Fly.

Who is talking to whom?

It should be obvious that in order to analyse the executional elements in an ad requires some rather subtle analysis. An invaluable starting-point to the process is to ask two questions:

- Who is the ad talking to? and
- Who is doing the talking?

The way we experience a commercial depends on what role the ad casts us, the viewers, in. This in turn influences who is seen to be talking to whom.

Lecture-style ads

Consider ads like 'This week only at Merv's supermarkets we have the following red-hot specials . . .' 'I'm Fred Bloggs and have I got a deal for you.' Who is speaking to whom? These ads take a relatively traditional form in which it is clear that the advertiser (Merv's or Fred Bloggs) is talking to us, the viewer in front of the TV set.

We process these lecture-style ads in terms of the relevance of the information they convey. The advertiser hopes we will listen to what is said, find it of interest and see its relevance to us, then remember the information and act on it. For this to happen the ad has first to capture our attention and our interest. In advertising jargon, it has to 'cut through the clutter'.

Look who's talking: Face vs voice-over

Ads that reason with us often feature a presenter putting the case for why we should try or buy this widget rather than some other widget. (Comparative advertising is the most direct method but the least used in Australia.)

One important way in which lecture-style ads vary is in whether or not we can see who is talking; whether we can see the face of the advertiser. In the typical supermarket ad announcing the week's specials, the advertiser is usually unseen. The focus is on the specials. The person doing the talking is invisible. He or she is merely a 'voice-over'. If there is any real sense of a human being in the commercial it is merely a disembodied voice informing us how much we will save. Car dealer ads, on the other hand, often have the dealer himself as the on-screen speaker. The words come out of the dealer's mouth. In the advertising jargon, the ad has lip-sync.

These ads are like lectures and the person doing the talking is like the lecturer. Some lecturers and some ads stick in our minds much more than others. Some lecturers like to work in a darkened room, hidden behind a lectern, with the audience's attention focused on a screen. Other lecturers are more lively. They work the audience from up-front, doing demonstrations and interacting with the audience or attempting to get participation from them.

So it is when we have a lip synched, on-screen presenter. Professor Julius Sumner Miller worked magic in this way for Cadbury's Dairy Milk chocolate. Such presenters engage us visually and verbally while they communicate.

Lecturers who stay in the background tend not to impress themselves, or their message, upon us and we feel less warm towards them. Similarly advertisers who communicate with us only as disembodied voice-overs are frequently less effective. In tracking lecture-style ads of this type over the last 10 years, the ones with an on-screen human presenter and lip-sync emerge as the ones that almost invariably outperform those in which a disembodied voice-over is used.

This is no doubt related to why many people don't like talking on the telephone and prefer to talk to people face to face. Talking to someone on the phone is just not the same when you can't see the other person's face and expression. This type of news or lecture style communication where the advertiser is imparting information usually comes across as more meaningful and more effective when there is a human face, a personality who is doing the talking. That is why so many car dealers are persuaded to appear in their own ads—because somebody whose face we can see is talking to us. It helps when the organisation that is talking to us has a human face.

Presenters

This raises the question of whose face? Some advertisers choose to use a human face but not their own. Just as governments use ambassadors to represent them overseas to be the human face of the government, some companies prefer to use a presenter to represent the organisation. So the presenter is not always the advertiser. He or she may be a model or actor with the 'right kind' of face. AAMI insurance for years used an anonymous, pretty woman who urged us to 'call me, call Amy'.

Or the presenter may be a famous person. The use of celebrity presenters is widespread. Carpetcall [*sic*] used Dennis Lillee, Heinz used Penelope Keith and the Bank of Melbourne used Jack Thompson. Years ago Winfield used Paul Hogan, Esso used Mike Willesee, Custom Credit used John Newcombe, St George Building Society used Julie Anthony and Voca used Gough Whitlam as their spokespeople. You will no doubt recall one or more of these old ad campaigns—testimony to the durability of the memory trace that the use of such presenters can create. Celebrities and actors act as surrogates for the advertiser. They can put a human face on our image of an organisation.

Apart from giving the advertiser a human face, the use of a presenter also acts a mnemonic device to increase the salience of the brand. Paul Hogan was ultimately prohibited from doing Winfield ads because of his huge popularity with kids and his mnemonic association with Winfield cigarettes. Just as the 'Winfield music' reminded us of Winfield, so too did Paul Hogan, whether in a movie, a variety show, or being interviewed on TV.

The use of a presenter instead of the advertiser to do the talking in an ad seems to create a lessened sense of someone with a vested interest talking directly to us and doing a hard sell on us. We receive the message, from the company but through a congenial and familiar figure (e.g. John Laws for Toyota, Paul Cronin for Mitre 10) and who presents the advertiser in a favourable light. This is almost always more effective and more memorable than the use of anonymous, disembodied voice-overs. Even when the presenter is not a celebrity or is the advertiser, the ad is more memorable if the presenter's own voice is used, (e.g. the lady in the white dress for Panadol, Ken Morgan for Ken Morgan Toyota, Jacko for Duracell).

Musical voice-over vs lecture voice-over

If we go out to an entertainment event like *Phantom of the Opera*, we clearly approach and assimilate the experience quite differently from a university lecture. One way that an ad can vary and improve markedly on the traditional voice-over is to set it to music. Take for example the ads for Meadow Lea ('You oughta be congratulated'), Schweppes Cola ('Time for a change') or Gillette ('The best a man can get'). These are more entertaining and enjoyable than spoken voice-over commercials. They are processed differently—i.e. more as an experience—and their effects are more subtle. In setting the voice-over of an ad to music it seems to subtly change the way the ad is cognitively processed by the viewer. The way we process them is more akin to the way we mentally process drama or musical drama.

Who is the ad talking to?

What is important in an ad is not just who is talking or singing but who they are singing or talking to.

Take the Colgate Fluoriguard ads featuring the schoolteacher Mrs Marsh, for example. Ask yourself who is Mrs Marsh talking to?

The answer is that she is talking primarily to the children on the screen. At the same time the children and adults on our side of the screen are also experiencing the commercial and getting the message, but in the role of bystanders or passive observers.

The difference between being a bystander and being the obvious target of a communication was demonstrated in 1962 in an experiment by Walster and Festinger.[4] Subjects listened in on a conversation between two graduate students. Some subjects believed the students knew they were listening. Others believed the students were unaware of their presence. The first group believed what the students said could conceivably have been directed at influencing them, the listeners.

The second group were more influenced by the opinions expressed in the students' conversation. In other words, being in bystander mode seems to reduce the motivation for us to engage our defensive reactions and reduce our tendency to be as critical of what is being said.

The classic 'Madge' ads for Palmolive detergent cast us in bystander mode. Madge is not addressing the viewer directly. She is talking to the lady on screen, the one who is 'soaking in it'. Similarly, with Castrol's 'Oils ain't oils, Sol', the message was aimed not at the viewer but at an on-screen character—the mechanic.

We as viewers get messages from these ads indirectly rather than directly, much as we do when viewing a play or a soap opera or a movie. Our minds are not set to get a message but to be entertained.

This contrasts with the traditional type of ad which addresses viewers directly. The most common examples of this type of ad are the many retail ads (for Sussan, K mart etc) in which the two main components are:

- voice-over and
- illustrative visuals (usually of the products).

Such ads clearly and unambiguously talk to the viewer. Most early TV advertising was like this, and we still tend to think of it as typical, probably because advertising's heritage is in the print medium. Straight words with illustrative visuals is an approach very much in the style of, and a carryover from, print advertising. But if you watch today's TV ads closely you will see that this style has developed considerably. Often the (off-screen) voice-over appears to be talking not so much to the viewer but talking to, or about, an on-screen character.

Voice-over talking to on-screen character

Having the voice-over in the ad appear to address an on-screen character is one of the primary ways in which a shift can be induced in our mental processing. It is one of several elements that invite us to take a bystander perspective.

The Caro (coffee substitute) ad is just one of the many ads in which the voice-over appears to be addressing the product-user character. In it, the man on the screen is told by the off-screen voice-over that there are many people just like him who now drink and enjoy the product. The viewer is a bystander and the viewer's 'focus of processing' is the bystander's perspective.

The difference between being a bystander and a target is the difference between overhearing a conversation and being told something directly. What is different in overhearing information in a conversation between two other people is that our attention and cognitive processing are focused differently (see Chapter 7).

When we are being told something directly we are more likely to engage our defensive, counter-arguing mechanisms. We are more on the alert and ready for counterarguing. The information gained from overhearing someone else's conversation may or may not be the same. However, the defensive processing applied to it is likely to be quite different.

The on-screen character as receiver

A seemingly strange but interesting question to ask of any musical commercial is 'Who is the voice singing to?' Who is the object of this communication? Sometimes the answer will be 'the on-screen character'. For example, the Meadow Lea commercial 'congratu-lates' the woman on screen for using the product.

Setting the words of the voice-over to music can impart a sense that it is the on-screen character who is being sung to. This style helps further disengage the viewer from acting the role of defensive customer. It engages the viewer more as a passive observer, a bystander enjoying the entertainment. The musical voice-over is not selling, talking nor even singing *to the viewer*. Rather, it seems to be singing to the on-screen character—as in 'You oughta be congratulated.'

To the extent that viewers identify with the on-screen character, they also receive the message indirectly and see it as relevant to themselves. In this type of ad, the pronoun 'you' occurs often (e.g. You oughta be congratulated, You're looking good). This style engages us as passive observers and invites us to enjoy the ad while being invited to interpret the 'you' as referring to the on-screen character. However if we identify with the on-screen character, we can simultaneously interpret the 'you' as referring to us.

Tuning in to the on-screen character's thoughts

In ads such as: 'I feel like a Tooheys', 'I'm as Australian as Ampol', and Australian Airlines' 'We're lifting up our tails', it is as though the characters on screen are *thinking* the sentiments expressed in song. Viewers have the impression of sharing what the characters are thinking or feeling. In these ads the words *could* be being sung by the characters, but they aren't. Instead the message seems to come from the characters' thoughts. If setting a message to music lessens the sense of being lectured to, this technique probably lessens that sense even more. We seem to be simply overhearing someone's thoughts.

The on screen characters in all these commercials are depicting doing other things while simultaneously we are hearing what seems to be their thoughts, desires or remembrances coming through the audio track.

The style is frequently characterised by use of the pronoun 'I' or 'we' ('I'm as Australian as Ampol.' 'We're lifting up our tails.' 'I feel like a Tooheys.'). To the extent that we find ourselves sharing the feelings of these characters and identifying with them, the pronoun 'I' or 'we' can be taken as referring to us as well.

Characters

When developing a commercial, ad agencies consider what is the target audience for the product (i.e. who buys it) so they can make decisions about the characters. 'Young products' (e.g. jeans) usually feature young people and 'older products' (e.g. superannuation) usually feature older people. Similarity in age between characters and audience is usually a plus.

The ad maker attempts to weave roles and characters into the ad that we will welcome—that are consistent with the way we see ourselves or would like to see ourselves. Roles and characters that we can easily identify with.

The closer we feel to a character and the greater the similarity between that character and ourselves, the more effect a commercial is likely to have on us. This is why ads for Mattel toys usually star children, ads for Coca-Cola feature teenagers, and ads for All-Bran breakfast cereal show the whole family. The age, sex and lifestyle of the characters are chosen to maximise the probability that the target audience for the brand will identify with the character.

Multiple target audiences

Many ads have one specific target audience and the target character is designed accordingly. It is possible, however, for one commercial to address multiple target audiences and still achieve identification.

An example is the original Telecom 'bunyip' commercial, in which the boy phones his grandfather and asks 'Are bunyips fierce?' Almost anyone could identify with at least one of the three character-targets this ad contained.

Children could identify with the boy whose parents have let him call his grandfather, prompting requests for permission to phone their grandparents. Grandparents could identify with the grandfather and hope their relatives would call them, or perhaps be motivated to make a call themselves. Parents could identify with the parent characters. Their thoughtfulness in suggesting that the child make the call allows them to experience the joy of both the boy and his grandfather. Any parent who doesn't relate to this would have to be a hard case.

Successful identification, then, should lead to suggestions for similar calls in similar households. This ad (which ran for two years) invited viewers to step into one or other of the roles by identifying with the actors' words, actions, feelings or thoughts.

Two questions are therefore pertinent when we examine an ad and its characters. First, are we members of the target audience for the ad? Or is it aimed at people in some other age, sex or socioeconomic group? Tampon ads are not aimed at me, nor are women's fashion ads. Often, however, it is not that obvious. Assuming we are in the target audience for the ad, then which character or characters seem to be most like us? Which character in the ad do we feel some identity or empathy with? If the ad is working on us it is most likely to be through that particular character.

The person playing the character

Michael J. Fox, the actor in the Pepsi ads mentioned previously, is liked and admired by most adolescents. Ads which feature already admired characters generally have a head start in getting the audience to identify with, and project themselves into, the character. Almost every adolescent 'wants to be' a Michael J. Fox.

What if an unknown actor had been used in that commercial? It would probably still have worked—but almost certainly not as well. Viewers would have taken longer to develop a feeling of familiarity with the character. This would have necessitated many more repetitions of the ad and possibly even the making of multiple ads. The identification process would not have been anywhere near as immediate or as intense. In other words, where the character has to be introduced and developed from scratch, the advertiser has to spend much more money for on-air time to elicit the same degree of identification effect.

When advertisers develop identities and establish characters in their ads they therefore regard these as an accumulating asset. They have an investment interest in the development of these characters. It is important for them to have in their ads attractive, recognisable characters that we the audience will want to identify with—whether these are known entities or (initially) unknown. This explains the advantage in ad campaigns of maintaining continuity in the star character. It is why we are beginning to see more sequels of successful ads. Advertisers are discovering that there are advantages to be gained in not changing the characters with every change of commercial. (See Part B, 'Using sequels for greater effect'.)

Animated characters

Fictitious characters in shows like *Sesame Street, Home And Away* or *Neighbours* get fan mail all the time from people who empathise or identify with them. The fan mail is addressed to the character, not the actor. Why does this happen when everybody knows the characters are fictitious? It is because even though they are only characters they are real enough for us to identify with and empathise with.

We can even feel warm towards cartoon characters and puppets. A generation of people felt empathy, if not identity, with the *Peanuts* character Charlie Brown, the born loser. A different generation warmed to Big Bird and the Cookie Monster.

Animated characters have also been used as negative role models. In *Sesame Street*, for example, watching Oscar the Grouch is fun but acting like him is clearly absurd. Who wants to be perpetually grouchy? Oscar is the negative role model in *Sesame Street*; others, such as Big Bird and The Count, are positive role models.

Like 'drama' ads, ads with animated characters such as Mr Sheen or Louie the Fly seem to be most successful when the on-screen character does the talking.

Animation can be used to change the whole feeling and tone of a commercial. In particular it can be used to 'lighten up' what might otherwise be a serious, unpleasant message such as 'killing flies before they spread disease' (Louie the Fly). The US advertising agency Doyle Dane Bernbach, in an ad for Kit 'N Caboodle cat food, needed to show a cat chasing a mouse. Although mice are the 'gold standard' in cat food they come in only one flavour, but Kit 'N Caboodle comes in a variety of tastes. Instead of having cat owners watching their darling pussy on TV threatening the life of a real live, grey mouse, the ad agency used animation. The agency wanted people to respond to the realism of the cat so they mixed live footage of a cat with an animated mouse.[5] The ad was a delightful example of animation's ability to lighten an otherwise unpleasant scenario.

One appeal that animated characters have for advertisers is that they are in total control of characters' behaviour. Their investment is protected. Advertisers using real people always have to hold their breath and hope. The character may get into trouble and develop a bad reputation which can cross over to the brand. (Any advertiser using Mike Tyson would have been running for cover when he was charged and convicted for rape.) With cartoon characters this can't happen. As one US film-maker put it: 'Animated characters are . . . appealing because they don't age like regular characters and won't be caught in a crack house and then try to gang rape the arresting officers . . . They give advertisers control.'[6]

Length of commercial

A 60-second TV commercial is about one-hundredth the length of a movie. This means that getting us to project ourselves into it and identify with a character is much, much harder to achieve. In the time it takes to screen a movie you could watch about one hundred 60-second commercials. So any identification that does occur is much more fleeting with advertising. This is one reason drama commercials seem to work better at 60 seconds or 45 seconds than at 30 or 15 seconds.

Time is both an enemy and a challenge for drama commercials. There is extremely limited time in which to develop the characters, depict the situation and get a message across. (See Part B, 'Learning to use 15-second TV commercials'.) It takes time to build involvement and identification with characters. This is why sequels can work so well—because the characters have already been developed in an earlier ad.

Negative roles or characters

Some ads deliberately use a character designed to be a negative role model. For example, in an attempt to get people to save water, Melbourne Water uses a thoughtless, mindless character named 'Wally' in its ads. The theme is 'Don't be a Wally with water' and we are urged not to be like Wally. Another negative role character was 'Lucky' Phil in an ad for random breath-testing. 'Lucky' Phil's luck had run out. When he was caught by the breathalyser he was over the limit and lost his licence. The implicit message of the ad was: Don't delude yourself. Don't be like 'Lucky' Phil.

Interestingly, some ads, in an attempt at humour, do this inadvertently. They depict the target character as something of a 'goat', yet the advertiser still hopes that we will react positively to the character and what he or she is saying. An example a few years ago was Bert Newton in an electric hot water ad. Referring to his own fall from fame, he proudly announced that the water 'will still be hot when you're not'. Another example was the Fosters drinker who failed to recognise the person he was drinking with at the bar. This was the cricketer Graham Wood in the first commercial and the golfer Bob Shearer in the second. As the audience we squirmed in embarrassment at this character's naivety.

A commercial is supposed to be fostering (if you will pardon the pun) a positive image of the product user. This is negative role-model stuff. It should be the kiss of death for an ad. It inhibits identification and the ad must rely on other psychological mechanisms to work—if it is going to work at all. When we were kids we identified with the goodies, not the baddies. We wanted the attractive roles, not the embarrassing ones. Who wants to identify with the baddies, the losers or the naive?

So do ads like this work? I have yet to see one that did, unless it was strongly informational. I suspect the Mrs Marsh ads for Colgate and the Madge ('You're soaking in it') ads for Palmolive dishwashing liquid worked—because they were informational. A number of non-informational ads of this type that have been observed in market research tracking have in fact had *negative* effects on the brand's image. In many of these cases the advertiser remained unaware that the ad was having negative effects. The effects of advertising, whether positive or negative, rarely reveal themselves unambiguously in a company's overall sales data. Other, more sensitive, tracking measures are necessary.

Summary

Music and jingles make an ad more memorable and are mentally processed in a different way from spoken words. Our focus of processing also differs in 'news' and 'entertainment' commercials. Commercials don't necessarily have to be liked if they are imparting news. When there is no news and everything else is equal, entertainment commercials are often used. A brand's advertising is one attribute of its personality, so if we like the ad there is a greater chance we will like the brand. This is a 'feather'. With entertainment commercials we tend to record any incidental information or message that happens to get conveyed while the focus of our attention is on being entertained.

One important question is, 'Who is doing the talking?' Straight 'news' ads and lecture-style ads have more effect when we can see the person talking to us on the screen with lip-sync. Using a presenter character as a surrogate for the advertiser seems to lessen our sense of a hard sell. The presenter character also acts as an important mnemonic device.

The other important question is, 'Who is the ad talking to?' When it appears to be talking to an on-screen character, we tend to mentally process the ad as a bystander. The closer we feel to the character, the more effect the ad is likely to have on us. 'Overhearing' something can be more influential than being told it directly because we tend to apply less-defensive processing to it.

9   Limits of advertising

It should be clear from previous chapters that advertising's effectiveness has been much exaggerated. At the same time, this effectiveness is based on what seems to be powerful psychological mechanisms: learning without awareness, making brands into symbols, having people see a brand in different ways, the influence of conformity, and the use of brands to express identity. So why is advertising not more powerful than it is?

This chapter explores the many factors that severely constrain and often frustrate the power of individual advertisers to influence us. It shows how difficult it is for advertisers to make these psychological mechanisms work and how their unbridled use in any wholesale manipulation is virtually impossible. Just as democratic political systems have various checks and balances to constrain the power of elected governments to dictate to us, so too are 'checks and balances' inherent in the competitive environment in which advertisers operate. In addition, we consumers vote with our feet—the most powerful constraint of all. When the brand or the product does not live up to its promise, when it does not meet the expectations created by the advertising, then we simply don't buy it again. So as we shall see, advertising's power is constrained as much by practical limitations as by absolute limitations.

Competitors' advertising

One of the most important limitations on any advertiser's power to influence us is the activity of its competitors. Competitors' advertising, more often than not, severely blunts an individual advertiser's efforts. If Meadow Lea was the only advertiser in the margarine or butter category, its advertising power and market share would undoubtedly be much greater than they are. For every advertiser there are at least one and usually several other advertisers in the same product category. These create a lot of advertising 'noise' and clutter. The 'noise' of competing claims often neutralises or at least greatly dilutes the effect of any individual campaign. It also makes it much more expensive for any individual company to advertise at a level and frequency that can be heard above the competitive 'noise'. This imposes a limitation of its own.

Money: Limitations of budget

In the competitive environment it takes huge sums of money, sometimes over long periods, for such mechanisms to be really effective. Even the largest companies cannot afford the advertising that would be necessary to manipulate us in the way that many opponents of advertising fear.

This is especially true when the brand has no unique benefit or difference over other brands and the difference has to be created by advertising. Even when the brand does offer a substantial benefit over its competitors, it must be prepared to spend very heavily to get the message across. L'Eggs pantyhose is a case in point. L'Eggs had a benefit or difference, a super-stretch pantyhose that had no shape until pulled onto the leg and which then moulded itself to the shape of the leg. It also differentiated itself with unique packaging. When it launched in the US, L'Eggs had to be prepared to spend $10 million on advertising for the first year. This was double the total spent by all advertisers in the pantyhose category in the previous year.[1]

Even dominant brands like Coca-Cola rarely account for the majority of advertising in their product category. Coke, for example, accounts for between 25 per cent and 40 per cent of the total advertising for soft drinks in Australia. The proportion is even smaller if we take into account other beverages which are less-direct competitors of Coke, such as fruit juice, milk, tea and coffee. So even the huge brands rarely have the advertising field to themselves.

'Creating' needs

People who are 'anti advertising' often feel that advertisers create needs and manipulate us into buying things we don't really need or want. To what extent can the psychological mechanisms of advertising be used to create needs or manipulate us to buy things we don't really need or want? Before answering, we should answer two related questions. What do we really need, and what role does advertising play in bringing new products to our attention?

Advertising announces new products. It is generally quite effective in at least making us aware of new products and new brands. This role of advertising people rarely object to—unless the new product is trivial. Most people see this as a positive role—informing us of new events. In this sense it is like news, which is valued because it is informative.

People who are 'anti advertising' do not focus on the awareness role so much as the persuasive role of advertising—on its ability to make us buy things that we don't need. I have largely dismissed persuasion in earlier chapters and pointed out that of the many psychological mechanisms underlying most advertising, persuasion is often the least relevant. If it were truly relevant its record would be rather poor. Estimates vary but everybody agrees on this much— at least 40 per cent of all new consumer products fail! The proportion is much higher if we take into account products that are not launched because they have failed in a test market.[2] There is a real interaction between what advertisers and marketers would like to sell and what we as consumers can relate to, and in the end feel we want or need.

Advertising does not create these products. What it does do is to help accelerate their diffusion into the mass market. The more truly new and beneficial a product is, the more informational its advertising tends to be. We have a choice. Are we interested in this new benefit or not? Can we afford it? Are we prepared to pay the price?

Every household today needs a refrigerator, a TV and a telephone. Even the severest critic of advertising is likely to have one of each. What else do we really need? At the time of writing about 50 per cent of all homes in Australia have microwave ovens. Ten years ago almost nobody did. Almost every home in Australia today has a calculator. Twenty years ago none did. Many today have a dish-washer. Ten years ago almost none did. Many have a video recorder. Twenty years ago none did. Central heating, air conditioners, home computers, video cameras, compact disc players—the list goes on and on.

Yesterday's inventions and luxuries become tomorrow's necessities. Today 98 per cent of homes have a television set. More than 90 per cent have a telephone. Almost all have a refrigerator and a washing machine. But do we need them? Those who argue that we don't need all these material things are right. We could live without them. But do we want to?

These are acquired needs, not biological needs such as hunger, thirst and sex. Were they created by advertising? No, they were created by inventors. Advertising's primary role is creating awareness of these inventions in the mass market. There is no doubt that without such advertising, innovations such as microwave ovens or combined shampoo and conditioner would diffuse through the economy much more slowly.

How advertising accelerates mass markets

Communicating the existence of a new product (e.g. calculators, digital watches) to the mass market, even without persuasion, expands the demand for that product because just on the probabilities alone, some proportion of us will always be interested in buying an innovation. These purchases then have the effect of increasing the size of the production run for the new product, which in turn reduces the unit cost of production. This creates economies of scale in production and translates into a lower price tag on the new product that is offered for sale. When the product is advertised at a lower price, some of us who had previously decided against buying it because it was too expensive become interested. It has now become available to some of us who otherwise could not afford it. This expands sales further, which increases production runs further, which reduces price further, which makes the product more available and affordable by even more people. Electronic calculators and digital watches are classic examples.

The whole effect is circular. Advertising, in communicating first the product and then the affordable price, accelerates the diffusion of the innovation into the mass market. Without advertising the process would probably still happen, but at an infinitely slower pace. My mother might still be using a wringer washer. I would still be using a manual typewriter, and computers would probably be something that only businesses could afford.

The critics of all this often seem to be nostalgic for the simplicities of the past. Nostalgia is an attempt to create an idealised past in the present.[3] It tends to gloss over the unpleasant aspects of the past and focus only on the pleasant aspects. However, there is no argument for staying where we are. I don't accept that primitive man was happier in his cave. I don't accept that my mother was happier when she was doing her washing in a kerosene tin boiled over an open fire than she is now, 60 years later, with her modern washing machine, her refrigerator, her telephone and her many other creature comforts.

Ads for brands or ads for products?

The vast majority of advertising attempts to get us to buy one brand instead of another and not new products per se. Earlier chapters focused on the low-involvement effects of advertising, which can tip the balance in the weighing up of brands when everything is equal or can influence which brands get weighed up. But only a very small proportion of advertising is directly aimed at affecting our decision as to whether to purchase a product or not, as distinct from which of the various brands to buy. (The main exception seems to be advertising of primary food products like cheese, rice, milk, butter, bananas and avocados.)

Persuasion is not involved in the great majority of brand advertising that we are exposed to. To the extent that most brand advertising does influence our feelings of need for the product category itself, then this result is more a side-effect than a primary focus of the advertiser. That is not to say that it is unimportant. Clearly, enough people think it is important to have banned cigarette advertising.

Research into the ability of brand advertising to create demand for the category as a whole is sparse and remains frustratingly inconclusive. My own suspicion is that research will eventually show the spin-off effect to be substantial and that its mechanism is based primarily on agenda-setting by creating an image of popularity and social acceptance for the product category—but only if enough advertising for enough brands is aired for long enough.

If this turns out to be true, it still implies very severe constraints on the power of advertisers to foist just anything onto us. Unless a new product finds reasonable acceptance quite quickly, it is likely to be discontinued before the agenda-setting process has time to take hold. There are limits to how long advertisers are able or willing to keep advertising a product that is not selling enough to pay for the cost of production, simply in the hope that it will eventually 'catch on'. This is why market research tries to determine beforehand what consumers would like to have, or at least what is likely to meet with ready acceptance rather than resistance.

Resistance to change

There is another limitation on advertising's ability to exercise unbridled influence and this is reflected in our resistance to change and the natural way our minds work. Our minds seem to have inbuilt in them a strong need for cognitive consistency. We tend to reject that which is not consistent with what we currently know or have come to expect. To succeed, an innovation usually has to find a line of least resistance.

For example, for years after it was developed, many people rejected instant coffee, which was advertised on the basis of ease of use. Research revealed that household food buyers (mostly housewives in the 1950s) saw the so-called convenience benefit as reflecting directly on their performance. Buying instant coffee (as distinct from coffee beans) was seen as the mark of 'a lazy housewife who did not care for her family'. Remember, female role models in the 1950s were quite different from today's. This negative association slowed the rate of acceptance of many innovations pitched at convenience and time-saving, including dishwashers, microwave ovens and automatic washing machines.

Another example was a noiseless food mixer, which was rejected for quite a different reason—because it seemed not to have much power. We tend to believe powerful machines are noisy. A noiseless food mixer is a contradiction. A machine that is both powerful and quiet is inconsistent with our experience, so we find it difficult to accept.

Perhaps the most telling example of this effect is dishwashing detergent. Before detergent was invented, when we washed dishes in soapy water in the sink, it was lack of suds on the top of the water that we used as a cue to tell us when to add more soap. Dishwashing detergent does not naturally foam, but manufacturers eventually had to add foam to the product to get it accepted. Without foam the detergent was not seen to be working. Unless new products fit with, or at least do not clash with, what is already in our minds, their advertisers are likely to encounter substantial resistance to the innovation. They are likely to face a long, hard and very costly battle over many years before the product eventually, if ever, achieves widespread acceptance.

Dishwashing detergent as a new product initially clashed with (was not consistent with) something that was well established in our minds—namely that sudsing indicated when washing up water was working and lack of suds indicated when it was not and it was time to add more suds. For a product to get widespread acceptance, the product may also have to be made consistent with consumers' existing beliefs or expectations. This reflects a more general psychological principle which is often known as cognitive consistency.

Cognitive consistency

Our minds seem to have a need for consistency, in our attitudes and beliefs, and between these attitudes and our behaviour.[4]

Let me illustrate the general mechanism that is at work here. If we believe that Volvos are very safe cars and we read in *Choice* magazine a consumer report that more people have fatal accidents in Volvos than in any other car, what happens? A motivation is automatically set up in us to try to resolve the apparent contradiction. Either our original belief is wrong or there is something wrong with the report. We are experiencing the need for cognitive consistency. We either have to start to change our mind about Volvo cars being safe or we have to find something wrong with the consumer report—to discredit it.

When information comes in which is in conflict with, or is inconsistent with what we believe, then we are likely to experience cognitive inconsistency. Our minds automatically try to resolve this. We humans try to keep our attitudes and beliefs consistent, as well as our attitudes and behaviour. This is not a voluntary mechanism but more an unconscious one that goes into action automatically. It was first demonstrated by Leon Festinger in a classic series of experiments. During the Vietnam war, for example, Festinger gave experimental subjects who were opposed to the war an incentive to argue a position that was contrary to what they believe i.e. to argue for the war. He found that these people's attitudes to the war tended to change in the direction that they had been paid to argue, i.e. in favour of the war.

This demonstrated that when we perform behaviour which is inconsistent with our attitudes, then those attitudes begin to change. Just as importantly, the same thing happens if we hold two attitudes or beliefs and then find out that they are not consistent. For example, what happens if I dislike Nissans and my closest friend, whose judgment I respect, tells me he has just bought a Nissan? I have two attitudes, one positive and one negative. My attitude towards my friend is positive. My attitude towards Nissans is negative. The two attitudes are inconsistent or out of balance. When this happens and we cannot avoid facing the inconsistency of two positions, then our minds automatically begin to change one or other of them in order to bring them into balance.

Advertising is the weaker influence

Advertising is usually the weaker influence compared to what we already know or have in our minds. Any ad campaign is most likely to lead to advertising failure if the message is inconsistent with our existing beliefs. Advertisers have to strive to put a position that is credible, or at least is not inconsistent with what we as consumers already know and think.

For example, light beer has struggled for years in Australia to gain acceptance among young (18- to 24-year-old) male beer drinkers. It has always been much more accepted by older drinkers. The young tend to be searching for identity, and self-expression symbols play a role in this. Despite successful efforts by advertisers to get light beer accepted it has nevertheless tended to be strongly resisted by the younger people for a number of years. For them, the image of light beer as a product is inconsistent with the strong male image that drinking beer has traditionally been identified with. Light beer will probably and ultimately be accepted in this age group but it will have been a very long haul.

It is rare that advertisers can afford to engage in protracted efforts to change such entrenched attitudes by confronting them directly. Usually, they have to look for an approach that will be readily accepted because it fits neatly with existing beliefs. One example of this is the famous 'Avis—we try harder' campaign. This capitalised on the widespread belief that monopolies and big companies tend to become complacent. Companies which are still trying to get to the top probably will try harder. The ad is cognitively consistent with what is already known, so it is more likely to be accepted.

Our need for cognitive consistency means that advertisers who simply try to persuade us against our will, who try to get us to accept something that goes against our existing information or attitudes, are almost certain to fail (unless they also have unlimited time and money to hang in for the long term). This is a big constraint on advertising's power that is contained in our psychological make-up. Like most of the other limitations, it is not an absolute constraint. Finding ways around it poses a real challenge to advertising agencies.

Positioning for cognitive consistency

Chapter 2 pointed out that humans have the ability to see the same thing (whether it be the same product or the same advertisement) in different ways depending on our frame of reference. The challenge for advertising agencies is to position the ad or the product in such a way that it is seen to be consistent with, rather than to clash with, our existing mind set. This is one of the great challenges for advertising and one where it is all too often unsuccessful—as evidenced by the fact that so many new products fail. It is a creative task and those charged with the responsibility for it in the advertising agencies bear the title 'creative director'.

It is difficult to give examples of this 'creativity' at work without breaching client confidentiality, so let me illustrate how it works with a hypothetical example. Suppose John West wanted to market a fish paste to compete with other fish pastes like Peck's. 'It's the fish John West rejects that makes John West the best' is the slogan which this brand has used very successfully for many years. The new fish paste would naturally have to be positioned on the quality dimension to make it consistent with the John West quality image. So it would be 'John West superior quality fish paste' in order to fit with pre-existing beliefs and work in harmony with the pre-existing image of quality that the John West brand has developed. So far so good. A real limitation however lurks below the surface. If there is a widespread belief among consumers that 'fish paste' is made of left-overs, all the good parts of the fish having been used for something else, 'John West superior quality fish paste' is likely to translate unconsciously in our minds as 'John West superior quality leftovers'. This is hardly the desired image. It would also be disastrous for the product. The cognitive inconsistency is likely to doom the product to failure from the start.

What can an advertising agency do in this type of situation? One way here would be to rename the product and market it as John West Fish Pâté. Pâté is also a spread, but it has associations that are consistent with the quality positioning of the John West brand. This strategy is more likely to succeed than a strategy of directly confronting entrenched negative attitudes to fish paste.

Much of the art of advertising, then, lies in finding ways to play the focal beam of attention on the attributes of the product that are consistent with what already exists inside our minds. That which already exists inside our mind is a limitation or an inhibitor on what advertising can do.

When everything else is not equal

Advertisers are beginning to find that advertising seems to work best when it communicates some positive benefit, or when the brand is at least equal to other brands on the market. Rarely can advertising succeed if a brand is inferior to the competition or if its qualities are cognitively inconsistent with the consumer's mind set. In other words, advertising is not magical. It is just one influence among many and when there are real differences between brands the truth generally wins out eventually. Advertising may get us to *try* a product, but our experience with the product then overrides anything that advertising may tell us. If the product does not live up to the promise, we don't purchase it again.

Conversion/persuasion vs reinforcement

This highlights the fact that advertising's principal effect is to reinforce rather than persuade. That is, it reinforces us in the decision we made to purchase the brand and increases the chances of buying it again. Using panels of consumers reporting on what they purchase each week, Professor Andrew Ehrenberg in the UK has studied the effects of advertising on purchasing probably more than any other person in the world. His conclusion is that 'advertising's main role is to reinforce feelings of satisfaction for brands already being used'.[5]

This is consistent with my observations in Australia. Advertising has frequently proved quite ineffective at getting people to buy a brand for the first time. To achieve widespread trial of a new brand, advertising usually has to be heavily supplemented by promotions, in-store displays and free sampling. With supermarket brands this is very much influenced by simple locating behaviour. The new brand has to stop us walking at 2 km/h and cut through the clutter and get noticed. There are limits to how much advertising alone can do here. (Advertising does seem to be more effective at getting people to buy a truly new product for the first time than at getting them to try yet another 'me-too' brand in an established product category. But again, with supermarket products it often takes in-store displays and promotion to achieve widespread trial reasonably rapidly.)

Reinforcement is the reason why some campaigns, the ones conducted by the smart advertisers, talk to their own consumers. One of the best examples of this is Meadow Lea's 'You oughta be congratulated'. Note how much weaker this ad would be if it said, 'You will be congratulated if you switch to Meadow Lea.' That would be making a promise or a claim. Rather the communication was directed at reinforcing the behaviour of those who already used Meadow Lea and it told them 'You oughta be congratulated' which helps in keeping them buying it. Instead of the typical promise type form i.e. 'buy x brand and you will get y result', it provides a verbal 'pat on the back' to its own customers. At the same time, it casts people not using the brand as bystanders who 'overhear' a communication between the manufacturer and the buyers of that brand. As we saw earlier, this can be even more effective than when it is addressed to that person directly.[6] And should the bystander eventually try Meadow Lea, the commercial is then saying directly to them 'you oughta be congratulated'. The bystander does not look to prove or disprove a claim or promise. There is thus nothing in the ad that non-buying bystanders are likely to be motivated to refute or object to. The ad's effect is a feather.

One of the best examples of this technique was a US commercial for Toyota trucks. It featured vignettes of Toyota truck owners saying what they were doing when their truck clocked up 100 000 or 200 000 or 300 000 miles. It closed with an invitation to Toyota truck owners to phone a free number 'and tell us where you were and what you were doing' at these milestones. This ad undoubtedly reinforced the repeat buying of those who already owned a Toyota truck by reminding them of the durability of their truck and the number of miles it had endured. Just as importantly, however, it also got the message across indirectly to the 'bystanders', to those who had never bought a Toyota truck that these must be very, very durable machines.

The long-running 'I can't get by without my Mum' campaign for Mum deodorant is another example of using a brand's own customers talking about their product in such a way that the viewer is cast as a bystander rather than the target of the message.

Deighton, in a brilliant new twist on this, has pointed out that advertising tunes up our attention to a brand's key attribute(s) *at the time that we are consuming it*.[7] It is more likely that we will think of some aspect of the advertising at the time we use the brand, and consequently take greater notice than we otherwise would have of the advertised attribute. In the same way as I can direct your attention to the noises going on around you right now that you were previously not consciously aware of, so can advertising draw our attention to or remind us to notice the advertised attribute when we are consuming the brand. As a result of repetition of the advertising, when we consume the brand we may think to confirm that the brand does indeed have the advertised attribute. The advertising sensitises us to experiencing those advertised attributes and confirming them. It therefore has the potential *to transform the consumption experience*. Without first experiencing the advertising we might simply consume the brand without noticing the differences between it and its competitors.

Confirming that a brand has the advertised attribute has two effects:

- It reinforces the consumption experience and makes us more likely to buy the same brand again.
- It makes us feel more positively toward the advertiser and the truthfulness of their advertising. (People use their experience with the brand to judge an ad's truthfulness and therefore its informativeness. Whether people regard an ad as 'informative' is greatly influenced by their satisfaction with the brand.[8])

Ads that work or ads that win awards

Far from being omnipotent ogres who can manipulate us at will, companies which advertise often struggle desperately to produce an ad that works. They are often frustrated by the inability of their advertising agency to give them a campaign they are looking for, one that has a measurable impact on sales and market share. What they too often get instead are clever pieces of art.

Companies which advertise want to sell product. The people who are primarily responsible for making ads for them, the creative directors in advertising agencies, are artistic people. Many of them are making ads not because they choose to, but because they can't do what they most want to do—make feature films.

Denied the opportunity to make full-length films, it is natural that they will get at least some satisfaction from producing 30-second feature films instead. The result is that advertisers often end up with 30-second feature films disguised as TV ads and many of these win awards. Now 30-second feature films may look nice and they may be very clever and entertaining, but if the brand is used merely as a prop and little regard is given to the main purpose as a commercial, then the chance of it succeeding in its real purpose is very small. If it does work, it is likely to be more by accident than design.

Until 1990 in Australia, awards for advertising were based solely on subjective judgment of quality and/or artistic merit. Objective measurement of effectiveness in selling the product was not considered. Indeed, many advertisers in the past have not known whether these mini-films worked or didn't work. More often than not, they could not gauge effectiveness by their sales alone because there are too many other things (price promotion, what competitors do) that also affect sales, and as we have seen, reinforcement rather than sales is often the primary effect. Advertisers have been able to do little more than grope towards effective advertising.

However, this is now beginning to change. With the advent of new market research technology and a more educated breed of product managers, marketing managers and marketing directors, companies are becoming less and less reliant on their advertising agency simply winning artistic awards to reassure them that their advertising is working. Awards introduced by the Advertising Federation of Australia in 1991 made objectively measured effectiveness the main judging criterion.[9] More and more, the advertisers themselves are putting in place the market research mechanisms which will allow them to assess what is working and what is not.

Summary

Most advertising tries to get us to buy one brand instead of another and is not concerned with new products *per se*. It tips the balance in the weighing up of brands when everything is equal, and it can influence which brands get weighed up.

Advertising for new products announces more than it persuades. To the extent that persuasion is involved its record would be extremely poor, because at least 40 per cent of all new consumer products fail. When advertising does influence our feelings of need for the product category, this is more a side effect than something that the advertising is primarily focused on.

The effect of advertising more often therefore is not persuasion but reinforcement. That is, it reinforces us in the decision we made to purchase the brand and increases the chances of our buying it again.

Much of the art of advertising lies in finding a way to play the focal beam of attention onto the attributes of the brand that are consistent with our existing mind sets. Positioning a product in this way is no easy task.

Advertising's power is constrained as much by practical limitations as by absolute limitations. These include:

• The fact that consumers vote with their feet.
• Competitive advertising.
• Money: limitations of budget.
• Economic reality.
• Resistance to change and cognitive consistency.
• The fact that advertising is usually the weaker influence compared to what we already know or have in our minds.

None of these limitations is absolute but taken together they make advertising much less able to influence us than would be thought by the average consumer. This notion will probably not convince those who want to believe in the manipulative power of advertising, because advertising is one of those things that some people love to hate. The reality, however, is that the power and mystique of advertising and the people who make it have been much exaggerated.

Part B

What works, what doesn't, and why

Introduction

We saw in Part A that we can gain an important insight into advertising by asking the question, 'Who is the ad talking to?' The same applies to books like this one. Who is this book talking to? If it is aimed at the general reader it will have a different feel and style, than if it is aimed at advertising practitioners or students of marketing or mass communication. Part A talked primarily to the general reader.

At this point in the book the general reader will sense a change of key. The articles that make up Part B were written for the trade publication *Advertising News*. Its readers are advertisers and marketers who want to know more about how to make advertising work more effectively.

While this section talks primarily to these professionals, general readers should find it an interesting 'bystander' experience. In fact they may like to imagine themselves as advertisers. By looking briefly through the advertisers' eyes they will develop a greater understanding of advertising at work, and see the obstacles that advertisers strive to overcome in their attempt to influence us.

Most of these articles appeared between 1990 and 1992. Some updating and merging has been done for this book but by and large the content remains the same.

An understanding of only three technical terms is necessary for reading Part B. The first of these, 'ad execution', has already cropped up in Part A. A brand like Coke will often have several different ads on air in the same week. While the brand and the essential message are usually the same, the characters, dialogue or general scene may be different in each case. Each variation is referred to as an ad execution. Alternatively, you may see a 30-second ad and a 15-second one which is recognisable as a part of the larger ad. These are regarded as two different 'executions'. The creative execution, then, is the way that a particular ad is carried out or executed.

The second technical term is 'flighting'. Some advertisers schedule their brand's advertising to appear every week. This is known as a continuous advertising schedule. Others prefer to 'flight' their advertising, in other words to have a burst of several weeks of the same advertising followed by a few weeks off air, then go on air again with another few weeks of the same advertising and so on. This is known as a flighted ad schedule. Each new burst of advertising is regarded as a separate 'flight'.

The third technical term is TARP, short for Target Audience Rating Points. Loosely speaking, it is a measure of the exposure that an ad gets. Indirectly, it reflects the amount of audience exposure and the number of exposures that the advertiser pays for. The number of TARPs is a measure of how many people from the target market were sitting in front of the TV set when the ad was shown.

Let me explain this with an example. Kleenex might define its primary target market for tissues as females 18 to 45 years old. If the ad for Kleenex tissues went to air on Channel 9 at 6pm last night and 20 per cent of this group were watching the channel at that time, the ad has 20 TARPs. If the ad is shown again several times in the same week, each time the percentage of the target market that is watching that channel at that time is added to the accumulated TARP figure. So the ad might accumulate 210 TARPs for the week. Note that this is merely the gross total of people exposed at each sitting. Some of these will have seen the ad when it was shown earlier in the week but they are nevertheless counted *again* in the TARP figure. The total TARP figure is therefore calculated from the percentage of the target market that has seen the ad at least once, or *the net reach*, and average the number of times they saw it, which is known as *the average frequency*.[1] A total of 210 TARPs for the week could represent a variety of combinations of reach and frequency. The table below shows only a few of the possibilities.

Table Part B Introduction   Calculation of TARP figure

Net reach (%)	Average frequency	Total TARPS
100	2.1	210
50	4.2	210
35	6.0	210

For example, the whole target market may have seen the ad during the week and they may have seen it on average 2.1 times. Or perhaps only 50 per cent of the target audience saw the ad but they saw it on average 4.2 times. This still accumulates to 210 TARPs. In other words an ad can accumulate 210 TARPs through any combination of net reach (percentage of the target audience who saw it at least once) and average frequency (the average number of times these people did see it) that when multiplied together totals 210.

The majority of ad campaigns in Australia run at 100 to 300 TARPs a week. Fifty TARPs would be a light weight while 400 TARPs would be a heavy weight of advertising in any one week.

10 Continuous tracking: Are you being followed?

I estimate that maybe one in five major packaged goods makers, as well as some durable goods manufacturers and semi-government utilities, are now tracking their competitors' as well as their own activities continuously with customer surveys. These are not once a year or once a quarter surveys. They are conducted every week— on small samples each week which accumulate over the year into a large database and provide a total, continuous picture.

Every week these organisations capture, in their computers, fresh information on a new sample of consumers. The information covers all players in the market. It covers the state of play for that week in regard to people's behaviour, attitudes, brand awareness, brand image as well as direct communication effects such as advertising recall, advertising recognition and message take-out. This is then related to other information such as media data indicating what advertisers were on air during that week, at what times and at what advertising weight.

This market research technology is rapidly becoming accepted as the best way to accurately assess advertising effects and diagnose why an ad is or is not working. Before its development, from the 1950s through into the 1980s, market research was characterised by the large-scale, large-sample survey representing a single point in time. 'Ad hoc' surveys, as these were known, were conducted before an ad campaign and then again after it. Any differences in key measures between these two surveys (such as in the levels of peoples' brand awareness, ad awareness or market share) were supposed to indicate possible effects of the advertising. This 'pre-post' survey technique, as it is known, is slowly but inevitably giving way to the new technology of continuous surveying.

Conducting ad hoc surveys or pre-post surveys is the 'old' way of trying to understand what is happening in a market. It is like taking a couple of still frames from the beginning and end of a TV commercial and trying to get a sense of the whole commercial from just those two pictures. The difference between ad hoc surveys and continuous surveying resembles the difference between still photography and moving pictures. Without continuous moving pictures, the dynamics of what is happening can only be guessed at.

Take the case of the now famous Decore commercial. The plot unfolds as follows: A new, different ad hits the tube: the 'singing in the shower' Decore ad. It is clearly an exciting and different commercial. The advertiser is putting quite heavy expenditure behind the 60-second commercial. Quickly we see, to no one's surprise, that this ad successfully cuts through the clutter of shampoo advertising and delivers a message. We see this in the first two weeks of data (see Figures 10.1 and 10.2). So far so good, but will the ad sell product? If you are a competitor, do you react? Panic? Sit tight? You recall a previous ad for Decore which cut through very well, but ho-hum, it didn't sell. Maybe this will be the same. Let's not worry too much yet! The key issue is will consumer *behaviour* change?

The continuous surveying that you are doing in the field asks as a matter of course which brand the respondent last bought and the answers come in each week in the weekly sample data. You wait and watch agonisingly. Will brand purchase behaviour move in response to the ad?

Figures 10.1 and 10.2 tell the story. Within a month of the ad coming on air, you know the hair-raising truth (see graph B). By the third or fourth week of the new advertising, Decore's market share is clearly moving. By the fifth week it has doubled from 2.5 per cent to around 5 per cent. There is now no doubt this new ad is working. If Decore is a competitor, you had better move fast to try to find a way to counter it. Or start revising the annual market share projections for your brand *downwards*.

In fact, nine weeks after the launch of the new ad, Decore has successfully increased its market share in this group to more than 10 per cent—a phenomenal achievement. If you are a competitor of Decore the news you are getting from your tracking is depressing. The upside of this, however, is that you know at the earliest possible moment. While it may be cold comfort, you do have more time to formulate a retaliation strategy.

I have also seen situations like this where the ad, while very visible and attention getting, did not sell the product (sometimes because there was no relevant message or the ad failed to correctly communicate the brand and link it with the message). In the absence of such weekly information, it is sometimes overwhelmingly tempting to react when in fact there may be no need to. It is comforting

Figure 10.1   Decore advertisement awareness

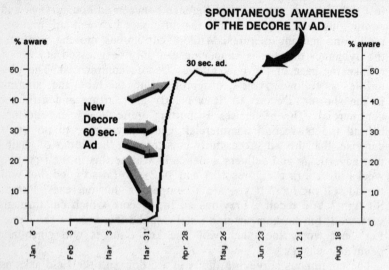

Note: Graph A. Continuous tracking of people's spontaneous awareness of the Decore advertisement.
Source: MarketMind® Continuous Tracking. Sutherland Smith Research.

Figure 10.2   Decore 'market share'

Note: Graph B.
Source: MarketMind® Continuous Tracking. Sutherland Smith Research.

to know at the earliest possible time that you *don't* need to react to a competitor's move.

With this Decore commercial, you have just received the clearest possible evidence that advertising can work in this market. Additional analysis over time allows you to draw conclusions as to the *type* of advertising that works and how it works in this market (because not all markets work the same way).

For example, in this market, did attitude change before behaviour, or did behaviour change before attitude? Did the advertising impact on image then attitude then behaviour? What was the direction of the chain of events?

Product managers and marketing managers want to know what works in their market and what doesn't. If a competitor implements a new action, should they react? How do they judge what to react to and what not to react to?

While continuous surveying as a 'rear-vision mirror', has been around for a while, I am beginning to discern among some of our own clients a new trend in its use. That is, they are not just using it to see where they have been and evaluate the effectiveness of their moves, but to address the much larger question of *how the market works*. Increasingly, they are using it before making their important moves—to study their competitors' activities as well as their own. Their objective is to know what works and what doesn't *before* they make any important move in the market. The idea is to formulate the right move and ensure the maximum chance of success.

Not all are using it in this way but an increasing number are. They are not so much interested in tracking their own brand initially (although they do that too). They are very interested in studying their competitors and *their* actions and the effectiveness of those actions. By getting a handle on what is effective and what is not, they move towards closure on the question of what works and what doesn't in the particular market.

They address such questions as:

- Does advertising work in this market?
- What type of advertising works?
- How does it work?
- Does the advertising change attitudes and then behaviour? Or behaviour then attitudes?
- Should we have advertising that primarily reinforces behaviour ('You oughta be congratulated')? Or do we need advertising that will primarily generate trial ('Four good reasons to try brand x')?

In other words, 'What works? And what doesn't?'

It is important to note that we are not just talking about advertising here. Product managers and advertising managers are also interested in promotions, changes in media flighting, different media weights, a switch to 60-second ads, a free sampling campaign, a change in pricing, new positioning, a new presenter, or new creative advertising ideas. (The graph shows what happened when Decore switched from 60-second to 30-second commercials. The flattening out of the growth in ad cut-through is very common after such a switch. It also happens after a switch from 30s to 15s. Almost any action or event that takes place in a market can be plotted on the time line and subjected to this type of effectiveness analysis.

Snapshot, single-point-in-time surveys do not cope with this. Dynamics are needed. Snapshot pictures are too slow, and they don't capture unexpected events—such as the launch of this new ad campaign by a competitor. Pre-post or periodic-snapshot surveys of the market every quarter or half year or so are yesterday's technology. The problem with them is that the time dimension is missing.

With dynamic measurement, market modelling and market knowledge accumulate over time and let a company know much more than its competition about how the market works, what works in it and what doesn't. The objective is to do more of what works and less of what doesn't.

It is no accident that Ronald Reagan was the most popular president ever—or that George Bush came from miles behind to take out the presidency in 1989. The Republican party discovered some years ago the 'missing link' in research. The missing link was the time dimension. (Bush was ultimately defeated in 1992 by Clinton which demonstrates the point made earlier—there are real limits to what advertising and promotion can do when the product does not perform or is looking old and tired.)

Traditional market research has often failed to produce actionable results. It has often been difficult to assess its value, precisely because the time dimension, reflecting the dynamic nature of markets, was either missing or very much mistreated. The time dimension has to be treated as a continuous variable and factored into marketing research methodology instead of being ignored or treated as a dichotomous variable.

The problem with traditional market research is that with the time dimension missing, it is like taking still-camera snapshots. It is equivalent to taking the first and last frame of a television commercial and trying to guess from that what went on in between. With the time dimension included, you get the full dynamic picture. The research becomes richer and its value is much more easily demonstrable in terms of:

- Its role as an 'early-warning system'.
- Its ability to reveal changing patterns in a market.
- Its ability to tease out inferences about causation and relate these to assessment of the effectiveness of advertising, promotions etc.
- Its ability to capture unexpected events.
- Its asset value as a cumulative data-base resource.

Markets are dynamic. They are a moving picture and they need dynamic—not static— techniques to capture their richness. Tracking on a continuous basis puts the missing dimension of time back into market research.

If you are not tracking your competition using continuous tracking, is your competition tracking you? Are you being followed?

11 New product launches: Don't pull the plug too early

Why do so many new products fail?

Using MarketMind® Continuous Tracking*, we have monitored more than 50 product categories in Australia alone over the past several years, and in many of them we have been able to observe a range of new brands or products being launched. There is no single reason for the high rate of new product failure but there is one fairly common one. This has to do with the fact that the care and attention evident at the pre-launch stage are not carried through after the 'go' button is pushed.

Not enough companies closely and continuously monitor what is happening at the product launch and in the immediate post-launch period. The result is that many of the all-important fine-tuning adjustments necessary to marketing success, fail to be made. And the product crashes.

Most companies these days put a lot of money and careful attention into development of a new product. They do the same with the development of the advertising and the promotional program to back it up. They pre-test the advertising and the acceptance of the product concept and try to put everything in place for the launch to succeed.

But then a funny thing happens. The launch button is pushed. And in this crucial immediate post-launch stage, the tendency is to do little more than take a deep breath, pray that they have done everything right, and wait anxiously for the judgment—the judgment of the market . . . Will the product be a success or a failure?

If NASA launched space shuttles the way manufacturers launch new brands, there would be fewer astronauts!

* MarketMind® Continuous Tracking is a proprietary system of continuous surveying and databasing which is conducted under licence from MarketMind Technologies Pty Ltd.

Durable products

Many new durable products fail because early sales do not come up to expectation. Pessimism then spreads within the company and often results in management 'pulling the plug' too early and abandoning the product.

Figure 7 shows a new brand of durable product which was launched with a continuous advertising schedule for seven weeks. At the end of that time the company took the advertising off air 'because sales were not up to expectation'. The whole mood of the company and its marketing team projected disappointment and an expectation of looming product failure. This is a real danger point in new product launches because the gloom is likely to be self-fulfilling.

Fortunately in this case, and for the first time in this company's history, not only sales but also the effect of the campaign on attitudes towards the brand were being monitored continuously. On the basis of the continuous tracking data, we were able to argue that the company should keep going; that just because sales had not yet responded was no reason to abort the advertising or to give up on the new product.

As a result the company went back on air with advertising for the product. The graph clearly shows that since then, each time there was a burst of advertising, attitudes toward the brand improved (with one exception, when the launch of another new, competitive brand muddied the picture somewhat). Three months after the launch, the brand, far from being a failure, had a 15 per cent market share. The same brand is alive and well today, but if the abort decision had been made it might well have ended up in the annals of product history as just another new-product failure.

This case also illustrates the importance of continuous measurement—not just snapshot surveys. The market is a movie and its richness cannot be captured by a couple of snapshot surveys with a box Brownie. It needs continuous measurement.

Consider the situation in the first eight months of the product's life. If a snapshot-type survey had been conducted on 3 February, it would have shown that 10 per cent of people were prepared to seriously consider the brand next time they bought that type of product (i.e. were 'short-listers' for the brand). A good result. If another snapshot survey were conducted on 18 August after 6 months of advertising, it would have shown no change as a result of all that advertising. Without continuous measurement, these snapshot-type surveys might well have given the false impression that

Figure 11.1 Advertising influence on intentions

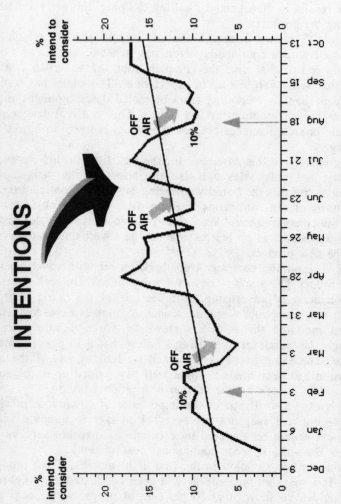

Note: Intention to buy new brand increases when on-air and decays when off-air, resulting in an overall upward trend.
Source: MarketMind® Continuous Tracking. Sutherland Smith Research.

further advertising bursts were having no further effect on people's attitudes.

However, as the trend line in the continuous data clearly indicates, there was a long-term positive effect of continuing with the advertising for this brand. Each time it went on air it was developing and strengthening attitudes towards the brand—it was strengthening the brand's consumer franchise. Between those on-air times, the mental territory that the advertising had previously captured would begin to erode because of the lack of advertising reinforcement, but overall, in the long haul, the product was gaining more than it was losing.

Repeat-purchase supermarket products

Measurements of sales, profit and market share are not enough to enable you to know what is going on in new product launches. It is crucial to monitor various other things—among them awareness (the proportion of people who are aware of the new product) and trial (the proportion who have ever tied it)—and to do this continuously.

Why is this so important? It is because a 10 per cent market share in supermarket-type products can come about in either of two extreme ways.

- Ten per cent of people have ever bought the new brand and they are buying it 100 per cent of the time—that is, they are completely loyal.
- One hundred per cent of people have bought it, but they are only buying it 10 per cent of the time—that is, they are buying that brand only about one in every ten times they shop for the product category.

Depending which situation the new brand finds itself in, the strategic implications are quite different. In the first case the company needs to get more people to try the brand if it wants to increase market share. In the second case, the company has managed to get people to try it but the only way it is going to increase market share is to increase their repeat buying.

So it is vitally important in the lift-off stage to measure not just market share but also how many people have ever bought or tried the new product. Incredible as it may seem, some companies fail to do this. And when it is done, a reading is generally only taken in a survey repeated every six or twelve months.

This is not enough. Companies need to know how the trial is progressing *continuously*. NASA monitors its space launches continuously. It doesn't press the button and then come back after lunch to see how things are going. It knows that anything may have happened in the meantime. Things occur that need correction, adjustment or fine-tuning! By the time some manufacturers come back and do a survey one month, two months or six months after launch, it is too late. What they frequently find is that the product is out of control or has crashed—or sometimes, that it never even got off the ground.

A well-known biscuit manufacturer several years ago launched new biscuit products this way all the time. The company spent huge resources developing new varieties of biscuits and then conducting in-home placement tests in which consumers were asked which one(s) they liked best and therefore which were the best candidates to put on the market.

This type of testing revealed which varieties people liked, how much they liked them, and how likely they were to repeat-buy those varieties. The problem that this company failed to come to grips with was how to get people to buy and try the biscuits in the first place.

Typically, after launching one of the new biscuit products, the company would look only at sales. If sales were not up to expectation in the first three months or so, it would simply abandon the product. While it had some successes, it had many more 'failures'. The main reason for the failures continued to go unrecognised and the company continued to make the same mistake over and over.

The problem in most cases was not that the new variety was rejected by the market. It was to do with the inadequate level of marketing support put behind the launch and the over-reliance on advertising alone without promotional activity to generate that key first trial.

The company failed to monitor closely what was happening immediately after the 'go' button was pressed and the launch had begun. Because it didn't know exactly what happened between the launch and the crash it kept having crashes, largely as a result of the same problems. Many other companies only look at profit, sales and market share to indicate new product performance and then make these critical decisions. Therein lies a common problem with new-product launches.

In one case in point a new biscuit was launched but discontinued after about four months. When the decision to abort was made, this variety had about 3 per cent market share, which was regarded as 'not enough'. Like so many of its previous new product attempts, the company regarded this as a failure.

When the decision to abort was made the variety had only about 3 per cent market share but this was primarily because only about 10 per cent of people had ever tried it. Its repeat buying rate was in fact quite good. The people who had tried it were buying it about one in every three times they bought biscuits—which is not bad in the biscuit market, where there are so many varieties to choose from.

The company had tested the product by in-home placement, i.e. 'forced' trial, and this had accurately predicted that people would accept and like the product one they had tasted it. The key words are 'once they had tasted it'.

Remember, only 10 per cent of people had tasted it before the launch was aborted. It was not the *product* that failed. It was the marketing activities that were designed to get it trialled that failed! Not enough resources were put into the launch to ensure successful communication of the product's qualities to enough people to prompt them to try it the first time.

The company aborted this variety and went off to develop a new one that it hoped would do better next time!

The point here is that initial trial is a key ingredient in new product launches for supermarket products. Even if the product was the greatest-tasting biscuit ever and got a repeat buying level of 100 per cent, it could not have gone above 10 per cent market share if only 10 per cent of people had ever tried it. On the other hand with a 30 per cent repeat buying level, if the company had got another 60 per cent of people to try it, the product would have gained a potential market share of 18 per cent (i.e. 30 per cent of 60 per cent).

Our biscuit manufacturer wasted a lot of money trying to find outstanding product formulations that would guarantee success. But once you look at its activity in the light of the very low trial figures for its new products, the lesson is clear. The world will not beat a path to any company's door, whether it develops a better mousetrap or a better biscuit. The product has to be effectively marketed. The company has to get people to try it.

Instead of looking for ideal product formulations, the urgent need is more often to address the level and fine-tuning of marketing support for new products. To ensure that these are adequate and functioning as they should requires that companies closely monitor their launches, making appropriate adjustments, fine-tunings and corrections as required. Failure to do this is one of the most important causes of new product failure. Too often, marketers have too little information and pull the plug on the new product too early, i.e. before they have achieved the necessary awareness and trial.

Trial needs to be gained early, while the product has a newness and freshness about it. If it does not achieve good penetration in the first six months it is unlikely to succeed. This is particularly important for seasonal products such as new varieties of canned

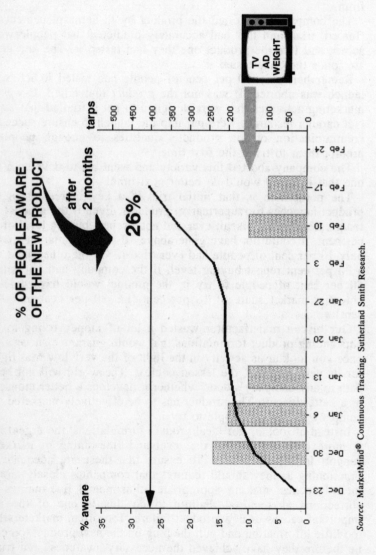

Figure 11.2 Awareness of a new food product

% OF PEOPLE AWARE OF THE NEW PRODUCT

after 2 months

26%

Source: MarketMind® Continuous Tracking. Sutherland Smith Research.

soup or chocolate biscuits in winter or of ice blocks in summer. If trial is not achieved quickly and in the first season, the 'new' product has to come back next season as an old product and yet try to pretend 'newness' in order to get interest and trial. Generally, it doesn't work. (See Chapter 16: Seasonal products)

If the new product is going to succeed it has to get trial as quickly as possible before it loses its image of newness; that usually means in the season in which it is launched.

An obvious part of getting this first-season trial is making people aware of the new product and getting them interested in it. This is a communications task and, like everything else, needs monitoring.

Figure 11.2 shows response to a new product two months after launch. Only 26 per cent of consumers have heard of the brand, which means that advertising to this point has failed to communicate the existence of the new product to more than half of the potential market.

The implication is clear. It would be foolish to abort the product. What is needed is a change in the advertising or promotional strategy. Either the ad targeting and scheduling is ineffective, or the ad itself hasn't got the creative touch to cut through clutter and get people to try the new product without more promotional support.

Launching new products should be like launching space shuttles—the successes should outnumber the failures. It is not an inevitable law of marketing that in the launching of products there needs to be more casualties than successes.

12 Planning campaign strategy around consumers' mental filing cabinets

Ads are like alcohol: the more you have the less you remember. After only two or three drinks your faculties start to become impaired. After exposure to only one or two competing ads, your memory, for the first one, starts to become impaired. What is true of alcohol is surprisingly true of consumer memory for advertising—at least for competing brands in the same product category.

Over a period of a week, the more competing commercials that are aired for a product category, the less the average person will remember about any one of them. Most people think that forgetting is simply the fading of memory with the passage of time. However, it is now well established that forgetting is due not to the passage of time alone, but to additional learning that takes place during that time. (In an extreme example, a 1924 experiment in psychology showed that people remember much more over a period of time when the interval is filled with sleep rather than normal waking activity.) When time passes but little or no further (competing) learning takes place there is very little forgetting.

On the other hand, where a lot of activity and new learning—especially competitive learning—fill the time interval, these 'interference effects' become very great indeed. These effects are one of the clearest of findings on the way human memory works. They are also one of the most frequent findings to emerge from continuous tracking of advertising.

Memory, the ability to retrieve an event or message, can be severely impaired when a person is exposed to other similar events within a short time. While this is a well-established finding in psychology, it is not widely recognised in marketing. Few people take account of it in planning advertising media schedules or when they are assessing why their ad campaign may have 'failed'.

126

Models of memory and forgetting

At a crowded party, if you want to communicate you have to speak very loudly. The more voices and the more competition, the louder the din gets. You have to shout to be heard above the clutter. On television you also have to shout for your ad to be heard. The greater the clutter the more you have to shout. In other words, the more competitors you have advertising against you, the more effort and money you will have to expend to get your message across.

Even when you shout, your communication may still not register successfully, especially if the target is distracted or tuned in to someone else's conversation, or is musing on something else. How many conversations can you tune in to at one time? Two? Three? How many commercials for different brands in a product category can a consumer hang on to in his or her mind? There is no single threshold. Rather, each subsequent input progressively diminishes the memory for any and all others.

The popular view of memory is that a trace of the remembered thing is either there or it is not. You can either remember it or you can't. This model of memory is demonstrably wrong. How many times have you been unable to remember someone's name even though you *know* that you know it? Forgetting has more to do with 'inability to retrieve' than with failure to store the memory. It is usually not failure to store the memory that is the problem. It is inability to remember it when you want it.

I find it helpful to think of memories as being stored in one of several mental filing cabinets. If you carefully file a new memory, a new ad, in a particular filing cabinet you should be able to retrieve it quickly and easily as needed. However, if you were distracted enough or unmotivated enough to casually stow the new memory away without paying any attention to what you were doing or which filing cabinet you were stowing it in, the chances are that you will have great difficulty retrieving it. More to the point, you will be unable to retrieve it quickly. The only way you can retrieve it will be to painstakingly look through every cabinet and every possible file.

With memory, the problem is usually not inability to retrieve, but inability to retrieve in any reasonable or functional time. So for all intents and purposes, the information becomes 'functionally lost'.

Information can become functionally lost because it is a long time since you filed it. It can also become functionally lost as a result of interference effects—the competing exposures discussed earlier. You can think of interference effects as the outcome of trying to store several similar memories all in the one file. The more cluttered the file becomes, the longer it is going to take to look through it and to retrieve any particular one.

When a consumer is exposed to competing commercials, this is what happens. There is interference from previously stored ads, often exacerbated by the fact that the consumer is often fairly unmotivated or uninvolved when storing them. These types of memory inputs and the interference effect is all the greater when the viewer has low involvement.

Another way of thinking about it is that exposure to competing commercials is like laying down tracks on a two- or three-track tape. After you have recorded the first one, two or three, the next one is laid down partly over the previous ones. And subsequent ones are laid down on top of that, thus setting up increasing interference and distortion in the memory play-back.

Advertising application

It is for this reason that the 'effectiveness' or impact of a commercial is very much influenced by how much competitors spend advertising against it in a particular week. It is rarely just a simple function of how much an advertised brand spends on advertising time (its media weight) in any week.

An advertiser cannot effectively plan or monitor a brand's ad strategy without information about competing on-air activity. This is why anyone who is serious about maximising the effectiveness of their ad strategy needs to have access to weekly data (monthly or quarterly is not good enough) on which advertisers were on air in that week and at that weight. Such data is available through AIM-Data.[1]

It is always worth looking at the raw relationship between the amount spent on a brand's advertising and indicators of effectiveness such as sales, market share or advertising awareness. But don't be surprised or disappointed if you don't see any clear relationship. This does not mean that the advertising is not working. Try looking not at the total amount of advertising for the brand but at the brand's *share* of advertising in the product category, week by week. A strong relationship may then emerge.

Figure 12.1 illustrates the point. The bars indicate the weeks when this brand's advertising campaign was on TV. Their heights indicate the brand's share of the total TV advertising in its product category (share of media weight or share of voice).

The product is a consumer product and its share of voice is plotted against a measure of people's spontaneous awareness of the ad. This latter is a relative measure and is called the brand's TV share of

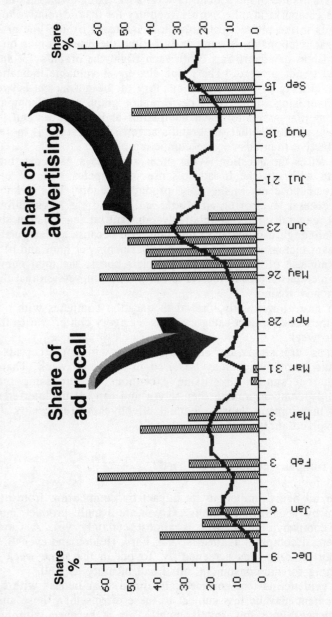

Figure 12.1 Television share of mind and share of voice

Note: For this brand a clear relationship is evident between its share of advertising and its share of advertisement recall.

Source: MarketMind® Continuous Tracking. Sutherland Smith Research.

mind. This is the brand's share of total advertising awareness in the product category; in other words, memory for that ad relative to all other ads in the product category. It is indicated by the line graph.

A clear relationship is evident each time the brand comes on air with a flight of advertising. With each flight the brand's TV share of mind trends upward. (The graph also gives valuable indications of how quickly or how slowly memory of the ad decays between each advertising flight.) This performance graph can be compared with a similar graph for each competitor and inferences can then be drawn about whether the brand's advertising strategy is more or less effective than ads for the competing brands.

This raises the question: What other ads does a particular brand compete with? In the broadest sense it competes with all other ads—even those not in the same product category. This is known as the general level of on-air clutter and any ad has to cut through it. This general clutter is relatively constant, at least in the short term—although it grows over the long term because a) deregulation has meant increased numbers of advertisements per hour and b) the increasing use of 15-second commercials boosts the total number of commercials seen and increases the general impression that there is more advertising.

Even more importantly, the ad in question competes with other ads in the same product category. This 'category clutter' varies from week to week.

Perhaps surprisingly, our ad also competes with any other ads for the same brand which may be aired in the same week. That is, multiple but similar advertising executions for the same brand frequently compete among themselves and can set up interference effects that impede their individual effectiveness (especially with low-involved audiences).

Can a company compete with itself?

Is your ad being limited in its impact by competition from other ads run by your own company? If you are a multi-product, multi-brand company, the answer is almost certainly yes. A Corolla commercial competes against Nissan, Ford, Holden and even BMW ads. But all other ads screened by Toyota in the same week are competing for the consumers' mind and memory as well.

The evidence is that commercials aimed at audiences with high involvement may be less subject to these effects than those aimed at audiences with low involvement. This is because with high-involvement situations the consumer may consciously and deliberately process the message in such a way as to make it more resistant to forgetting. That is, he files it in a way that anticipates a future need to retrieve it. With high involvement messages, unlike low involvement ones, the viewer anticipates a future need to use the information.

The key point here is the level of involvement of the target audience. If car ads are aimed at people intending to buy a new car in the next two or three months, then these people are likely to be highly involved. However, around a third of all new-car purchases are made by people who did not intend to buy a new car but were overtaken by events. These include people whose old car suddenly gave them problems and the growing number of people who separate from their spouse and find a need for another car. Such people are likely to be low-involved at the time of exposure to the advertising—at least up to the point before the 'need' is triggered by the unforeseen event.

So advertising for high-involvement products such as cars may need to address an uninvolved target audience as well as a highly involved one.

In summary, successful advertising planning and evaluation demands detailed analysis of more than just one's own ad expenditure. It especially necessitates an understanding of consumer memory processes in regard to interference effects as well as memory decay. The on-air effectiveness of an ad is influenced by several things—not necessarily in this order:

- The execution. Is it a great ad?
- The dollars spend. How much 'weight' was put behind it that week?
- The flighting. How is the ad being flighted from week to week?
- The number of competitors who are on air in the same week and how much they spent.
- The number of different ad executions for the same brand that you have on air in any one week.
- The number of commercials for the same umbrella brand that you have on air in any one week.
- The level of involvement of the target audience and the complexity of the message that needs to be communicated.

13   What happens when you stop advertising?

In tight economic times, the pressures are always on to cut advertising. Can a company do this? Can it get away with it? What will be the effect on the company a bit further down the track? These are the questions that start to be asked when the recessionary animal starts to bite.

If the company stops advertising and sales stay at the same level, the cessation of ad spending generates an immediate improvement in the bottom line. Hence the strong temptation to cut advertising in tough times and make the company's profit performance look good. What are the consequences? What do we know about stopping advertising?

What happens when advertising stops?

We do not know a lot about what happens when advertising stops but what we do know is enough to warrant caution. Most companies don't know what happens when advertising stops because they only look at the immediate sales figures. If sales don't go down, they breathe a sigh of relief.

So it could be a smart decision. But then again, it could be a time bomb. A doctoral thesis on milk advertising in the US in the 1970s revealed the nature of the time bomb. It underlines the fact that maintenance of sales in the short or medium term is no reason for complacency.

In a prolonged series of test market experiments, it was found that when advertising of milk was stopped, nothing happened to sales. Nothing, that is, for twelve months! After a year of no advertising, milk sales suddenly went into a sharp decline and continued to decline at a sickening rate.

Advertising immediately re-started. But it was too late. It took another eighteen months to halt the decline and then begin to reverse it. So beware of the delayed time bomb. 'To regain a favourable position lost during recession costs more in the long run than to retain it by continuing advertising at a satisfactory level.'[1]

For how long can a company afford to stop its advertising?

Rather than ask the question 'Can we stop advertising?', it may be more meaningful to ask: 'For how long can we pause our advertising without risking everything?'

The answer seems to depend on how much residual or carry-over effect the current and past advertising has had. Some campaigns have amazingly strong residual memory effects. Other ads have almost none. They are forgotten almost as soon as they go off air. Continuous tracking of campaigns and advertising flights can reveal how much 'residual capital' has been built up and how quickly it gets eroded once the advertising is stopped.

Some Australian experiences

Figure 13.1, 13.2 and 13.3 demonstrate some Australian experiences with stopping advertising. Compare the first two graphs. They show what happened when two brands (from different product categories) stopped advertising.

Brand A and its advertising had a lot of residual recall even after the ads stopped. There is almost no memory decay of the brand or the advertising after three months. In the case of Brand B, on the other hand, the brand itself had good residual recall but the advertising didn't. When the advertising stopped, recall of the advertising declined rapidly while awareness of the brand held up well.

Brand A had been off air for four months. Brand B had been off air for seven months. Market share did not show any decline in either case. But that is where the complacency ends. When we look more closely, the indications are that other things are going on which could be very detrimental in the longer run.

Erosion of brand franchise

The third graph shows total advertising exposures (TARPs) in one of these markets. Advertising stopped in this market three months previously. There had been no marked changes in sales or market shares for any of the brands in this market—*at that point*.

Figure 13.1   Spontaneous awareness—Brand A

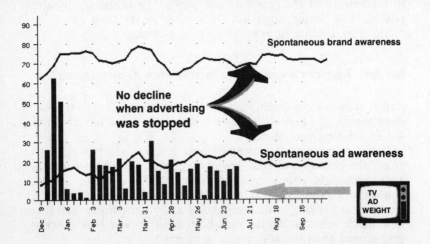

Note: When advertising was stopped for this product no significant decline was observed in spontaneous awareness of the brand or for spontaneous awareness of its advertising.
Source: MarketMind® Continuous Tracking. Sutherland Smith Research.

Figure 13.2   Spontaneous awareness—Brand B

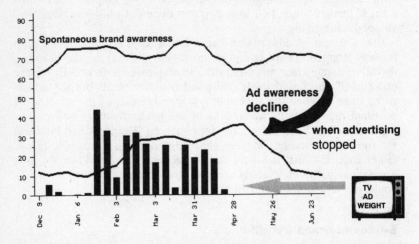

Note: When advertising was stopped for this product the spontaneous awareness of the brand did not decline significantly but a rapid decline in spontaneous advertising awareness took place.
Source: MarketMind® Continuous Tracking. Sutherland Smith Research.

Figure 13.3 Size of market segments

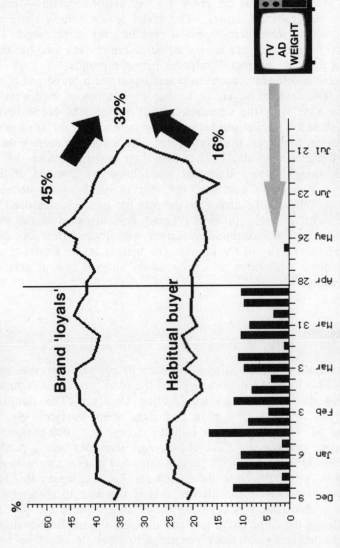

Note: When advertising stopped there was no visible effect whatever on sales. But after two months the 'commitment' of buyers eroded rapidly. The absence of reinforcement created habitual rather than loyal buyers, leaving the brand vulnerable to attack.

Source: MarketMind® Continuous Tracking. Sutherland Smith Research.

However,. if we look further below the surface we find a worrying trend emerging. Brand loyalty is declining. People are still buying the brand but any feeling of 'commitment' that they may have to the brand is eroding.

The market shown in the graph has two major segments—'brand loyals' and 'habitual buyers'. The brand loyals believe there are differences between brands and always buy the same brand. The habitual buyers also tend to buy the same brand each time but they believe there are no real differences between brands.

There is a difference between repeat buyers of a brand and brand loyals. The habitual buyers repeat-buy for reasons of inertia rather than loyalty. With the cessation of advertising, the brand loyals diminish in the market and habitual buyers increase. While sales do not change, the major brand(s) in the market become more vulnerable—more open to attack. They lose their brand franchise.

Even though sales and market share have not changed, if this trend is allowed to continue, the market itself would be very different. Whereas the market in the past has been characterised by brands with strongly promoted brand franchises, it could well become more of a commodity market with little differences perceived between any of the brands. The market leader's sales could thus become wide open to a price attack from a new or existing competitor.

Opportunity

'Rather than wait for business to return to normal, top executives should cash in on the opportunity that the rival companies (who are stopping their advertising) are creating for them. The company courageous enough to stay in and fight when everyone else is playing safe can bring about a dramatic change in market position.'[2]

Now we can see why. The above case illustrates how a market can be made vulnerable even though sales and market shares do not appear to have changed in the short term. For a company that is a smaller competitor in the market, this is the time to go after the market leader. Like a pilot taking off in an aeroplane and picking out holes in the cloud cover to climb through, the smaller advertiser can take advantage of these situations to steer its brand up to a higher level of market share. At such times there is less advertising clutter and the smaller advertiser, even with a small ad budget, is more likely to be heard when the large advertisers are silent.

Reinforcement effect of advertising

So the effects of advertising must not be looked at just in terms of increasing or holding sales. To do so ignores the fact that advertising has a very important reinforcement effect.

One of the most important effects of advertising is consolidating and protecting what has already been built. It reinforces behaviour. People are more convinced of the 'rightness' of their brand choice if they see the brand advertised. And, all other things being equal, they are more likely to buy that brand again.

Some of the most avid readers of car ads are people who have just bought that brand of car. The ads provide reinforcement of their decision. This may not make a whole lot of rational sense, but that's the way we human beings are.

Alternatives to stopping advertising

A key question should be whether to take surgery to the advertising or simply eliminate it. Which way will improve the bottom line without jeopardising the brand in the long run?

We have seen the dangers of stopping advertising altogether, so if you are not going to stop but are under budgetary pressure to economise, is there anything else you can do? Yes! You need to consider some belt-tightening strategies for tough times.

Some belt-tightening strategies for tough times

You need to make the available, though limited, ad budget work more efficiently. Rather than stop the advertising, consider these ways of trimming the waistline and tightening the belt:

- A 'drip' media strategy, i.e. rather than stop the advertising altogether, use reduced exposures (reduced weekly TARP weights) to at least try to hold the ground you have already captured.
- Examine the feasibility of having longer gaps in your advertising flighting pattern. How long can you afford to stay off air between flights without jeopardising your brand franchise?
- If you are using several ad executions on air at the same time, cut back to just one ad and put all your media weight behind it. Be very single-minded. Most companies use too many executions anyway and put too few exposures (TARPs) behind each execution. In other words, avoid 'executional anorexia'. (See Chapter 17, 'Stopping execution anorexia'.)

- If you want to cut back, consider 15-second commercials—but use them not as attack forces but as occupation forces to hold the mental territory that has already been captured. Make sure you build ad awareness to a high level with longer commercials before you switch to 15s. Don't just use 15s as substitutes for 30s. (See Chapter 14, 'Learning to use 15-second TV commercials'.)

14 Learning to use 15-second TV commercials

In the past five years we have tracked numerous ad campaigns, of which an increasing number were beginning to use 15-second commercials. In some cases we have had the opportunity to compare the performance of a 30-second ad in one city with that of a 15-second version of the same ad running simultaneously in some other city.

Conventional wisdom has it that a 15-second commercial is two-thirds as effective as a 30-second commercial. Conventional wisdom is all too often wrong, as our experience with continuous tracking of commercials over time has underlined. We now have a greater understanding of how shorter commercials work.

When they work, 15-second commercials seem to work very differently from 30- or 60-second commercials. Simply trying to use them as cut-down versions of a 30-second ad to save money doesn't work. They need to be used in a different way.

Memory activation vs new learning

We know from psychology experiments that it takes much less time to recognise and process something that is familiar. The more we prime (or activate) something the more familiar it becomes. It is like priming a pump. The more it is primed the quicker it works.

The more familiar something becomes, the faster our minds can process it. Conversely the more unfamiliar something is, the longer it takes our minds to process it. Even with English, the less frequently a word occurs in the language the longer it takes our minds to recognise or process it. Look at Figure 14.1. This shows the time it takes for us to recognise words (measured in fractions of a second).

If I flash a word like 'bagpipes' on the screen for 0.1 second you

139

Figure 14.1 We recognise the familiar more quickly

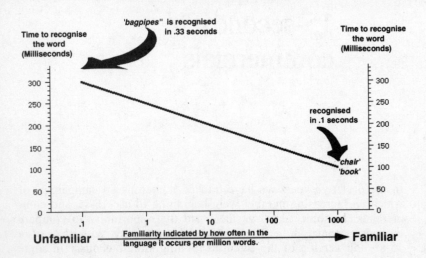

Note: It takes about three times longer for our minds to register and process relatively unfamiliar words like 'bagpipes' than it does to register common words like chair or book.
Source: Adapted from *Journal of Experimental Psychology*, 1951.

will not be able to identify it. The exposure is too fast. It takes an exposure about three times longer (almost 0.33 sec) for your mind to register it.

On the other hand, if I flash your name, or a very familiar word like 'book' or 'chair', your mind will register it in about 0.1 sec. This is because it is familiar to you. We require less time to 'see' and mentally process things that are familiar—including commercials. This points to an underlying principle to guide our use of 15-second commercials.

Getting into people's heads vs staying there

A general principle in the psychology of learning is that it is harder to get into people's minds than it is to stay there. In other words, there are two processes: the process of learning and the process of priming and reinforcement. One is original learning; the other maintains and reinforces the freshness of that learning. The process of reinforcement is not the same as the process of originally communicating something. It usually takes more repetition, or a longer commercial, to get an ad into people's minds in the first place than it does to keep an ad and its message there.

Shorter length commercials are the occupying forces. They are best at occupying and holding the mental ground that has already been captured by the 30- or 60-second attack forces. Thirty- and 60-second commercials are the attack forces. They are good for bringing about learning. They are good for getting a message into people's heads in the first place.

We have found 15-second commercials to be quite effective in holding mental ground *after* 30-second commercials have been used to capture it. However, when used on their own, these shorter commercials often prove disappointing and ineffective (see Figure 14.2, for example).

A telling example

One day, while browsing through information on which advertisers were on air in the previous week, I noted that one advertiser went on air with a single ad but with a huge media weight of 450 TARPs for the week behind it. This means a lot of exposures and a lot of money, so you would expect it to be generating a reasonable return. I was amazed when I saw the data on this advertiser's ad awareness and market share. Figure 14.3 shows what they were. Have a look yourself. Note that ad awareness and market share did not go up. They actually went down—despite all this advertising! Crazy!

I was intrigued by this, so we got hold of the ad. I wanted to see what ad could possibly be that bad. Fifteen seconds later we knew! It was a 15-second commercial, it was being aimed at a low-involved audience, and it was being used on its own.

We had known from past experience that 15-second commercials, when used on their own with low-involved audiences, almost never work. Here again was vivid proof. Even with 450 TARPs this ad seemed all but invisible. It did not cut through, it was doing nothing for market share and nothing in the way of reinforcing people's feelings about the advertiser. It was a waste of money. The advertiser might as well have not been on air.

Lost in the clutter

Fifteen-second commercials, when used on their own with low-involved audiences, have great difficulty cutting through the clutter. Usually the first thing you want an ad to do is to cut through the clutter and get noticed. Time and time again, we have found that 15-second commercials are generally incapable of cutting through

Figure 14.2   A 15-second advertisement failure

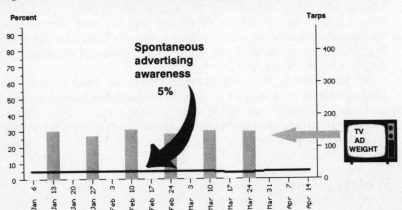

Note: The percentage of people who were spontaneously aware of this 15-second advertisement never rose above 5%.
Source: MarketMind® Continuous Tracking. Sutherland Smith Research.

Figure 14.3   Another 15-second advertisement failure

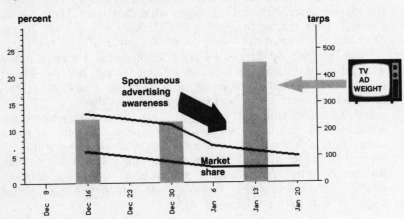

Note: The percentage of people spontaneously aware of this 15-second advertisement actually declined while it was on air as did the brand's market share.
Source: MarketMind® Continuous Tracking. Sutherland Smith Research.

on their own except when the audience is highly involved with the product.

This is surprising, because 15-second ads are usually screened at greater repetition levels than 30-second commercials. One of the seductive attractions of 15-second commercials is that advertisers can get more exposure for the same ad budget than they can with a 30-second ad. Even at very high exposure levels like this one, however, 15-second stand-alone ads often fail to register at the level of conscious ad recall.

There have been amazingly few exceptions. And the exceptions are usually due to the great creative idea in the commercial or to the audience being highly involved with the product category. You need exceptionally creative ad people, or a highly involved audience or an extremely simple message, if you are going to use 15-second commercials on their own. Otherwise they just seem to disappear into the ether.

Prompted ad recall

Some people have said to us: 'But that's *spontaneous* ad recall.' People may not be able to recall the ad but they might be able to recognise it if prompted. Well, what about prompted ad recall? Do 15-second commercials perform better on this measure? The answer is that 15-second stand-alone commercials have also tended to perform badly on prompted ad recall.

Prompted ad recall is an 'easy' test. When a 30-second ad execution is shown or described to a respondent with the brand blanked out, 70 per cent or more can usually claim to have seen it—provided the ad has had a few weeks on air at reasonable reach and frequency. Performance at 70 per cent or better on this 'easy' measure is regarded only as the 'bare minimum' that is necessary. It provides evidence of 'mental reach' without which it probably has no chance of working. It is very easy for people to claim to have seen an ad. (In fact in one case, we had 43 per cent claiming to have seen an ad before it had appeared on air.)

The graphs in Figures 14.4 and 14.5 show prompted recall for two ad campaigns that used stand-alone 15-second commercials. The significant thing is that neither of these campaigns achieved anything like 70 per cent recall. In fact in neither case did more than 30 per cent of people claim to have seen them—despite the large expenditure in airing the ad and the number of exposures.

To make things worse, the lower line on each of the two graphs reveals an even more depressing picture. These lines show the proportion of people who claimed to have seen the ad *and who*

Figure 14.4   Prompted advertisement recall

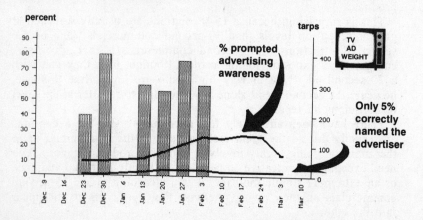

Note: This 15-second advertisement never achieved more than 30% of people claiming to have seen it and less than 5% could correctly name the advertiser.
Source: MarketMind® Continuous Tracking. Sutherland Smith Research.

Figure 14.5   Another prompted advertisement recall

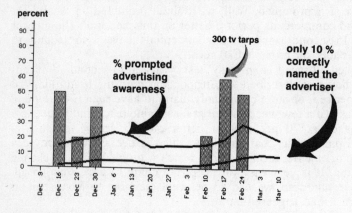

Note: Another 15-second advertisement where only about 30% of people claimed to have seen it and only about 10% could correctly name the advertiser.
Source: MarketMind® Continuous Tracking. Sutherland Smith Research.

could correctly tell us the name of the advertiser. They barely reach 5 per cent in one case and ten per cent in one other. This means that barely ten per cent of the target audience claimed to have seen these ads and knew who the advertiser was: the ads failed to correctly communicate the brand to 90 per cent or more of the target audience.

Message communication

At a second level, capturing mental ground means not only cutting through but also correctly delivering a message or an impression. We have found 15-second commercials when used on their own to be extremely weak in message communication with low-involved audiences. So when they do cut through (which is rarely), they seem unable to communicate anything but the simplest of visual messages.

Table 14.1 shows the results of yet another 15-second ad campaign. Compared with a 45-second campaign for the same product category but run at a different time, its performance is abysmal.

This 15-second commercial campaign went for six weeks with a huge number of exposures (a total of 1850 TARPs, or over 300 TARPs per week). Despite this heavy media weight it achieved only 25 per cent prompted recall and only 4 per cent correct message take-out.

This dramatically illustrates that a key weakness of 15s is in getting across a message. Their main function is one of priming, i.e. reinforcing an already learned brand or message. When they do cut through, 15-second commercials seem unable to communicate anything but the simplest of visual messages. Fifteen-second commercials won't communicate unless the message is extremely simple or the 15-second ad is a reminder ad following from a longer one (i.e. where the message is one which the audience has been exposed to and internalised previously).

Again, this is when used on their own, when the message is

Table 14.1 Comparison of advertisement campaigns

	45 seconds	15 seconds
Length of campaign	2 weeks	6 weeks
Total TARPS	400	1850
Prompted recall	49%	25%
Share of voice	28%	19%
Correct message take-out	30%	4%

anything more than a visually supported, very single-minded statement, and when the audience is not highly involved.

US researcher agrees

Researcher Lee Weinblatt was one of the first to openly question the merits of 15-second commercials in the US.[1] He says: 'You can't communicate a believable message in so short a time, unless you started with 30-second commercials and built a case of communication, then brought in a 15-second commercial as a reminder.'

Fifteens as cost-efficient reminders

The implications from both Weinblatt's and our research are clear. If we need to get across a message then the preferred strategy is to use 30- or 60-second commercials to get it across. Firmly entrench it, before switching to 15-second (*reminder*) commercials.

Fifteen-second commercials can definitely give us reinforcement and reminders at lower cost, but only if the main message has first been communicated with the longer commercial. This is because it takes less time and effort to reinforce or revise a message than it takes to understand and learn it in the first place. (A lecturer can successfully shorten his delivery if the audience is already familiar with the topic.)

Audience motivation

How does the level of motivation of the audience change things with 15-second commercials? How are the principles any different if we use them to advertise to a highly involved audience?

People who are highly involved also have low thresholds. To go back to our flash-card experiments, people who have not eaten for several hours recognise food words (like apple, bread, cookie etc) faster than those who have just eaten. Hunger makes them process faster, and be more involved in any stimuli that may be relevant to that need.

Most of the tests we have done of 15-second commercials have been with low-involvement, fast-moving package goods. Funnily enough, there seems to have been less inclination to try them in higher-involvement product categories such as cars or business products and services. Yet it is precisely here, with the more highly involved audiences, that 15-second ads seem to work best.

It is less demanding to get through to an interested, motivated audience. The communicator has to work less hard to get his message across because the audience is predisposed to put in more effort to understand and internalise the communication. Highly motivated students are likely to pay more concentrated attention to the lecturer and work harder at trying to understand and internalise what he has to say. There is less onus on the lecturer and more on the student.

We rarely find this level of involvement in advertising. However, when aimed at highly involved groups, a 15-second ad *can* work in its own right—if the message is simple. It may apply, for example, to a business ad with something new to say that is aimed at an involved audience watching, say, *Business Sunday*. Or a Toyota dealer advertising a red-hot price on Corollas to people actively shopping around for a Corolla. The key here is involvement, which affects not only attention but also the amount of work the recipient is prepared to do to take out the message.

Various ways 15s are used

Fifteen-second commercials have been used in a variety of ways:

- As a *reminder*: e.g. a 30-second ad followed, after an initial burst, by 15-second reminder ads. This works.
- As a *fast-follower*: e.g. 30s and 15s in the same commercial break. The 30-second commercial shown first up with the 15-second shortened version used last in the same break. The jury is still out on this one.
- As a *'sequel'*: e.g. a 30-second commercial first up in the break with a 15-second *sequel* commercial appearing last in the break. There is increasing evidence that 15-second sequels used like this, can work well.
- As a *mixture-ingredient*: e.g. 30s and 15s randomly scheduled in the same week. The jury is still out on this one but there is little encouragement.
- *'Back-to-back'* e.g. two 15s in a 30-second pod. Why would anyone do this? I don't know, but it is happening in the US. It is unlikely to work unless perhaps the ads are for two *related* products (e.g. toothbrushes and toothpaste for the same brand— say Colgate). These have the potential to appear as almost a 'seamless' 30-seconds of advertising for the brand's dental hygiene products.

- As a *stand-alone*: e.g. 15s used entirely on their own. The evidence is overwhelming. As Figure 14.2 shows, these almost never work.

Summary

1 Some agencies continue to waste their client's budgets on stand-alone 15-second commercials which are used inappropriately with low-involved audiences.

2 If the audience is not highly involved and/or the message is not visually simple, then *don't* use 15-second commercials as stand-alones.

3 Consider 15s as cost-efficient *reminder* ads after the mental territory has been captured with 30s, 45s or 60s.

4 Or consider using them as a sequel, topping and tailing them with a 30-second ad at the beginning and a 15 at the end of the break.

5 Remember that 15s have extreme difficulty cutting through the clutter. *They also add to the clutter.* (A three-minute ad break could conceivably consist of three 60-second ads or up to twelve 15-second ads.)

15 Fifteen-second ads: Play it again, Sam!

When the previous chapter on 15-second commercials was published in *Advertising News*, it aroused a lot of reaction. Some people accuse me of beating a drum on 15-second commercials, and I suppose they're right.

I am not saying that stand-alone 15-second commercials can't work—I'm saying that they almost never do. We have tracked an awful lot of commercials and it has been the exception to come across a stand-alone 15-second commercial that worked.

We found one recently that worked. It had a lot of media weight behind but it did work exceptionally well. Why? How did this campaign differ from the overwhelming number that we have seen fail? One difference seemed to be that it was extremely simple and single-minded, both visually and verbally. It did not try to do too much. The message was strongly communicated in both the visual and the verbal medium and it was an extremely simple message.

Its effects are shown in Figures 15.1 and 15.2.

So 15s can work! It's just that those that do are the exception and not the rule. But why is this?

Blame the creatives?

Some people take the view that it is the fault of the creative teams. They argue that when 15s fail it's because of poor creative work, and not the length of the ad. This argument says that any commercial will work if the creative and the media are right.

In light of the many stand-alone 15s that we have seen fail, I think it is unjust and far too simplistic to blame it all on the creative teams. To do this ignores what is widely acknowledged—that there are inherent limitations to shorter ads. It ignores the fact that 15

Figure 15.1   A 15-second advertisement campaign that worked!

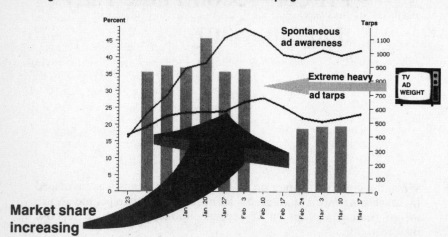

Note: This 15-second advertisement had an extremely simple and single-minded message along with extremely heavy advertising weight. It worked and market share increased—while it was on air!
Source: MarketMind® Continuous Tracking. Sutherland Smith Research.

Figure 15.2   Percentage of people associating the brand with the advertised image

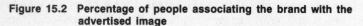

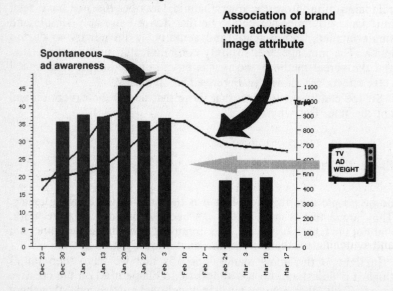

Note: The same 15-second advertisement also increased the percentage of people associating the brand with the advertised image attribute.
Source: MarketMind® Continuous Tracking. Sutherland Smith Research.

seconds may be an impossibly short time to get across the great majority of messages—at least from a standing start.

Yes, part of creative teams' job is to cleverly package messages in such a way that they communicate easily, quickly and entertainingly. Their success in this has made Australian advertising among the best in the world. But 15 seconds is an extremely short time in which to successfully communicate anything. In those few instants the ad has to:

- Tune people *out* of the previous commercial or program that they are watching
- Lock their attention onto the ad
- Communicate the brand name
- Get across an effective message
- Consolidate the memory trace before the next ad comes along (with the potential to interfere with the mental processing of what has just been said).

I suspect that the first and last of these may prove to be very important reasons why stand-alone 15-second ads turn out to be less effective than we think they should be. It takes time for people to tune out of one thing and in to another. This applies to ads, conversations or abrupt changes in our stream of thought.

It takes time, however brief, for people to switch from what they are currently thinking about or attending to and re-tune their thoughts to something else. All of us can relate to the experience of being interrupted while doing something and then having to ask the interrupter to repeat what they have just said.

It is easy to be deceived by the fact that we are talking about only very small amounts of time for this mental switch to take place. It may only be a couple of seconds, but this is a couple of seconds out of our mental processing time. And in a 15-second commercial a couple of seconds represents 13 per cent of the total exposure time.

The problem may exist in the final seconds of the commercial as well. The 'interruption' interference effect on mental processing may also apply to the last second or two of the ad content. The memory trace for this has the potential to be interfered with by the next commercial. Psychological experiments show that interruption by, and switching to, the next event (the next ad) attenuates the mental processing and memory of what went on in the few seconds immediately before the interruption.

So for up to a quarter of the 15-second ad, the viewer's mental processing may be subject to interference effects of one kind or another.

One swallow doesn't make a summer

My critics on 15-second commercials have pointed to one or another 15-second commercial and said that since this one worked, the argument against 15-second commercials is wrong.

I don't say 15s never work or that they can't work. What I can say is that we have tracked an awful lot of them and on the basis of this it is extremely difficult to find examples of stand-alone 15s that have worked. (I might add that in the case of several of those that the critics claim have worked, the evidence they present would hardly pass the test criteria for the AFA ad-effectiveness awards. But that's another story.)

Re-triggering old memories

It is interesting that a number of 15-second campaigns that critics cite as having worked turn out not to be 'stand-alones'. Instead, they coincide with what I said previously about when 15s seem to work or are most likely to be effective.

An example was the 15-second ad campaign for Rheem. We didn't track this, but the agency believes that it worked. This would not surprise me at all, because the campaign was re-triggering old memories. The ad is built around a Rheem jingle which goes way, way back:

Rheem comes on hot and strong . . .
When your old heater's had the gong . . .
Install a Rheem
Install a Rheem
Install a Rheem

This has been firmly established by many past ad campaigns. The point is that it takes more to get into people's heads in the first place than it does to stay there—or re-trigger memories that reside there and are well established. In such situations 15s can work well. This is not what I mean by 'stand-alone' 15s. This is building on or re-triggering what has gone before. It is advertising that ties closely back into, and re-occupies, the mental territory that has already been captured.

Fifteen-second commercials are the occupation forces of the mind. Thirties and 60s are the attack forces and are much better at capturing the mental territory in the first place. Fifteens are good at holding the mental territory once it has been captured.

Involvement

Another thing I said previously was that 15s may work well with audiences who are highly involved—but at the time I said it we hadn't had the opportunity of tracking many 15-second campaigns for such audiences.

A 15-second campaign that one critic believed worked well was the launch of the *Sunday Age* newspaper in Melbourne. In a city where the population had been deprived of Sunday newspapers for decades, the launch of not one but two Sunday newspapers was something of a news event. It was augmented by articles in daily newspapers and news items on TV and radio that publicised the event. The involvement level of audiences in this type of situation is probably very high. High-involvement markets are a niche where stand-alone 15s may perform well. The key word here is involvement, which impacts not only on attention but also on the amount of work that the recipient is prepared to do to take out the message.

Summary

In Japan 80 per cent of TV spots are 15-second ads, whereas in Australia the proportion is only about 30 per cent and increasing. Australia is not Japan, however. There are fundamental cultural differences as well as apparent differences in the way we process ad information. As one ad agency has pointed out, in Japan to be tight-lipped is to be trustworthy. Product demonstrations and user testimonials are generally not well received. 'The harder you try to explain something, therefore, the pushier you will appear . . . Where our TV commercials tend to progress from beginning to end, the Japanese often dispense with chronology altogether.'[1] In a culture like Japan, the 15-second stand-alone commercial may work. In Australia, with low-involved audiences, it almost never does. What needs to improve in Australia is the ability of advertisers and ad agencies to more realistically select those brands and strategies which lend themselves to 15-second commercials and to use these in ways that maximise the chances for effectiveness. Let's not ignore the growing evidence on 15-second commercials in Australia—let's recognise it. Ad agencies can then use it to build better campaigns that give their clients' advertising greater chances of success.

16 Seasonal advertising

All advertising is not created equal. And all product categories are not the same. It is clear to me from tracking the numerous ad campaigns in Australia that there are important seasonal influences on advertising.

Sometimes these things are pretty obvious, but all too often, we realise this only in retrospect. It is easy to fail to be aware of them or to be distracted from them in the product management process.

Seasonal product categories

Products that are to a greater or lesser extent seasonal include:

Summer: ice creams, suntan lotions, soft drinks and swimwear.

Winter: canned soup, chocolate bars, chocolate biscuits, cough and cold preparations.

Seasonal events: electric razors (most of which are sold for Father's Day and Christmas), children's shoes (start of school year), greeting cards etc.

In addition, some public-authority advertising campaigns may be distinctly seasonal, for example: save water (summer), prevent bushfires (summer), speed kills (holiday seasons) etc.

Perceived popularity

I referred earlier to the 'perceived popularity' of a product and the role that advertising plays in it. Brand popularity can be self-fulfilling. If people see something as popular the chances are enhanced

154

that, provided everything else is equal, they will follow suit and buy the brand. Perceived popularity can tip the balance.

Sometimes products gather momentum through their advertising. The brand is seen as increasingly popular. And just when it is about to really catch on, the visibility and impetus suddenly stop. Why? Because 'the season' is over. This points to one key difference in marketing seasonal products—especially in the way one goes about developing a new brand.

The need for accelerated trial

With product categories that are seasonal, advertisers have limited time to build momentum. They have to make the product 'catch on' in much less time than they would normally have for a non-seasonal product. They are always racing to beat the seasonal clock.

Even with non-seasonal products there is an unwritten rule of thumb that you need to aim for maximum trial for a new brand in the first three to six months. Otherwise, it loses that sense of newness. It risks acquiring an image of having been around for a while and not having taken off. If this sets in, it makes gaining further trial all the more difficult to achieve.

With a seasonal product the problem is acute. If the ad can't create a sense of the brand having taken off in the first season, chances are that by its return in the second season the brand will risk being perceived as 'old hat'. People will remember that it was around last season but 'didn't seem to catch on'. This can be the kiss of death.

Maximising the proportion of people who try the product is crucial to success. Remember, a 20 per cent market share can be achieved in two very different ways:

- If only 20 per cent of people have tried the brand but they are buying it 100 per cent of the time.
- If 100 per cent of people have tried the brand but are buying it only 20 per cent of the time, i.e. one in every five times they buy the product category.

To give a brand the maximum chance of success it is important to aim for maximum trial as early as possible. If the trial rate at the end of the first season has only reached 25 per cent it means the brand is relying on a very high repeat buying rate to achieve satisfactory market share and viability. More to the point, it will not be until next season that the brand will get a crack at the 75 per cent of consumers who have not yet tried the brand. By that time it may be too late.

The off-season pause

With seasonal products, the off-season period of inactivity is regarded by many advertisers as a temporary interruption. When it is over they expect to simply resume where they left off last season, in the same way as, when you re-start a video after pausing in freeze frame, you expect it to resume exactly where it left off.

But does it? It is dangerous to assume that even if it always has done that, it will do so again next time. Memories fade, attitudes change, people change and competitors may try to influence the market during the off season. If you have spent real effort and a lot of money during the season to capture the mental territory of the consumer's mind, can you leave the opening round of next season's battle to chance?

It is worth considering occupation strategies that attempt to hold on to the mental territory you captured during the peak season.

Extending the season

In Victoria, the 'speed kills' and '.05' campaigns were traditionally seasonal. Now they run throughout the year, with obvious benefits. The same goes for consumer products like Kit Kat or Lipton's tea. Kit Kat, a primarily winter product, extended its season from winter into summer by promoting the 'Cool Kat'—keeping Kit Kats in the refrigerator and eating them cold. Lipton in the US has expanded the tea 'season' into summer by promoting iced tea. Most Australians would be surprised at how widespread iced-tea consumption is in America.

The idea is to find ways to maintain during the off season that which has been built up in the season. This may be in people's minds or behaviour or both.

An example

Figure 16.1 shows one example of a highly seasonal campaign. This was a public authority campaign which ran over two months (January and February) each year. It was very successful. Note that it achieved about 48 per cent spontaneous advertising awareness in the first season. I can't reveal the advertiser, but the campaign was analogous to the 'speed kills' campaign.

The campaign was very successful . . . *while it was on air*. But it was on air for only two months of the year. Why that should be is beyond my understanding. This campaign built extremely good

Figure 16.1 Seasonal advertising campaign

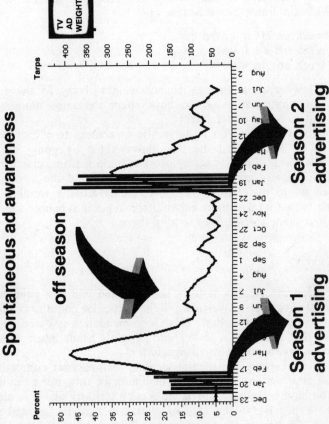

Note: A seasonal advertising campaign that is successful but its effect is very shortlived.
Source: MarketMind® Continuous Tracking. Sutherland Smith Research.

awareness but by the end of April its effect was virtually gone. Like the 'speed kills' campaign, it was aimed at influencing people's behaviour. The need for this is more acute in January and February, but it is also present throughout the year—albeit at a lower level.

A better strategy would be to have built the awareness in January/February (to 48 per cent) and then, instead of going off air completely until the next year, to implement a low-cost maintenance advertising campaign to run through the other ten months of the year. With a maintenance schedule of

- one week on air followed by
- one week off air followed by
- one week on air, etc

and at a low exposure (a maintenance weight of say 75 TARPs per week), this organisation would have spent the same amount of money but to much better effect.

The point is that if you build public awareness to a high level and then let it come all the way down again by going off air completely, it takes just as much effort to build it from scratch next time. It is usually much more economical to build the awareness and then try to maintain it with lowered advertising weight. The principle is that it takes more expenditure to get into people's minds in the first place than it does to stay there.

Get in early

If your product category is truly seasonal and you and your competitors always start advertising in a particular month, consider jumping the gun. Get in first. This recommendation is based on the principle that it is easiest to get into people's heads *when there is little or no competing advertising clutter*.

If you can capture the mental territory before your competitors come on air, your job is easier—a maintenance task, not a building task. You have already captured the mental territory and it is easier and less expensive in the face of clutter to hold the ground you have won. Getting in early can be an effective strategy. (But make sure you also send in the occupation forces in the form of a maintenance campaign when the competitors come on air.)

Who determines seasonality?

Is your product truly seasonal? For some products, seasonality is almost dictated by what the advertisers do—or don't do—in the off season. With wine coolers, for example, all brands seem to observe a conventional promotional seasonal cycle. The dictum seems to be: We only advertise in the season.

As some of the previous examples show, it is sometimes the marketers as much as the consumers that determine if something is seasonal. If marketers believe it is seasonal, this is likely to be a self-fulfilling prophecy. Products are rarely as inherently seasonal as we are inclined to believe.

Take the soft drink market, for example. Users consume primarily because they are thirsty. And it is true people get thirstier more often in summer. Hence the product is seasonal. However, brands like Coca-Cola and Pepsi Cola have been deliberately given a social overlay—an image that makes the drink function as a 'social lubricant' for teenagers and not just as a simple thirst-quencher.

This adds functionality and at the same time reduces the seasonality of these two brands compared to ordinary soft drink. Like beer, they tend to be consumed more in summer but are also drunk in winter in substantial volume for social reasons.

The changeover-to-daylight-saving trap

Advertising on TV at certain times of the year has problems. In the Christmas and New Year holiday season, there is significant doubt about how many people are going to be away on vacation and will therefore not be sitting in front of their TV sets being exposed to the advertising.

One problem that is too often unrecognised is the changeover to daylight saving. We first encountered this with a new brand that was advertised for the first time around the end of October 1987. This four-week ad burst seemed to be very *in*effective and everything indicated that the advertising, and hence the brand, was failing.

The ad agency and the advertiser's corporate personnel were consumed with gloom and the atmosphere could only be described as one of endogenous corporate depression. In all likelihood, this new product which everybody had worked so hard on would have to be abandoned.

Fortunately we were able to bring other information to bear. We were also tracking at the same time for many other product categories and advertisers. We found that in a number of other product categories, a similar thing seemed to be happening, but with brands whose existing ads had previously been shown to be working. Some of these ads were also showing signs of having taken a nose-dive in terms of their apparent effectiveness—and at precisely the same time as the new brand in the other category.

What this exposed was the 'changeover-to-daylight-saving' trap. It is especially a trap for a brand that relies heavily on advertising during the evening news between 6 p.m. and 7 p.m. The changeover to daylight saving in October means that a number of people who one week at 6 p.m. were sitting in front of their TVs are the following week not watching TV at all at that time. They are out kicking a football or swinging a cricket bat with their kids or doing something else in the new-found daylight.

When it was clear that the poor ad performance could be generalised across several products, the company had the courage to go back on air with the same advertising but at different times. And as they say, the rest is history: that brand is alive and well today. In fact, it is the clear market leader in its product category.

17 Underweight advertising: Execution anorexia

How many exposures does an ad need to be effective? And in what period of time? No one knows for sure. Another way of putting it is: Is there a minimum threshold of media weight (number of exposures) needed to make an ad campaign work? The answer seems to be 'yes' (at least for some brands and some product categories).

A case example

I once saw a new campaign come very close to being cancelled by the client. A whole battery of effectiveness-tracking measures said the campaign was having a disappointing and marginal impact. The client was close to the point of concluding that 'the ads are hopeless'.

The media weight for this campaign was around 150 TARPs per week. This means that the people who were the target market for the product were supposed to be exposed to it on average about 1.5 times a week.[1] At least that was what was planned. Before dubbing any campaign a failure or concluding that 'these ads don't work', it is crucial to look at the actual TARP figures, the actual *delivered*, as distinct from the planned, media weight.

Sometimes ads do not go to air because of some mix-up. Sometimes the buying of air time is not as good as it should be. Sometimes (as in the changeover to daylight saving, holiday periods etc) there are not as many people watching TV as there were the previous week. When these actual TARP figures were obtained (some two months after the campaign had started), it emerged that only about 60 per cent of the planned weight was in fact achieved (i.e. about 90 TARPs per week).

Corrective action was taken and in the subsequent weeks the planned exposure rate, the full 150 TARPs per week, was achieved.

With this weight the campaign went on to perform amazingly well in the test market and later nationally. The reason the campaign was not working originally had little to do with the creativeness of the commercials. It was like listening to a signal from deep space. The signal was too faint. The volume had to be turned up.

Here was a perfectly good creative campaign which could have gone down in the annals of 'great advertising failures'. The problem was not the ads themselves but a level of exposure that was too low.

Execution anorexia

Why was the difference between 150 TARPs (planned) and 90 TARPs (actual) so critical? Ninety TARPs was 40 per cent less than what was planned, but while it may be a light weight, many ad schedules have succeeded at only 100 TARPs per week. The difference between 150 and 90 TARPs a week may not seem like much. However, this campaign had three executions (three ads) being rotated on air in each week. This means that each ad was being exposed at the rate of only about 30 TARPs per week. This is a very low figure and evidently below a critical threshold for effectiveness—at least in that particular market.

There is a valuable lesson here. When planning a media schedule, the threshold TARP weights cannot be decided without taking account of the number of ad executions that will be used. The advertising weight must be set in terms of the number of TARPs per execution and not just in terms of an overall figure. Many advertisers use multiple executions (e.g. Coke, Fosters, Toyota) but recognition of this point is all too often the exception rather than the rule. The rule is that in media planning it important to factor into the advertising schedule the number of TARPs *per ad execution* in addition to the overall campaign weight. Otherwise the campaign can end up, like this one, with execution anorexia and underweight advertising.

One execution or many?

This raises an important question. What is the optimum number of ad executions to air in any one week? One? Two? Three? Is it better to have one execution or many?

I wish I could tell you that the answer was straightforward and simple. It's not. One thing is for sure, however. Multiple executions have to be considered carefully in terms of tightness of integration, media weight, flighting of each execution and particularly the degree of involvement of the target audience. Especially with low-involvement products, the use of multiple executions can be counter-productive. I have seen as many as six ad executions used for the same brand in one week. Were they effective? No! If there is a general rule that emerges it is this: For low-involvement products don't use multiple executions—or if you do, be prepared to back each one with substantial TARP weight in its own right.

There may be examples of tightly integrated campaigns where multiple executions have worked well (Hoover's 'Ahead of the rest' ads, perhaps?) but the general note should be one of caution. Being single-minded is usually best.

Low vs high involvement

How many TARPs you need to get effective response from advertising depends on the involvement of the audience as well as the number of ad executions you intend putting to air. Low and high-involvement audiences process ads, and the information in them, quite differently.

Communicating to a target audience which is highly involved in what you have to say differs from communicating with people who don't care too much. How? Here is a potted summary.

- Highly involved target audiences are more motivated and actively looking for information.
- As a result the ad may require less repetition, and print media may often work very effectively.
- Advertising to highly involved audiences has been shown to be less subject to interference in memory from their seeing subsequent ads for competitive brands. The implication of this is that you should be able to get away with a lower share of voice (i.e. a lower share of the total ad spend in the product category) than would be the case for low-involvement products.
- Some evidence suggests that advertising to highly involved audiences is not as subject to minimum TARP thresholds as is advertising to low-involved audiences.
- Advertising to high-involvement audiences is therefore thought to be less sensitive to the number of ad executions on air—but only relatively.

Some guidelines for the low-involvement audience

A crucial difference with low-involvement products is that the advertising has to capture the attention of the low-involved consumer. This is certainly the case with most packaged goods. Advertising for low-involvement products puts a premium on highly creative and sometimes bizarre ad executions to make the advertising cut through the clutter.

For low-involved audiences the overriding task is to cut through the clutter of other ads and force people to notice the ad and its message. If you don't cut through, the ad doesn't get noticed and the chances are that nothing happens. Consumers don't 'see' the ad and don't process the communication.

The ad and the message needs to be very single-minded. Once you have forced attention, you have only limited time and tolerance to get your message across and have it processed effectively. The message has to be simple. The temptation to incorporate several messages in the same ad or in different ads needs to be cut off at the knees. An uninvolved audience just won't work hard enough to take in all the elements of your communication. If it requires anything other than easy processing, you have lost them.

Even when you get your message across with low-involved audiences, the way it has been processed makes it particularly subject to interference and memory degradation *through subsequent exposure to competitive commercials* for other brands. This is why, with low-involved audiences, repetition is so necessary. With highly involved audiences the desired effect may often be achieved and maintained with much less repetition because a) the audience works harder on the message in the first place and b) this greater 'elaboration' as it is called, consolidates the information in memory, thereby rendering it less subject to subsequent interference and memory degradation from exposure to other competitive commercials.

With low-involved audiences you not only have to get the information in, you have to work to keep it there. This is where 15-second commercials come into their own, along with print media tie-ins with the TV commercial—that is, to provide repetition and reinforcement. (See Chapters 14 and 15.)

For all these reasons, the number of executions on air and the TARP weight behind each execution are critical for low-involved audiences.

Another case example

Research has revealed a number of occasions on which multiple executions have been a problem in effectively communicating a low-involvement product. Figure 17.1 illustrates one such case. This is a frequently purchased, low-cost and relatively low-involvement product.

This brand was advertised with up to five different ad executions i.e. five ads on air for the same brand. The company then cut back on the number of different executions being rotated on air.

Mixed-involvement audiences

To make things even more complicated, some product categories have *mixed* audiences—something that some ad agencies do not seem to explicitly recognise in the ad planning process. For example, with most durable goods (cars, PCs, appliances, telephone systems etc) you have at one time some people who are ready to buy and highly involved and some who may not buy for several months or years and who are relatively little involved.

Audiences are rarely homogenous. Some people will be highly involved and some will be less involved. In the planning process the advertiser needs to know the mix of the target audience.

To take one example, the audience for new car ads is often thought to be 100 per cent high-involvement because only people in the market for a new car are thought to be worth targeting. This is a mistaken view. A third of the people who will buy new cars in the next three months don't yet know they will do so. These people are unaware of what is just around the corner.

Some of them will find their present car starting to break down over the next three months; or if not their *car*, their marriage. So some will separate from their spouse and find themselves without the use of a car. Some will be relocated in their jobs; and still others will come in for some unexpected windfall such as an inheritance or a lottery win.

These are just some of the many things that put people into a market when they didn't expect to be. Right now they may be low-involved but very soon they may well be much more highly involved. So like it or not, in these categories an advertiser needs to communicate with both the uninvolved and the involved consumer. The ad strategy can ill afford to assume that the only people worth targeting and communicating with are the highly involved ones.

Summary

Not every ad campaign is going to succeed. But don't let your ad

Figure 17.1 The number of advertising executions

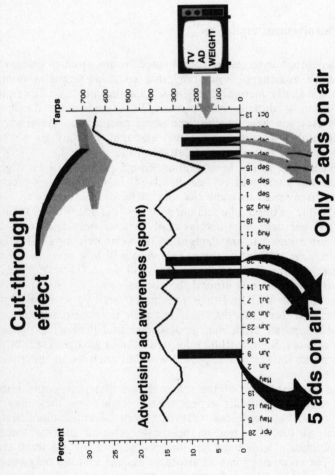

Notes: This graph shows greater overall advertisement cut-through associated with fewer on-air executions for this brand. Executions reduced from five to two in any one week had a dramatic effect on advertisement awareness.

Source: MarketMind® Continuous Tracking. Sutherland Smith Research.

campaign die from underweight advertising. Here is a small checklist:

1 Check that your planned TARP weights are in fact achieved.
2 Especially with low-involvement products, use a single execution unless there is a very good reason for doing otherwise.
3 If you are using multiple executions, make sure you check for the possibility of execution anorexia. Check the number of TARPs per execution per week. (Execution anorexia can be fatal to a campaign's health.)
4 As a rough rule of thumb, if you can't afford to put a minimum of 50 TARPs per week behind *each* execution, don't risk using a multiple execution strategy. Stay with a single execution and do it well.
5 Check the involvement mix of your audience.

18 Why radio ads aren't recalled

Why is a lot of radio advertising so poorly remembered? I know, it doesn't have pictures and it doesn't have the reach of television, but is there more to it than that? Even saturation campaigns don't seem to make it into the consumer's mental filing cabinet to the extent that one might expect. For example, one 'successful' saturation radio campaign which ran for a 16-week period in a specific target market was one of the highest-scoring campaigns we have seen in regard to radio ad awareness, yet it did not get more than 40 per cent of people to spontaneously recall the advertising.

Attention and pictures

Radio is not TV and it is not a substitute for TV. It could be used more effectively, but advertisers often seem to use it wrongly. The two main problems with radio seem to be listener attention levels and the fact that radio advertising doesn't have pictures. Advertisers can do something about both of these factors in designing more effective radio ads and media schedules.

Radio competes with its environment for the listener's attention—much more so than TV, which usually has its own, relatively quiet, exposure environment. When people watch TV they more often do so in silence and there are usually fewer distractions. That is not to say that TV audiences are glued to the set. Brands in low-involvement product categories particularly have to rely on very creative ad executions to grab and hold their audience's attention.

Radio, however, competes with all sorts of things. At breakfast it competes with the clatter of cutlery, the sounds of breakfast preparation and breakfast conversation. Again, in the morning and drive-time slots, radio has to work exceptionally hard to cut through a different kind of 'attentional clutter'. This 'clutter' is made up of the peak-hour traffic, the business of driving, and passenger conversation, as well as the person's own thoughts.

So at certain times of the day, many listeners just aren't listeners in any full attentional sense. Radio's traditional listeners, who in its early days sat glued to *Dad and Dave* emanating from the Bakelite mantel radio, have gone to television. Nowadays, peak-time radio listeners are a low-involved lot. They are schizophrenically pressured from minute to minute by the many stimuli that compete for their attention.

Whether it is radio, TV, or point-of-sale advertising, the ad has to cut through. Then it has to deliver its communication. At the same time it has to successfully register the correct brand. So it is important with radio and low-involvement advertising generally not to look just for people's ability to recall the ad. Advertisers also need to look for image or salience effects before concluding simply from the lack of recall that the advertising is not working.

Lessons for using radio

The message I want to communicate here is certainly not that advertisers should use less radio. That would be throwing out the baby with the bath water. Rather, I think the need is to use radio more intelligently and more effectively. Here are a few pointers.

- **Don't rely solely on recall as a measure of effectiveness.**
Also look for gradual image shifts and any influence on stimulating product-category consumption (as distinct from brand selection).

- **Use more selective time periods.**
Clearly advertisers are likely to have more effect with radio (and TV) if they choose periods (or programs or stations) that offer less competition in the environment—less likelihood that the audience will be distracted. These may be the times when the listener base is at its lowest. So each spot may be more effective in itself, but effective among fewer people. This means using more spots but at a lower cost per spot.

- **Create better radio ads.**
Put money into making better ads—ads that demand attention and cut through. Too many radio ads are awful. There is a logical reason for this. Radio is regarded as the low-budget medium. But keeping costs down at the expense of skimping on good writing and production seems to be the ultimate in false economy with radio.

- **Use radio for involved, dedicated listeners.**
Some segments (such as teenagers) seem to pay more attention to

radio. They are more involved with or more dedicated to the medium because it, and its content, are an important part of their own peer-group subculture.

- **Use TV first to provide faces and visuals. Generate reminder and reinforcement through radio.**

Most people process something more easily and retain it better and longer when they associate pictures and faces with it. Pictures or 'visuals' act as memory hooks of the mind. This puts the focus on concrete messages and imagery. Use TV to give people the pictures and then use radio as a retrieval cue, i.e. to *reinforce* the brand and the message that have already been associated with those pictures, for example the sound track or jingle from the TV commercial.

Fifteen-second TV commercials usually fail when used alone as attack forces. However, when used as occupation forces they can be remarkably effective. Radio can be used in the same way with low-involvement products. Establish the visual mental territory first with TV and then tie in radio as a reminder/reinforcement. It takes more to get into people's heads than it does to stay there. Use TV for the pictures and the attack. Use tie-in radio as the reinforcement/reminder.

- **Take advantage of the immediacy of radio.**

Data from the US confirms the intuitively obvious. Exposure to advertising is attended to more (processed more deeply) and has more effect the closer the customer is to the purchasing occasion. Schedule radio tactically to hit the maximum number of consumers immediately before the purchase occasion (e.g. Thursday and Friday after 10 a.m. is when a lot of supermarket shopping is done.)

- **Take advantage of the flexibility and immediacy of radio to stimulate consumption.**

For example, Campbell's Soups in the US sets aside $750 000 a year to run radio commercials on days when a storm threatens.[1]

- **Mention the brand name in the first eight seconds and a minimum of three times during the ad.**

This finding emerged from recent studies in the US of 30-second TV commercials. My guess is that it is probably even more important for radio than for TV.

Summary

The aim must be to cut through the clutter and get attention in order to deliver the ad message, or the chances are that your communication won't have anywhere near the desired effect. The more attention an ad gets, the more effectively it is likely to communicate and the more it is likely to be recalled. If it gets only a low level of attention it is likely to be at best inefficient and at worst ineffective.

There is scope for using radio a lot more intelligently and to greater effect. Radio is a medium that is rarely well done!

19 Closing the gap between the mailbox and the mind

It is about ten metres from the front door to the mailbox. It is a much greater distance from the mailbox to the mind. The gap between the mailbox and the mind is the biggest wastage problem in the letterboxing of catalogues, brochures and free samples.

In the course of tracking various markets week by week, we observe the effects of letterbox drops as well as ads on TV and in other media. Here I would like to share with you, in a general way, some of what we have learned about letterboxing.

My family has become a two-phone-line household in recent years. Soon we may have to become a two-letterbox family because of the congestion of the letterbox—especially around Easter, Christmas and Mother's Day. Every year, like most families, we receive hundreds of brochures and catalogues. In addition there are the occasional free samples of toothpaste, shampoo etc. These are crammed into our letterbox along with the newspapers and the ever-present note from the local real-estate agents who for some strange reason lust after my house.

Direct mailbox drops have really only been with us for the last twenty years or so. Compared to other media, this marketing technique is very under-researched in terms of effectiveness. Yet the cost in 1992 of a national mailbox drop to approximately four million households was in the order of $40 per thousand to deliver, i.e. about 4c per drop plus printing costs.

So the national drop of a four-page brochure, including printing, is likely to cost between $350 000 and $500 000, depending upon quality. This compares with, say, ten 30-second spots on prime-time TV. This is an area which deserves and no doubt will get more independent research and evaluation of its effectiveness.

As with any media there is a certain degree of wastage in catalogue drops and free sampling via letterboxing. But how much?

Figure 19.1   A national 'free sample' drop

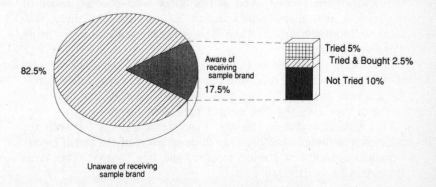

82.5%

Aware of receiving sample brand 17.5%

Tried 5%
 Tried & Bought 2.5%

Not Tried 10%

Unaware of receiving sample brand

Note: Case study: graph 1 shows that 83% of target buyers remained unaware of receiving the free sample.
Source: MarketMind® Continuous Research. Sutherland Smith Research.

Where does the majority of this wastage occur? And are there ways to minimise it?

A case example

Figure 19.1 shows the actual results of a national saturation drop of a free sample of a supermarket-type consumer product. This data was obtained as part of the normal tracking of this market week by week.

The figure shows that despite the 'saturation' drop to all households, nearly 83 per cent of target buyers remained unaware of having received the free sample. (Actually it was 75 per cent plus another 8 per cent who knew they had received a free sample but had forgotten the name of the brand.)

What happened to all these samples? One can only speculate. Some, no doubt, were never delivered. And we know that there are some people who regard everything of that kind as junk mail and put it all in the bin straight out of the letterbox. In other cases kids remove samples, and brochures can get blown away.

But possibly the biggest problem exists in the camouflage of the clutter. Just as a TV ad can get 'lost' in the clutter, so too can a letterbox brochure or even a free sample. After it has been taken inside by a family member, often a child, it may lie in a heap of other items, unnoticed by other members of the family.

When advertisers pay to letterbox a free sample or a brochure to a virtual 100 per cent of households they need to know how many

of their target buyers in those households will receive it and will
be aware of the receipt. And among those who become aware of
receiving it, how many will in fact try it—or, with a brochure, how
many will look through it? Then there is the bottom line—how many
will buy as a result?

In the case illustrated in Figure 19.1, only 17.5 per cent of target
buyers were aware of receiving the sample. The net result was that
7.5 per cent tried it, 2.5 per cent bought it, and 10 per cent were
aware of receiving the free sample brand but did not try it.

This indicates that by far the biggest wastage is between the
mailbox and the mind. More than three-quarters of the target buyers
remained unaware of having received the free sample. This turns
out not to be an isolated case.

Another case example

Figure 19.2 shows the results of a 'saturation' drop of a catalogue.
In this case we showed the interviewees the actual catalogue and
asked if they had received it in their mailbox in the last week or

**Figure 19.2 Percentage of people who claimed to be aware of
receiving a catalogue**

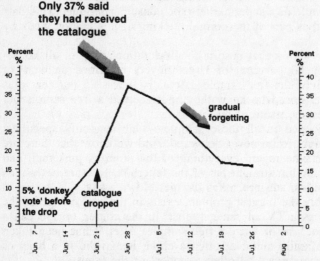

Note: Graph 2: Despite a 'saturation' mailbox drop, 63% claimed they had not received it;
5% claimed to have received it before it was in fact released.
Source: MarketMind® Continuous Tracking. Sutherland Smith Research.

so. Despite this, 63 per cent claimed they had not received it. Only 37 per cent said they had.

Non-delivery

Some wastage is in the delivery. But this looks to be the smallest part of the problem. Stories of 'walkers' (the people who put the catalogues in letterboxes) stashing their bags of catalogues in rubbish bins are well known. The major delivery companies have checking systems to try to control this.

It is nevertheless very difficult to know precisely what proportion of catalogues and brochures do not get delivered. Most big delivery companies claim a delivery rate of around 93 per cent. The only independent Australian auditing service, which operated several years ago out of Melbourne, has closed down. It claimed that the actual delivery figure was consistently between 75 per cent and 80 per cent. (An interesting by-product of that system was that its clients were able to negotiate rebates from the mail-drop companies on the basis of the non-delivery figures.) So the best guess as to how many drop items never get delivered is between 5 per cent and 25 per cent.

The average case

Suppose 40 per cent of people claim to have received your store's brochure or catalogue. What do you make of such a figure? Is it good? Is it bad? You need to know how to interpret it. This is not simple. There are a number of sources of confusion, so let's get some perspective on it.

Figure 19.3 summarises how we see the relevance of non-delivery in the average letterbox drop. The size of the gap caused by non-delivery is small by comparison with the gap between the mailbox and the mind. So compared to the average, and relatively at least, 40 per cent may not be that bad. In our experience from tracking, only between 25 per cent and 50 per cent of the target buyers at whom a mail drop is aimed ever become aware of receiving the item.

I stress that this is an 'average' figure. There are exceptions. As with TV, the level of involvement of the target audience plays a part and can heavily influence the results. For example, it is claimed that an independent audit of the national mailbox drop of 'the Tax Pack' on behalf of the Taxation Office in June 1991 achieved an awareness level of 95 per cent. When the target audience is involved

Figure 19.3 The gap between the mailbox and the mind

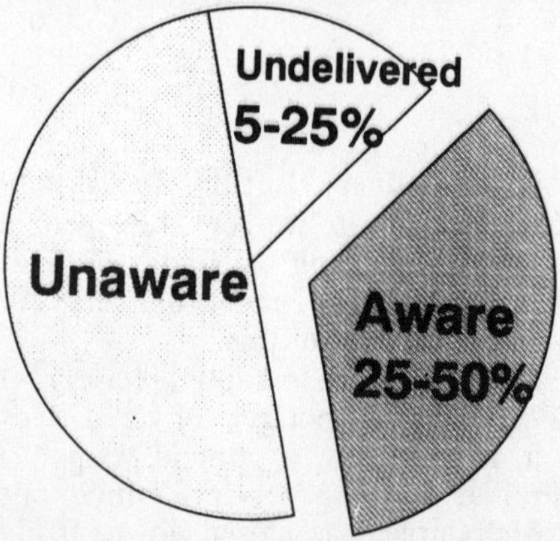

Note: The general rule is that between 25% and 50% of the target buyers at whom a mail drop is aimed, ever become aware of receiving the item.
Source: MarketMind® Continuous Tracking. Sutherland Smith Research.

and is anticipating the item, a mailbox drop does not have to work so hard to cut through the clutter and register its presence. Also, the Tax Pack, in its plastic 'envelope', looked more like mail.

Confusion

Figure 19.2 illustrates another interesting feature of catalogue drops—the confusion in people's minds about exactly what they have received and who it was for. In this case we began showing the colour catalogue to respondents before it was released but without telling them that this was the case. Eight per cent nevertheless claimed not only that they had received it but that they had looked through it. I repeat, this was in the week before the catalogue was actually delivered.

This is not something that happens exclusively with catalogues. The same thing happens with advertising in other media where the advertising for the various brands is very similar. For example, we once recorded 43 per cent of a sample group claiming to have seen a particular TV ad before it went to air. This was in the analgesics category in which for years every advertiser had a presenter who dropped a tablet into a glass of water, extolled the fast pain relief it gave and advised, 'If pain persists, see your doctor.' This 'sameness' is a sure recipe for brand confusion.

We have recorded as many as 23 per cent of a sample group claiming to have received a catalogue in the last seven days from a store that had not sent out a catalogue for six months. When ads for different brands in the same category have generic visuals or a generic style or a generic feel about them, consumers almost invariably get confused about which brand is which or which store is which. The individual identities get obscured in the clutter. So many catalogues are identical in style that the level of confusion is hardly surprising.

Research methodology

This points to the fallacy of evaluating direct-mail drops by means of figures from a single snapshot survey conducted after the delivery. You have to have a good fix on the 'donkey vote' before the mail drop or you may be misled. In Figure 19.2 only 37 per cent claimed to have seen the catalogue at the peak—a week after it was dropped. But considering that there was an 8 per cent 'donkey vote' (i.e. 8 per cent had already claimed to have seen the catalogue before it was released), the real net awareness was probably about 29 per cent (i.e. 37 per cent minus 8 per cent).

Objectives of mail drops

The objectives of retail brochures/catalogues are:

- To build store traffic
- To generate sales of the particular items
- To enhance the image of the store (e.g. its wide range).

Most retailers have a handle on the first and second of these from their sales figures. Transaction counts and sales of particular advertised items can tell you if the mail drop worked. The difficulty arises when it doesn't work. If it doesn't work there is no knowledge of the reasons. What is sorely needed is a diagnostic test, so that in the future you can do more of what works and less of what doesn't work. The American philosopher George Santayana once said: 'Those who cannot remember the past are condemned to repeat it.' Someone else once said: 'Experience is what you get when you don't get what you want.' Witty but not quite true. When something doesn't work we need to learn from it. We need to know why it did not work. Only in that way do we gain productive experience.

Summary

1 Australia needs an independent auditing service to monitor letterbox-drop deliveries.
2 Catalogues need more differentiation in executional style.
3 Strive to own a style. Integrate the store with the style.
4 Consider TV and other media to generate interest/involvement/awareness of the drop.
5 As part of ongoing tracking, include measures of 'recall receiving' as well as 'looked through' and 'bought anything as a result'.
6 Learn from each change of execution style or product-category inclusion what works and what doesn't.
7 Compare 'net awareness' results with advertising in other media rather than simply comparing cost per thousand items 'delivered'.
8 The biggest gap is between the mailbox and the mind.

20 Maximising ad effectiveness: Develop a unique and consistent style

Category conformity

Sameness, sameness everywhere! You can't see the bush for the trees. Too many product categories gravitate towards a single style of 'look-alike' advertising. The style becomes 'generic' to the category and we end up with entrenched category conformity.

As indicated in Chapter 19, until recently analgesics (aspirin, paracetamol) were one of these categories. Almost every brand's ad showed a glass with a tablet being dropped into it while the voice-over advised: 'If pain persists, see your doctor.' This is what I call the chameleon commercials syndrome. Instead of standing out from their environment, ads like this blend in with and disappear virtually into the background. The problem is that the ads are not distinctive enough to cut through the clutter in the category and deliver the brand and the message.

In one dramatic case, before the commercial went to air we showed several still shots from it to respondents and asked them if they had seen this ad recently. The ad was for a brand of pain-killer. Forty three per cent of the group claimed to have seen the ad on TV recently—before the ad went to air. Not surprisingly, most of these people said they had no idea who the advertiser was, or thought the ad was for some other advertiser.

How can people claim to have seen a commercial that has never been aired? What does this mean? It means that the visuals (and the audio) in the commercial were generic. They were similar to those used by other brands in the category. They could belong to anybody. If the brand were changed, it would do no violence to this commercial. One brand name could have fitted this ad just as well as any other. When it did go to air, it never achieved a recognition rate of more than 60 per cent. This was despite the advertising being

179

scheduled to reach more than 90 per cent of the target audience—a very disappointing but nevertheless predictable result.

Beware of generic visual or verbal elements in commercials. A high level of false recognition is a good indicator of this. It is telling you that the advertising is 'look-alike' advertising. If such advertising is allowed to go to air, many of those who do see the ad will not remember who the advertiser was.

So here's a suggestion to improve your advertising. Conduct a small test. Take your commercial, turn down the sound track and, as you watch it, imagine a competitor's brand being substituted for your own brand. Does it do violence to the ad execution? Or does the competitor's brand fit just as well as your own? If a competitor's brand would fit just as well, the chances are that your ad execution is lacking something and is suffering from 'category conformity'. The ad execution that works best is the execution that uniquely ties in to both brand and message.

Mistaken identity

One of my acquaintances wears a distinctive style of clothing. I can pick him out easily in a crowd. One day in a crowded Golden Wing lounge I caught sight of him, grabbed his arm and said 'Hi, Bob.' It turned out to be a case of mistaken identity: I realised that Bob had come to 'own' that style or position in my mind. Once somebody becomes inextricably associated with a particular style, it is natural to think of them whenever you see somebody dressed the same way.

Mistaken identity also occurs with commercials. If your brand is identified with a particular style, then anyone else who tries to use that style risks advertising for you.

'Owning' a style

Heinz for years achieved great cut-through with their ads by using high-profile presenters—first Robert Morley and then Penelope Keith. Along came Continental which, for one year only, tried to use a similar high-profile presenter in the form of Dame Edna Everage.

What happened? The commercials cut through. People remembered the Dame Edna commercials. But almost as many remembered them as being for Heinz as for Continental. They were mistakenly recalled as being ads for Heinz because Heinz 'owns' the 'high-profile presenter' style of advertising in the soup category. You can do a great job of advertising for your competitors if the competitor has an established style and you try to copy it.

In the pain-killer market, Panadol has established something of a consistent style. It may not be particularly clever or innovative but it is consistent. Various commercials over several years have featured the same woman as on-camera presenter, dressed in a single, clear colour (originally yellow and more recently all white). Any competitor to Panadol would be crazy to approximate that style. Suppose, for example, that a competitor were to make an ad with a woman presenter in a white dress. Guess who would get the major benefit of that advertising? Panadol! It may seem obvious but it is surprising how often this sort of thing happens.

Other chameleon categories

Pain-relievers are not the only category to suffer from a lack of individual style. Shampoo was beginning to fall into this trap until 1987, when Pears came along with Sue Smith as presenter and a different style of ad. The conformity in the category was then blown away a year or so later by the Decore 'singing in the shower' commercial.

Until a few years ago, car advertising almost always consisted of a cameo of visuals showing the car in motion accompanied by a male voice-over. The car was almost always red. A scene of it winding its way around a country road was obligatory. And then a few scenes would be cut in of it travelling in the city. Same. Same. Boring . . . sameness! Every now and again, however, an ad manages to break out. For example, GM-H broke out of this style in the 1980s with its first ad for the Holden Barina, featuring an animated character—the Roadrunner. Holden did it again in 1991 with a distinctive Holden Nova jingle ad which flouted car-advertising conventions.

The award for boring sameness in ads, however, has to go to the retail industry and in particular, supermarkets. This has begun to change in the 1990s but all too often we see ads where there is nothing distinctive to differentiate the advertised store from any other. In department stores and apparel stores there has been much more individuality.

John Singleton revolutionised a number of these categories in the 1970s with his 'Where do you get it?' ads and the early Norman Ross ads featuring the Reverend Barry Norman. These were two of the greats because they were total departures in style from the existing category conformity. In the late 1980s David Jones, in a softer way, also seemed to break out of the category conformity syndrome—not by a means of a unique style, but using one reminiscent of the perfume category in retailing.

To escape the category conformity trap it is useful to understand some of the key dimensions of style (See Chapter 8), then apply this knowledge in your search for opportunities to differentiate your advertising and develop a unique style. One key dimension of style is constancy. One of the important things about constancy is how it influences memory retrieval.

Style influences memory retrieval

Neil Savage is an artist who paints Australiana. So is Kenneth Jack, but their two styles are totally different. A style implies some sort of constancy. That is, the execution varies but some element remains the same. Kenneth Jack's style is almost photographic. A Neil Savage canvas, on the other hand, makes a feature of the brush marks. As a result, I don't have to be told that a painting is a Neil Savage. I don't have to inspect its signature. I know it from the style.

Can you pick a Ken Done design? Most people would say yes. There is a constancy in the style that acts as a memory trigger—a retrieval cue. It automatically retrieves from memory the identity (the brand) associated with it. Far too many advertisers have only one constant in their advertising from one campaign to the next and that is the brand or the logo. The brand or logo is important: it is the equivalent of the advertiser's signature. However, the most successful advertisers and the most successful artists don't rely on signatures alone: they have style!

What types of constants should you be looking to include in your advertising? Here are some thought-starters.

Slogans

A word, a phrase or a sentence can function as a constant. This is so common today that we even have a word for it—'slogan'. When we hear the expression 'Which Bank?' what do we think of? If we hear it in an ad, we don't need to be told who the advertiser is. We know the ad has to be for the Commonwealth Bank. The slogan is an obvious one. But there are other types of constants that we don't use frequently. It is more difficult to discuss them because we have no unique words, like 'slogan', to sum them up.

Action or gesture

Used very rarely but sometimes very effectively is the action or gesture. Anticol used this in the late 1980s and early 1990s and blended in a little fantasy. For several cough and cold seasons, Anticol's ads showed people with sore throats breathing fire. This highly visual and dramatic action device was uniquely associated with Anticol.

It is surprisingly hard to think of examples where a simple action or gesture has been used as the constant. Those of us old enough to remember will recall the famous 'Hey, Charger' campaign for the Chrysler Charger which showed people holding up two fingers in a V sign and saying, 'Hey, charger!' Anyone driving a Chrysler Charger could expect to be greeted by people making the 'Hey, Charger' gesture. The Toyota jump is probably the best known current example of an action as a constant. The freeze-frame jump that goes along with the lyric 'Oh, what a feeling' is a constant that has been incorporated into the signature sign-off for many years now.

Presenter

Sometimes a presenter—often a celebrity—is used as the constant. The celebrity also helps the advertising cut through. Penelope Keith for Heinz, Rod Quantock for Captain Snooze and James Dibble for Epson computers were all solid constants. It is worth noting, however, that the person as constant does not have to be a ready-made celebrity. There is an alternative—the 'Do It Yourself' celebrity (or DIY celebrity for short).

Some of the original DIY celebrities were cartoon characters: Chesty Bond, Freddo Frog, Tony the Tiger for Kellogg's Sugar Frosties, Snap, Crackle and Pop for Rice Bubbles. Successful DIY characters need not be cartoon characters. 'Lisa' the checkout girl for Coles supermarkets was one example. The Panadol lady is another. We may not know their real names, yet they may become consistent visual properties for the advertisers. There are many candidates for constants and many possibilities. Some have been used extensively; others have not.

Music

Music can function wonderfully well as a retrieval cue. While music is frequently used in commercials, it is used surprisingly rarely as a deliberate constant. Two of the most successful campaigns to use music as a constant were Winfield's, where the music always accompanied Paul Hogan, and OTC's which used Barbra Streisand's 'Memories' to great effect for over a decade (see Chapter 7).

Sounds

It is sometimes amazing what can act as a retrieval cue. We discovered this at one time while tracking for Nabisco. The sign-off for each Nabisco commercial was the brand. The brand name was sung, Na . . . bis . . . co . . . followed by a little ping. One could be forgiven for believing that the ping was irrelevant, incidental and hardly even noticeable. It was just a sound effect that punctuated the brand sign-off. However, when the ping was temporarily dropped to make room for a promotional tag to be included at the end of the ad, an amazing thing happened. The ads did not cut through as much. More importantly, they lost a lot of their ability to link the execution in people's minds with the Nabisco brand. The principle was crystal clear. Even a simple sound like a 'ping' can have far-reaching mnemonic effects.

Colour

What about colour? Can colour function as a retrieval cue? No doubt it can, but I can't think of many good examples of where it has been used in TV commercials as a constant. BP has certainly used the masses of green and gold to great effect in the redesign of its service stations. In commercials the only use of colour as a constant that I can think of is, again, the Panadol lady in her all-white outfit (but which was previously yellow for years).

Others

Various other factors could serve as constants but have rarely, if ever, been used. For example, there is no reason why one could not use things like i) a place—i.e. always incorporating the same well-known place in the executions for the brand, for example the Opera House, Como House, Parliament House, or ii) a feeling or an emotion.

These are all potential memory cues that could enhance the ability of an ad to automatically trigger recognition of the brand identity. The ad does not have to rely on the brand as the only constant.

When used consistently, such memory cues help develop a style that is unique to the brand advertiser because they become part of the brand identity—just as the flashy style of dress became part of my friend Bob's identity or image. They are symbols as well as memory hooks.

Voice-over . . . and over and over and over

One of the key dimensions of style is the use of voice-over. As discussed in Chapter 7, voice-over seems to be ubiquitous in TV advertising. While it has the advantage of being cheaper, using voice-over is almost always less effective than using on-camera presenters, whether direct or indirect.

Supposing that in the Panadol ad we had the same woman in white saying the same things but talking only as voice-over, what would happen? Would you get higher or lower cut-through? It is a sure bet: the ad would not cut through anywhere near as well.

Voice-over does not cut through anywhere near as effectively as using on-screen speech and we have seen this many, many times in the course of tracking various campaigns. However there is voice-over and voice-over. And just so we don't toss out the baby with the bath water, let me be clear that I am talking about traditional voice-over with on-screen demonstrations or illustrations.

The traditional voice-over style

This traditional style uses voice-over with on-screen illustration. In its loud form with fast cuts this is the classic retail advertising style (e.g. Sussan, Safeway weekly specials). In its more subdued form, with slower cuts and more extended scene shots, it is used by car manufacturers, perfume manufacturers and so on. This traditional voice-over, when used for packaged goods, cars and the like, does not cut through anywhere near as well as the voice of a person speaking on-screen. Examples of the latter variety of commercials include John Laws for Toyota, or the lady talking about Flora margarine—or the lady in the white dress talking about the benefits of Panadol.

Musical voice-over with visual illustration

This is typified by someone singing for the commercial, but not appearing on screen (e.g. Meadow Lea, Gillette—'the best a man can get', Schweppes Cola). This style engages the viewer as a passive observer, a bystander enjoying the entertainment. The voice-over is talking to the on-screen characters. The viewer is expected to identify with the on-screen character and hence the message is received indirectly. The musical voice-over appears to be addressing the on-screen characters rather than the viewer directly.

A subtle but important variation on this is where the on-screen characters are not speaking but the voice-over is meant to be what they are saying or thinking, for example: 'I feel like a Tooheys,' 'I'm as Australian as Ampol,' Australian Airlines' 'We're lifting up our tails.' The on-screen characters are 'sharing their thoughts' with the viewer. Because these are in the form of a sung voice-over, the sense of being 'talked to' directly is very much reduced and there is a feeling, a particular style about the ad.

The on-stage, all-musical singing commercial

There don't seem to be a lot of these in Australia these days. They were used in the launch of Diet Coke, and the Smiths Lites 'ballerina' ads were close to this style. But it seems to be used more frequently in the US than here: Pascall used it some years ago in a blatant 'knock-off' of the American commercial for Dr Pepper ('Pick a Pascall'). Sorbent also used it years ago ('What's the gentlest tissue in the bathroom you can issue?').

The choice of style

You, the advertiser, talk to the viewer through your ad. You probably think a lot about the message that you want to get across. But generally you leave it to your ad agency to execute it. In other words you leave it to the agency to choose the style and determine how the message is going to be conveyed.

Advertisers generally don't get involved in the choice of advertising style but the winds of change may be beginning to blow. There are many styles that can be used to communicate with the customer. At this stage of our knowledge we don't know a lot about them in terms of how they work or what works and what doesn't. Two things we do know are

- the style you choose can be a powerful form of nonverbal communication that identifies you and your ads
- voice-over ads are almost always less effective than on-screen speech. (The exception is when the voice-over addresses someone

on screen and not the viewer directly. Examples are Oral B's dentist 'Rob', or the Meadow Lea mother who gets the pat on the back.)

Summary

Style is such a subtle characteristic of advertising that language is hardly adequate for analysing and discussing it. To maximise ad effectiveness, it is useful to understand how style varies. Style is like hair. It needs careful grooming, it is crucial to your identity, and how you look depends on how you cut it!

21   Sequels

Why does every new campaign for a brand have to be a total change? If your ad or campaign is worn out, it usually means people are bored with it. So your ad agency develops an entirely new ad that bears little if any relationship to the old one. Out goes another baby complete with the bath water!

Why change *everything* when your ad wears out? All too often, ad agencies seem driven to come up with an entirely new ad concept. The message may be the same but the new execution is a total departure from the old. The advertiser may have just spent a year and a million dollars to break through the clutter—to build a strong awareness of the ad in people's minds. It has been a hard, competitive and expensive exercise but the advertiser has succeeded in taking the high ground. The ad now dominates the category in share of mind.

Then suddenly, for some reason, someone decides to change the ad. The focus is now on unleashing some other, entirely different ad execution. Why do so many advertisers make it hard for them-selves by being intent on doing it all over again from scratch?

'Wear-in'

Think of a new ad as having to 'wear in'. Like a new shoe, it may take a little time. The better the quality of the shoe the less time it should take to wear in. Some American coined the term 'advertising wear-in' as distinct from wear-out. It fits beautifully here. Some ads 'wear in' very quickly. A great creative execution can capture the mental ground very quickly with a minimum of media weight. Other ads are of lesser creative quality and require more time and media weight to 'wear in'. Unfortunately there are very few great creative executions. Most ads are more pedestrian and reliant on many media bursts over a period of time to build the assault and then hold the mental territory.

Residual recall barriers to mental entry

The more successful an old ad is in capturing and holding the mental ground, the longer it stays in people's minds even after the advertising is taken off. (This is one reason why it is difficult for a new competitor to cut through in the face of a long-advertised market leader.)

When a totally new ad for a brand is launched, it will be some time before the old one disappears from people's minds. In fact, the more successful and better-performing the old ad, the longer it will dominate and the longer it will take for the new ad to 'wear in'.

A truly great ad execution does not take much time to 'wear in'. But if it comes hard on the heels of another good performer, it will generally take longer. This is because it takes some time for the new ad to displace all those well-consolidated memories that surround the old ad and are linked to brand recognition.

The consumer's mind is not a vacuum. It retains for some time the residual memories of the last ad for a brand. And this can act as an inhibitor or a barrier to entry of the new ad.

An example of this is illustrated in Figure 21.1. An old ad dominated for seven or eight months after it came off air even while a new ad was being aired. The bars represent the weekly media weight (TARP) levels. The lines represent advertising awareness for i) the old ad and then ii) a new ad for the same brand. There are a few points to note:

1 The first ad peaked in August/September 1989 (at 32 per cent recall rate).
2 With no further screenings, its recall rate declined.
3 Despite not being on air it was still in people's minds five months later (at 12 per cent).
4 In the meantime, an entirely new ad had been introduced and aired.
5 Not until ten weeks later did the new ad break through and dominate over the old ad in people's minds, i.e. the old ad held sway in people's minds for seven to eight months.

We might note that while this 'fighting between ads' is going on in people's minds, the sum total of ad recall for the brand (i.e. the old plus the new) is very low. It is not until the new ad breaks through and begins to dominate that net ad awareness for the brand

Figure 21.1 Residual recall of old and new advertisements

Spontaneous advertising awareness

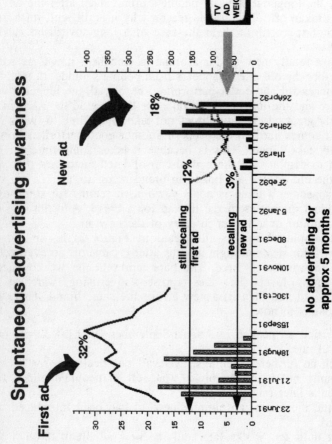

Note: Despite not being on air, the first ad was still in 12% of peoples' minds five months later. Not until about ten weeks after the new advertisement was introduced did it break through and dominate over the old one in peoples' minds.
Source: MarketMind® Continuous Tracking. Sutherland Smith Research.

starts to return to its previous levels. The implication of this is that considerable time and media money could be saved if only the advertiser could somehow bypass or avoid this transition period when there is 'infighting' in memory between ads. Is there a solution? Yes!

Greater use of sequels

Modern movie-makers such as Steven Spielberg know that it is better to build on something you have already established than to start from scratch each time. In movie-making the 1980s was the decade of sequels. There were a multitude, including *Rocky I, II, III, IV* and *V, Indiana Jones, Rambo, Mad Max* and *Superman*. They all testify to the success of the sequel strategy. It's the same with *Back to the Future, Lethal Weapon, Jaws, Star Wars, Gremlins* and *The Godfather*. The list goes on and on.

This strategy consists of harnessing the interest and familiarity that has already been built by previous movie 'executions'; of tying-in the next movie execution with the consumer recall of, and familiarity with, the last one. Ad agencies can't be unaware of this. So why do they launch totally new campaigns after the old one has had its day? Why don't they make more use of sequels, as has proved to be successful for movies?

A few great sequel ads

A sequel is one form of continuity of style. In advertising, continuity of style is the exception and not the rule (see Chapter 20). Nevertheless, over the years there have been some great sequel ads.

For example, who in New South Wales will ever forget 'Emily', the lovable housewife who featured for so many years in the St George Building Society ads? Emily was successfully followed by her daughter several years later. Similarly, Rob the dentist has been a great property for Oral B for many years. The sequel ads featured not only Rob but also his son. Mr Sheen is another 'sequel' that has been wonderfully successful because he is both the presenter and the product name. He seems to be the epitome of achieving immortality through continuity.

With a sequel the ad doesn't have to wear in. Nor does it have to displace what is already there. It just hooks in immediately to existing memories. No waiting. No delay!

Continuity seems to be the key

Like a good soapie, the above examples hold constant the main character(s) and vary the situations. When new characters are introduced they are introduced through their relationship or relevance to the established characters. Each new ad is like a new episode. It provides continuity in the form of an unfolding story.

The important thing is that the new ad has a meaningful relationship with the one before; it is encoded or linked into the existing memory like pieces of a jigsaw puzzle which fit together. In this way people can file the two ads together in memory and retain both.

I have previously likened this to storing things in a mental filing cabinet (see Chapter 12). Many people put off office filing, as I do. It's a chore. People are even less motivated to file ads in their mental filing cabinets, let alone file them carefully or correctly. They have little motivation to store a new ad in their mental filing cabinet at all—let alone under the correct brand name.

However, if something in the new ad immediately retrieves in people's minds something already stored there and clearly presents itself as a further development of the existing 'file', the job is done almost automatically for the consumer. Instead of having to store everything that comes in as a separate file, we will store anything new that is related to an existing item in the most obvious existing file. This saves us having to create an entirely new file for every new thing, every new ad, that comes in.

The more closely the contents of a particular file are related, the more it can act as a chunk—an integral whole in memory. *Human memory works best when new things that are introduced have an integral fit with, or can be related in some way to, old things that already exist in memory.*

Some advertisers achieve this sense of continuity in more limited ways. For example, instead of holding the characters constant, they maintain constancy in one or more aspects of style (see Chapter 20).

Add-on elements of continuity

Some companies try to achieve limited continuity through their tag lines or slogans (e.g. 'We drive your dollar further', 'Oh, McCain, you've done it again'). Others may do it with a visual executional sign-off. For example, the Toyota jump is like a tag line rather than an integral motif that runs throughout the commercial. These are add-on elements of continuity. They are undoubtedly effective in the main in improving the advertising's penetration into memory.

But they are not as effective as an executional element such as a character which is woven into the body of the commercial.

A great sequel? The Cointreau ads

The 1991 ads for Cointreau intrigued me as sequels. You know—the black-and-white ads in which the man summons the drinks waiter and sends a Cointreau to the lusty-looking lady sitting by herself at a table on the other side of the room. The man is momentarily distracted and she disappears. In the next ad in the series the situation is reversed. She sends the drink to him this time, and she disappears when he is momentarily distracted.

This ad didn't make a lot of sense unless you had seen the first one. Of course, some people would say that the first one didn't make a whole lot of sense either! But in retrospect the first one took on more meaning when you had seen the second one. It was made more memorable and intriguing by it. What's more, I remembered *both* and was doubly intrigued by both. A very memorable strategy. I always wondered, did he ever get the girl?

Owning an ad style

The Cointreau ads had a unique style. They illustrated how it is possible for a brand to own an advertising style. In the same way that a brand can own a unique position in people's minds, a brand or organisation can come to be associated with a particular advertising style. Kit Kat, for example, tends to have a particular style, as does Nobbys Nuts. So too do ads for Heinz, 7Up and the Commonwealth Bank.

The advantage in owning a style is that when a viewer sees that style of ad, it instantly triggers an association with the brand. The brand comes to stand for the style and the style comes to stand for the brand. So if a competitor should try to use the same style, he risks communicating the wrong brand (your brand) and doing an advertising job for *you*. It will be difficult for any other drink brand to use the Cointreau style without advertising Cointreau!

You see an ad that says 'Which bank?' What 'brand' of bank do you think of? 'Commonwealth', of course, has been clearly associated with that style or mnemonic. It now owns that execution style.

Not all ads are created equal. Sequels have a lot going for them. Too many ads start anew every time. There is scope for greater use of sequels to improve ad effectiveness.

Summary

1 If your old ad has been successful but is now wearing out, consider a sequel rather than a totally new ad.

2 If you do have to change horses and go for an entirely new ad, and if your past advertising has been very successful, then expect the new ad to take some time to 'wear in'.

3 If you hit on a unique style that works, then continue it in the next ad. Strive to 'own' that style in the consumer's mind.

22 Corporate tracking of image and issues

As we saw in Chapter 23, image is elusive. Your own image stares you in the face every morning, but do you have in your mind's eye the way you see yourself or the way others see you? Image is in the eye of the beholder!

The opponents of corporate image and corporate advertising argue that it is irrelevant; that people buy products, they buy brands, but they don't buy companies. Even if it were true that corporate image has no effect on consumer behaviour, corporate image would still be important because a well-known and well-respected company will always enjoy advantages in at least two non-consumer markets.

First, it will attract and retain better quality employees. A well-known and well-respected company is very different from a nonentity. When you are asked where you work, the importance of a corporate image is quickly apparent. If there is an instant recognition of the name and what it stands for the response is very different from 'Who are they? What do they do? Never heard of them.'

Second, corporate image can and does affect the company's price on the stock market. People do buy companies! Or at least shares in companies, and the price they are prepared to pay is influenced by the profile, the image and the respectability of the company. This has been very evident with companies such as News Limited, Ansett, G.I.O., Compass, Westpac and many others in recent years.

The basis of image

Before you can change or create an image in people's minds you

195

need to know what thoughts and associations are already there. The first step in image research is to find out

- which attributes are important in people's minds re the (product or industry) category?
- which attributes differentiate our company from companies generally?

In other words, the first step is to establish what things people associate with the particular brand or company. These associations may be blurred, half formed or even plain wrong. They exist nevertheless. For example, take a company such as BHP or Fosters. The associations here will very likely be blurred. In a sense they are in a fuzzy category of 'big companies'. It is not clear what category of companies they compete in, at least as far as the general public is aware. BHP is loosely associated with steel and mining while Fosters Brewing is associated with beer, BHP and the Japanese along with hangover associations with John Elliott.

The next step is to determine which image attributes the organisation wants to emphasise. What does it want people to think of when they hear the names BHP or Fosters? This is partly a research task, but it is not just a matter of asking people naive questions about what they think is important for a company. Positive attributes like credibility, stability, national interest, Australian, human, caring, responsible corporate citizen, non-polluter, environment-conscious—all of these are possible attribute associations that the company can position its image on.

But which one or ones? Trying to position on more than one or two at a time is fraught with the danger of image diffusion, i.e. trying to do everything and accomplishing nothing. The answer to the question has to relate back to the objectives. What are the company's priorities?

When an organisation decides on the image it wants to communicate, and confirms that it can deliver on that image, it should then track public perceptions and closely monitor the effectiveness of its corporate communications.

Changing an image

There are three elements in an image, whether it be a brand or corporate image. That image is a function of the attributes which are associated with it, the degree of those attributes it is perceived to have and how important that attribute dimension is in people's minds when they make a decision.

What advertising or corporate communications are trying to do is:

- *Move* the organisation *along* an attribute dimension, e.g. honesty or corporate citizenship, or
- *Add* a new attribute dimension to the image, e.g. environmentally responsible, financially secure, or
- Influence the perceived *importance* of an attribute dimension for the public in evaluating organisations, i.e. change the importance that people place on a particular attribute.

By monitoring each of these three elements over time, an organisation knows how well groomed it is and has an early warning system for change.

Tracking the agenda of concerns

In this era of environmental concern and corporate responsibility, the 'green' attack has had a real impact on corporate communication philosophy. Some organisations deliberately undertook to keep their heads down. Holed up in the trenches, they hoped that by keeping a low profile they would avoid being targeted by the environmentalists. Others, like the mining and timber industries, took a more proactive approach and mounted specific ad campaigns that took their case to the people.

I would argue that whatever approach is taken, there is usually a need to know what is going on outside the trenches—to at least know how many people are out there firing at you, and what they are most concerned about. To this end, a number of organisations (corporate, government and industry groups) track what might be called the agenda of concerns among the general public in regard to their particular organisation or industry.

By asking people what concerns if any they have in regard to organisation X (or industry X) an agenda of concerns is generated. For example, see Table 22.1.

This agenda is monitored continuously. It changes over time in response to the topicality of the environment, to strikes and to the

Table 22.1 Agenda of concerns

	% spontaneously mentioning the concern
1. Too big and uncaring	24%
2. Pollutes the environment	12%
3. Poor handling of its industrial relations	8%

organisation's own news releases and radio and TV appearances. The important thing about this is that the information allows the organisation to detect events that have had a positive or negative impact on people's perceptions and concerns. Furthermore, it allows the detection of these at the earliest possible moment. This is crucial if an organisation is going to take a proactive approach to managing corporate communications and corporate image.

Image: You can't leave home without it

Image is not something that companies can choose to opt out of. Nature abhors a vacuum, and so does the human mind. If an organisation doesn't effectively communicate the way it sees itself and its beliefs and what it stands for, then the public will do so for it. The environment will fill the vacuum and allow consumers to construct their own image of the organisation based on whatever evidence is around.

There is a lot to be said for a proactive approach to corporate communications and corporate image. Image is like grooming. It is something that needs constant care and attention, not a once-a-year examination. Especially in the current environment, where 'green' is very much the dominant colour.

23 Communicating the corporate

In the last ten years there seems to have been a corporate communications explosion. Why are so many people interested in corporate image? Why are companies spending so much money on advertising and promoting themselves instead of their brands?

Corporate communication plans and corporate image development are used strategically for both offence and defence. In this article I want to talk about the use of corporate image for pre-emptive defence.

It is not at all obvious that managing the corporate image is an essential part of defensive strategy for a public company. In this protective sense, corporate image is like a condom—both need to be used discreetly. By rolling on a strong corporate image and managing it effectively, management can get the prophylactic protection needed to keep out unwanted corporate invaders.

A company's share price, like any other price, is a subjectively derived value—what people are prepared to pay. People pay more for brand-name products than for generics. A Gucci toothbrush is 'worth' more than a Woolworths house brand. The physical product may be the same but perceptions of its value can be significantly affected by image. So too can share prices. People perceive more value in, and expect the price to be higher for, something that has a substantial image.

A healthy corporate image, along with a strong share price, is what keeps the corporate immune system intact. But why is so much corporate communication taking place these days? There are many reasons, and in the case of mining or environmentally sensitive companies the answer is obvious. However, a less obvious and more fundamental factor took root during the 1980s. That was the decade of the corporate takeover specialists.

Corporate raiders made a science out of hunting companies with undervalued or undermanaged assets. So top management, here and overseas, had its attention forcibly turned to corporate defence as well as corporate survival. To survive corporately, the management of public companies needed increasingly to keep the share price up and be seen to be effectively managing the company's assets. If the company became undervalued by the share market, compared to the true value of its assets, this invited takeover attention.

Corporate raiders try to target undermanaged companies where changes in strategic direction can dramatically increase the value of the shares. Or they look for companies with high liquidation values relative to their current share price. If the management of a company was seen to be weak, this implied that the company could be worth more under new management. This too could invite unwanted takeover attention. So it was important for the company not only to be well managed but also to be *seen* to be well managed. This naturally led to increased public-relations activities and corporate communication programs.

Perceived share value is not something that has been traditionally thought of as a marketable entity. But there is no better means of avoiding a takeover than a healthy share price.

The stock market as target audience

The most astute companies track the perceptions of their own shareholders—individual as well as institutional. They realise that it is important to know, week by week, month by month, how they and their management are perceived; what their strengths and weaknesses are. Is the company seen to communicate well with its shareholders? Is it vulnerable? What price would shareholders sell out at? What types of communications do they react best to?

Forewarned is fore-armed. This type of tracking provides an early warning system of any weakness or vulnerability and forms the basis for managing the corporate image and the corporate communications plan.

Corporations here and in the US are spending more on public relations aimed at the community generally and the stock market in particular, for example on 'advertising vehicles' such as their annual reports. The success of the company in communicating the effectiveness of its performance and, by implication, the fact that the management is doing a good job, can mean the difference between management survival and oblivion.

For management, superior performance in traditional accounting terms is no longer a guarantee of continued tenure. Nowhere is this more starkly illustrated than among the companies featured in Tom Peters' popular book *In Search of Excellence*.

In search of survival

If you managed to plough your way through that best-seller, you will know that it supposedly identified the key attributes of corporate excellence by studying the most successful American companies. These so-called 'excellent' companies were superior on all the traditional financial measures such as return on total capital, return on equity, return on sales and asset growth.

Since that book was published, however, a surprising number of these companies have taken a nosedive (e.g. Atari, Avon, Caterpillar, Digital, Levi Strauss, Texas Instruments). Strategic setbacks such as those encountered by these companies were flags that put them clearly in the corporate takeover specialist's sights. So today the emulation of these 'excellent' companies has lost much of its allure.

The problem was that many of these companies had overlooked their corporate 'achilles heel': public perception (i.e. the perceived value of their shares to shareholders). In terms of dividend performance and share-price appreciation these companies were, in fact, no better than average compared to the rest of the market.

In an original book entitled *Creating Shareholder Value*, Alfred Rappaport, Professor of Accounting and Information Systems at Northwestern University, exposed this, and analysed in detail the growing acceptance of shareholder-value orientation in companies.[1]

Major public companies have become especially aware of the importance to their share-price and investment rating of their image among the investment community—particularly large institutional shareholders and stockbrokers. A company's survival is based on marketing itself to the investment community in regard to two fundamentals:

- Its ability to generate cash (to satisfy the claims of its employees, customers and suppliers).
- Its credibility and reputation, i.e. how able it is to obtain any additional funds that it might need from external sources using debt or equity financing.

Positioning: The battle for the investor's mind

Like any good marketer, corporations are prepared to make modifications to 'the product' in order to reposition it and market it more effectively. In marketing to the investment community, this type of corporate modification or financial repositioning goes by the name of 'restructuring'.

Restructuring can take a variety of forms. The company may divest itself of businesses that are underperforming or products that do not fit. Restructuring can also take the form of debt swaps and other refinancing methods. Or it may involve getting rid of all-too-visible 'excess cash' by acquiring other businesses or buying back some of the company's own shares.

All of this is grist to the corporate communications' mill. Most of the so-called 'excellent' companies in Tom Peters' book have subsequently undergone 'restructuring'. In the US particularly, a country where 22 per cent of the adult population hold shares, the consumer is king but corporation management has now realised that serving the king is not enough. There is a growing realisation of the importance of a higher power—the shareholder—whose perceptions can, indirectly, make or break the company.

The disasters of many takeover specialists in Australia, together with the recessionary times, means that there seems to have been some easing up on corporate communications. The international takeover threat, however, probably remains as real as it has ever been. With the continuing threat of takeover attempts, it will be surprising if companies can continue for long to ignore their corporate communication programs. A healthy corporate image and a healthy share price are the prophylactic protection influencing survival.

Without that protection, what good are a company's new products? What is the value of consumer orientation? What does it matter if your traditional accounting figures are good? From management's point of view, these are all for nothing if the company gets taken over. The current board will not be around to enjoy the fruits of its efforts. As the old saying goes: 'When you are up to your backside in crocodiles, it's hard to remember your original objective of draining the swamp!'

24 Measurement of advertising effects in memory

Traditional measures of advertising effectiveness such as ad recall, ad recognition, message take-out, brand awareness, brand image and purchase intention confuse many advertisers. The question often posed is: What do these all mean? Which one should I use? Do they really indicate how effective my advertising is? This chapter and the next focus on these mental measures of advertising effectiveness. We look at what they mean and put them clearly into the modern perspective of how our memories work.

Diagnostic complementary measures

All these measures are mental measures. The only reason that mental measures are used at all is that measuring effectiveness through sales and market share changes is not enough. There are many reasons for this but it is partly a problem of sorting out what sales or market share changes are due to what causes. How much of any change is due to the advertising and how much to other things that happened at the same time (such as promotion, pricing, competitors' actions, etc)?

Advertisers want to know more than just whether their ad worked or not. They want to know how and why it worked. If it didn't work, they want to know why, in order to avoid the same mistakes next time.

Sales and market-share measures are crucial. They are the bottom line but by themselves they don't provide the necessary diagnostic ability. Mental-response measures therefore don't substitute for behaviour-change measures; they complement them. They help sort out what is causing what. They provide understanding of how and why the ad works or doesn't work.

203

To fully understand the way these measures work, to understand what they mean and how to use them, we need to jettison the traditional, old-fashioned view of memory. In the past 30 years there have been significant developments in psychological research into memory, many of which have not been picked up on by practitioners in marketing and advertising.

One reason for this is that some aspects of it are not all that easy to explain. It takes some effort to understand the full implications. So let me caution readers at the outset that what follows in this and the next chapter may not be fully grasped in a quick read. However, the main ideas should come across if a little time is taken to think about it. The effort will be repaid because an understanding of the modern view of memory is fundamental to understanding advertising's effects and to using mental measures diagnostically in the evaluation of an ad campaign.

The modern view of memory

In 1959, a neurosurgeon by the name of Wilder Penfield inserted a microscopic electric probe into a patient's brain while the patient was conscious. This will make your eyes water, but Penfield used local anaesthetic and the patient was able to converse with him while this was happening. The patient reported the most amazing things. He reported various memories being activated, like watching *Gone With The Wind* years earlier—complete with the smell of cheap perfume in the cinema and the beehive hairstyle of the person in front.[1]

When Penfield touched the brain at one spot the patient re-experienced or remembered a piece of music. Penfield then shifted the probe slightly and into the patient's mind suddenly came the vivid memory of an old childhood experience that had long been forgotten. Depending on the exact location in the brain that Penfield touched with the electric probe a different memory would be reactivated. Many were of things the patient had not thought about in many years.

Penfield's experiments eventually led cognitive psychologists towards what is now called the 'spreading activation' theory of memory.[2] This was developed in the 1970s and 1980s and today is the best-accepted theory of how memory works. Perhaps I should say it is accepted by cognitive psychologists, but there is often a gap of ten to twenty years between new developments in psychology and their dissemination and use in marketing.

Association

To understand 'spreading activation' theory, we first have to understand association. When you see 'Anyhow*' written, what do you think of? Chances are that it immediately brings to mind Winfield cigarettes. When someone says to you 'Which bank?' the chances are you immediately think 'Commonwealth'. This is because our minds work by association.

Things remind us of other things. For example we are often reminded, in the course of listening to someone else in a conversation, of something that we want to say. When I say the word 'cars', what do you think of? You may have thought immediately of 'roads' or you may have thought of a brand of car such as Toyota or Volvo. What underlies these associations in our minds can be thought of as a gigantic network of interconnected associations.

Mental network

Our minds consist of a gigantic network of billions of neurons which are all connected—some directly and others circuitously through other neurons. This is illustrated in Figure 24.1. It shows an over-simplified version of what part of this network might look like.

Just as the touch of Penfield's electric probe could activate his patient's networks and cause him to recall some memory, so may a word that we hear activate a point in our mental network and cause us to recall the meaning of the word. Hearing a word like 'car' or seeing a picture of one may both activate this meaning. The activation is like an electric current spreading outwards from the point and activating other close things that are associated with 'car'. This

Figure 24.1   A memory network

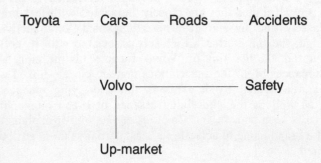

is why a word such as 'anyhow' is likely to trigger not only its own meaning but also any closely associated meaning, such as 'Winfield'.

'Spreading activation'

The network can be activated at any point. When we are exposed to words and pictures, each one activates a point in the network. A point does not have to be activated directly, however. It can be activated by 'spreading activation' from some near associate. This might be a picture, a word, an emotion or an expression.

This is one of the main reasons why the ad campaigns 'Which bank?' and 'Anyhow*' were successful. Both of these are frequently recurring expressions that crop up all the time in the normal course of our lives. So when we come across them in conversation it is the equivalent of inserting a Penfield-type probe into our minds and activating our mental memory network at that precise point. 'Spreading activation' then triggers off any close associates, including 'Commonwealth' or 'Winfield', that may have become connected to it. It gives the brand 'free registrations' and, as we shall see, it also helps the brand stay 'top of mind'.

Meaning and brand image

The fact that our memories work through a process of 'spreading activation' has far-reaching implications for advertising and marketing. It means much more than simply keeping something top of mind. In fact, it is the whole basis for the meanings things have for us, including the meanings of brands.

As Figure 24.1 implies, when 'Volvo' is activated it in turn activates any attributes that are closely associated with that brand, such as 'safety' and 'up-market'. These things that 'Volvo' activates in our mind, the things that are closely associated with it, collectively represent the meaning of 'Volvo' for us. This meaning takes in the resonances of all the associations that are closely linked with 'Volvo' and activated by it. This is the underlying essence of meaning as well as the underlying essence of brand image. It is why Volvo is seen as safe and Coke is seen as fun. It explains the ability of a brand name to activate (at least partially) these attributes in our minds.

Closeness of connections

Like an electric current, the further it spreads in the mental network the more the 'spreading activation' weakens. Memories that are closely connected are likely to be activated. Those that are less closely connected are not. So the more closely an attribute like 'safety' is connected to the brand Volvo, the more likely it is that activating 'Volvo' will spread activation to the attribute 'safety'. Conversely, the more distant something is from the point of initial activation, the less likely it is to become activated by the trigger.

Another way of thinking about this is in product positioning terms. Simply, it means Volvo 'owns' the safety position in people's minds. That is, Volvo is more closely connected to 'safety' than is any other brand. The 'spreading activation' view of memory thus gives advertisers a much richer way of thinking about product positioning as well.

Reinforcing connections

We all have leg muscles, but if we want to use them for running long distances they need to be strengthened and exercised. Like leg muscles, connections that are not exercised may be too weak to perform.

When those of us who experienced the Winfield campaign featuring Paul Hogan encounter the brand Winfield today, we rarely if ever think of Hogan. This is not to say that we are unaware that he once advertised Winfield. It is just that we don't think about it any more. The connection in a sense still exists but it has become so weakened by lack of use that it doesn't work of its own accord.

Contrast with the traditional view of memory

This all contrasts with the traditional view of memory that still dominates marketing practice. In this view, a memory trace is laid down. The memory is either there or it is not there. Either you remember it or you don't.

It is amazing that this model of memory has survived at all, because it is demonstrably wrong! How many times have you been unable to remember someone's name even though you *know* that you know it? Forgetting has more to do with 'inability to retrieve' the memory or, in other words, inability to activate it than it has to do with failure to store the memory in the first place.

Retrieval cues

Memories are triggered in our minds by retrieval cues. These are things that get us to remember other things. When we are trying to think of somebody's name, for example, and the name won't come to mind, we use retrieval cues. We may deliberately bring to mind the situation in which we last saw the person. That may help us remember the name. Why? Because we are hoping that the activation that spreads from the memory of the situation will suffice to activate the name of the person and allow us to retrieve (recall) it.

If that doesn't work, we may try other cues to help us spread enough activation towards the person's name to trigger recall of it. What we are doing is looking for a retrieval cue that will help us retrieve (activate) the name. Retrieval cues, then, are things that are so closely and strongly connected with something that they automatically remind us of it. They help pop it into our mind.

Purchase situation retrieval cues

The relevance of this to advertising is that advertisers want their brand to be cued into people's minds when they think of making a purchase from that product category. If you are an advertiser, you would no doubt like to tie your brand strongly to something (a retrieval cue) that is often in people's minds or in their environment—and ideally is also around at the time they buy the product category.

This could be almost anything. It could be visual (e.g. the pack or a dispenser label that we are likely to see at the point of sale). Or it could be verbal (e.g. 'Uh, huh' . . . You got the right one . . .). Or it could even be musical (e.g. the 'Winfield' classical music piece). So one test of whether an ad is working is to ask, Is it strengthening the association between a relevant retrieval cue (such as the product category) and the brand?

Consider as an example the Yakka ad that shows a cameo of people in hard-working, energy-expending situations with a voice-over chanting 'Hard Yakka'. The question here is, Does the ad strengthen the connection between the category 'work clothes' and the brand Yakka? When we think of the category 'work clothes' are we more likely to think of Yakka now than we were before we were exposed to this ad? If so, the ad is doing that part of its job successfully.

However, advertising is about more than getting people to think of the brand. It is also about getting them to feel good about the brand. This implies another type of connection. Again consider the

Yakka ad. In showing people in overalls and in hard-working, tough, physical exertion situations it is presumably designed to do two things: to get us to think of Yakka when we think of buying work clothes and to communicate that Yakka clothes are tough. In other words, Yakka wants to connect the attribute 'tough' in our mental network with the brand Yakka so that whenever we think of Yakka we will think of 'tough', and vice versa.

The Yakka ad, like many others, attempts to connect the brand with an attribute that the manufacturer thinks is important or at least influential with consumers.

Putting it all together

So the test of whether an ad like Yakka's is working is threefold:

- Is it strengthening the connection between the relevant retrieval cue—the category (work clothes)—and the brand (Yakka)? When we think of work clothes, are we more likely to think of Yakka than we were previously?
- Is it strengthening the connection between the brand (Yakka) and the advertised attribute 'tough'? Is the brand more closely associated with the attribute 'tough' than it was previously?
- If it is doing both these things, then it should be positively affecting our overall attitudes towards the brand Yakka and increasing our disposition to buy Yakka rather than some other brand—that is, if 'toughness' is an attribute that we see as important in work clothes.

To assess the effect of the ad, then, at least three things need to be measured—one to represent each of these effects. Readers will now recognise the rationale for three of the best-known and most-used mental measures. The first is *spontaneous brand awareness*. The second is *image attribute association*. The third is people's overall *attitudinal disposition* towards buying the brand (their purchase intention).

Note that all these are brand measures and not ad measures. They focus on the brand. What then of all the measures that focus on the ad itself, such as ad recall, ad recognition and message take-out? Why measure them? The measures that are focused on the ad itself supplement the critical three measures above that focus only on brand. The measures focused on the ad can help pinpoint exactly where an ad seems to be strong and where it seems to be weak and what action is necessary to fix it. As we will see in the next chapter, understanding this can help advertisers do more of what works and less of what doesn't.

25   The buy-ology of mind

The last chapter peeked inside our 'necktop' computer to see how memory worked. Memory consists of the firing or activating of an interconnected network of neurons. If our brain is touched internally at any point with an electric probe, our mental networks are activated and we recall a particular memory. Seeing a word or a picture does the same thing. It activates a point in our mental network and causes us to recall the meaning of the word or picture.

Like an electric current, the activation spreads out in all directions from the original point of activation, gathering up the meaning of the stimulus as it goes. The meaning of something is therefore represented by the total pattern of the 'spreading activation' that a word or picture initiates. Knowledge can be retrieved (or recalled) by activating the appropriate network in memory.

However, there are two types of memory. The first is 'knowledge' memory, or what psychologists call 'semantic' memory. But not all memory is knowledge of this kind. There is another kind of memory containing all the things that happen to us. This is more of an autobiographical memory than a knowledge memory. We remember episodes in our life—the things that have happened to us. For example, we remember driving to work this morning. Or perhaps we remember tasting a new brand of coffee this morning. And we remember, last night when we were watching the Channel 9 movie, seeing that Mrs Marsh toothpaste ad again.

These are events or episodes that are retained in memory at least for some time. They form memory networks that can be activated in our autobiographical memory. So our autobiographical memory consists of all the things that have ever happened to us that we can recall or recognise. Psychologists distinguish this type of memory by calling it episodic memory, as distinct from knowledge memory.[1]

Ads that are in our episodic memory, such as the Mrs Marsh

toothpaste ad, usually have four distinguishable components. These are:

- the product (category)
- the ad execution
- the brand
- the message.

The first component here—the product category—is obviously toothpaste. The execution is Mrs Marsh, the teacher, talking to a group of children, breaking a stick of chalk and dipping one end into blue ink. The third component is the brand. What was the brand? What toothpaste was being advertised? Before reading on, what's your answer? If you answered 'Colgate', ask yourself where this information came from. Note that in the description above I have not once mentioned Colgate—yet I'm sure that many readers will have thought I did.

When your memory network was activated at two points simultaneously (i.e. the product category and the execution) the 'spreading activation' triggered off anything else that was closely connected with those two points. As a result, many readers will have automatically thought of the Colgate Fluoriguard commercial. To the extent that this happens, then, here is one ad that clearly induces strong connection between the product, the execution and the brand. In fact, the ad execution communicates the brand so well that the connection in our memories between the two components (the ad execution and the brand) has become so strong that the two are almost synonymous. To find such a strong connection between these three components is all too rare.

What of the fourth component? What was the message in that ad? It was 'Makes teeth tougher—because the fluoride gets in.'

So episodic memory for this ad can be depicted as shown in Figure 25.1, where each of the four components is represented—the product, the execution, the brand and the message.

The execution is the creative vehicle that hopefully makes the viewer sit up and take notice; that makes the commercial cut through the clutter so that, having got some attention, it can deliver a message. Having cut through the clutter, what message takeout has the execution registered in memory? Is it what the advertiser intended to communicate? And if it is, did the consumer connect all of this in memory with the correct brand and the correct product category? (If not, the advertiser could be doing a great job of advertising for some other brand or product.)

Figure 25.1   Spontaneous advertisement recall—episodic memory

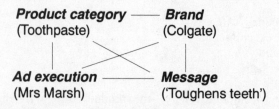

Arguments about ad effect measures

In the past, some advertisers have placed great store by people being able to recall their ad. Others did not believe in ad recall but thought it important that people be able to indicate that they had seen the ad by at least recognising it. Some advertisers have put the focus on communication of the message rather than the ad itself, while others have argued that consumers' ability to parrot back a message is not relevant to the ad's sales effectiveness. There is a resolution to all this. To arrive at it we must first understand that the effect of an ad is a process and that evaluating the effectiveness of an ad is also a process.

The process of evaluating an ad

Suppose that an ad like the Mrs Marsh toothpaste ad, when first put to air, is not showing clear and obvious effects on behaviour (as measured by sales, market share, trial, repeat buying). The first part of any doctor's diagnosis is to determine first if there is a real problem and, if so, to locate the source of the problem.

As has been made clear in earlier chapters, advertising does not just make us 'run out and buy'. In order to capture its intermediate effects we need indicators of its impact on more than just behaviour. For each strategic point in this attempted influencing process, we should aim to have an appropriate measure to indicate what is happening. When sales and market share movements as well as other behaviour measures do not react immediately to advertising, the advertiser needs urgently to diagnose what is happening. Is it at this point that the other measures assume centre stage, because it is necessary to trace back through the intermediate effects to see where the ad is having an impact and where it is not so as to make a judgment about what to do.

In the last chapter we touched briefly on three of the most common measures of ad effectiveness: brand awareness, brand image and brand attitude. We saw how the activation of structures in memory was related to these three measures. Now it is time to look at the full range of measures, including ad-focused measures.

The main measures

The measures that are most often used fall into two broad categories:

Brand-focused	*Ad-focused*
Brand attitude/purchase intentions	Ad recall/recognition
Brand awareness	Correct branding
Brand image	Message take-out

The first set focuses on the brand rather than the advertising, i.e. on people's overall attitude to purchasing the brand, their brand awareness and the image that they have of the brand. The second set focuses on the advertising itself, i.e. advertising recall, advertising recognition, 'message take-out' and liking of the ad.

The brand-focused measures that we touched on in the last chapter will be further investigated here but we also want to see how measures like ad recall, ad recognition and message take-out are related to memory networks and the spreading activation process. In short, we want to see where they all fit in the total picture of advertising evaluation.

Use of these measures

These measures are used in a process of elimination to try to assess if the ad is working and if not, to isolate what is going wrong. The questions that are asked about the effectiveness of an ad (such as the Mrs Marsh Colgate ad) will call for information derived not only from the brand-focused measures but also from the ad-focused measures. As we will see, the crucial difference that having all these measures makes is that it enables the pursuit of a full diagnostic interpretation.

Brand-focused measures

Assuming that sales and market share show no signs of reacting (and this is always the first step), the question that is usually asked is: Is the ad showing any signs of affecting people's overall attitudes to the brand or their disposition towards purchasing it? The answer can be provided by the first of the brand-focused measures, brand attitude/purchase intentions.

The earlier it is in the campaign, the more likely that the evidence from this may still be 'fuzzy' and inconclusive because the effect may as yet be a small one. So the next diagnostic level comes into play and calls for information from the other two brand measures. These provide the early-warning indicators that can tell the advertiser if the ad is likely to work and if not, where it may be going wrong.

One of these indicators is spontaneous or category-cued brand awareness. The one thing that is almost always in our minds when we are about to buy something from a particular product category is the name of the product category itself. So the product category (e.g. toothpaste, work clothes, margarine, beer etc) acts as a retrieval cue to bring the brand to mind in the purchase situation.

When market researchers measure spontaneous brand awareness they ask people what brands in the product category they can name. Which one can they easily bring to mind? This measure, known as spontaneous brand awareness, is a gauge of the degree to which the product category acts as a retrieval cue to bring the brand to mind; it indicates how closely the brand is connected to the product category. An increase in spontaneous brand awareness therefore provides an indicator of a strengthening in the connection between the relevant retrieval cue—the category—and the brand. This is shown as Connection 1 in Figure 25.2.

If spontaneous brand awareness is increasing, the ad is achieving at least that part of its aim. But if it isn't, then it signals the need to explore why the ad is failing to produce this part of its effect.

In the same way, the brand's association with the key image attribute featured in the advertising (e.g. 'tooth toughness') should also be showing signs of strengthening. If the image attribute association is improving (Connection 2 in Figure 25.2) then the ad is doing this part of its job. But if it is not then it signals the need to explore why the ad is not achieving this part of its intended effect.

It is in order to explore the where and why of something breaking down that gives rise to need for the ad-focused measures.

Ad-focused measures

The ad-focused measures are diagnostic supplements. Ad recogni-

Figure 25.2   The two key memory connections

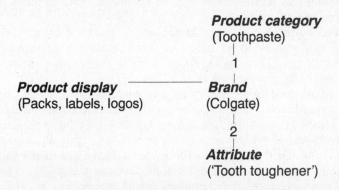

Product category
(Toothpaste)

1

Product display ———————— Brand
(Packs, labels, logos)   (Colgate)

2

Attribute
('Tooth toughener')

tion, ad recall and message take-out do not substitute for brand-focused measures but complement them. They assist in pinpointing which components of the ad are not performing and which ones are. They also indicate something about the nature of the remedial action(s) that might be taken to redress these problems.

For example, suppose we found that the connection (1 in Figure 25.2) between the retrieval cue—the category (toothpaste)—and the brand (Colgate) was not being strengthened, in other words that spontaneous brand awareness was not increasing. Naturally the advertiser wants to know why. There are two possible reasons.

First, the ad may simply not be cutting through—it may just not be being attended to. Alternatively, the ad may be cutting through but the execution, while commanding attention, may be weak in communicating the link (between the product category and the brand). To take remedial action, the advertiser needs to know if it is the attention-getting characteristics of the ad that need to be changed or the communication content itself. It is at this point that the ad-focused measures assume centre stage and allow us to trace back through the cognitive effects to see where the ad may be falling down.

Episodic memory and knowledge memory

We not only store ads as events or episodes in autobiographical memory, we also learn from our memory of our experiences and from other communications that we have been exposed to. This gives rise to the other type of memory, 'knowledge memory' or 'semantic memory'. For example, if an Australian terrier bites us we not only remember the episode but we also learn that this cute type of dog can be fierce and that we should be more cautious the next time we see one.

In other words, the episodes in our autobiographical memory also add to our 'knowledge' memory. They establish connections between things. These connections form a 'knowledge' network which might be represented as in Figure 25.3.

Our autobiographical memory already contains networks that represent experiences. These experiences may have some similarity to being bitten by an Australian terrier. Or they may be experiences that we have had with brands (such as trying Colgate Fluoriguard and liking it). Or they may be experiences we have had of ads (such as seeing the Mrs Marsh Colgate toothpaste ad last night). There are memory networks that represent brand experiences as well as memory networks that represent ads.

Such ads and brand experiences not only register in our autobiographical memory but also affect the various connections between things in our 'knowledge' memory networks. We don't know exactly how these two types of memories interact and affect each other but we do know that activating two items simultaneously (such as the category toothpaste and the brand Colgate) in one memory (Figure 25.1) also strengthens the connection between the same two items in the other memory (Figure 25.2). The 'spreading activation' primes or strengthens that connection as well as any other closely associated connections.

Armed with our newly acquired perspective on memory and the process of 'spreading activation', we can resume our examination of the role of the diagnostic measures of ad effect. It is time to examine, one by one, the more common measures that focus on the

Figure 25.3 'Knowledge' network

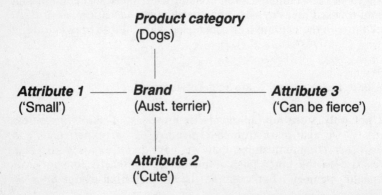

ad itself and outline the role of each, how it is used, its strengths and weaknesses and where it fits into the overall diagnostic armoury.

Ad recognition

Ad recognition is measured by either showing people the ad or describing it. For example, people may be asked if they have seen an ad for Yakka that showed a cameo of people in hard-working, energy-expending situations and with the voice-over chanting 'Hard Yakka, Hard Yakka'. A 'no' answer to this type of question has a clear implication. The ad has not been seen—or if it has, then it has failed to command enough attention to be noticed.

Such advertising will fail to show any observeable effects on behaviour, or on any other measure, if it is not being seen. So this type of recognition measure is an indicator of 'mental reach'. It indicates whether the ad is being seen.

When an ad *is* aired the advertiser can expect between 70 per cent and 90 per cent of the people it is aimed at to claim to recognise it. For most campaigns with reasonable media weights this figure should be reached after only a few weeks on air. Recognition of an ad is therefore not a very demanding test at all. It gives a valuable indication of what proportion of the target audience has been 'mentally reached' by the ad. This is a minimal measure of whether the ad feels new or familiar.

Ad recognition can be a good measure of 'mental reach' only if precautions are first taken to set benchmarks and control for the tendency to 'yeah'-saying. A new ad can look or feel familiar even if people have not seen it before. This is particularly the case if the new ad is generically similar to other ads. We have observed as many as 43 per cent of people in benchmark periods claiming to have seen an ad before it even went to air. It is amazing how many market research companies ignore this and fail to benchmark recognition measures.

Recognition is especially helpful as a diagnostic measure when it is low. If people don't recognise a particular ad after a few weeks on air, the advertiser can be certain there is something very wrong with the ad (or with the media schedule). The low recognition exposes the ad's inability to be seen or noticed (assuming it has been given sufficient media weight exposure).

The reality, though, is that low recognition figures are rare. Most often between 70 per cent and 90 per cent of people do recognise an ad and claim to have seen it. This may give a warm feeling to the advertiser but it is important to recognise that it reveals nothing about the strength of any mental connections that have been established. This is because ad recognition is in a sense an 'easy' test. It confirms that the ad execution does have some representation in consumers' memory networks. But establishing this is one thing. Measuring the strength of the mental connections within that network is another.

This difference is very easily demonstrated with old ads but it applies to new ones as well. Those of us who are old enough will recognise that we have a mental connection between Stuart Wagstaff and Benson and Hedges. Stuart Wagstaff was the presenter of Benson and Hedges' advertising for many years. We can remember this when we are prompted, so the connection is there in our minds. But ask yourself how many years it is since that memory saw the light of day. How long is it since it was last activated in your mind?

In the same way when we (who experienced the Winfield TV ad campaigns) encounter the brand Winfield today we rarely, if ever think of Paul Hogan. We are aware that Paul Hogan once advertised Winfield but we don't think about it anymore. The connection still exists but has become so weakened by lack of use that it doesn't work of its own accord. The connection is dormant.

So recognition measures can tell us that the connections exist but tell us nothing about their current strength or the likelihood that they will be activated by everyday events—and especially at the point of purchase. The fact is that there are many, many connections in our minds, most of which lie dormant and never influence us because they never get spontaneously reactivated. Even though we may recognise an ad, this recognition reveals nothing about the likelihood that the right connections will be activated in the purchase situation. Ad recognition is therefore a diagnostic measure to check if the ad has been seen—nothing more.

Most often the problem that emerges with an ad is not that it fails to be recognised. It is not the absence of connections, but the ad's inability to strengthen the appropriate connections that is more often the problem. This is an important point that is all too often missed. An ad with a high recognition score can still be failing to strengthen the necessary memory connections even though it is being seen and noticed. It is for this reason that the next two measures, spontaneous ad recall and ad-brand association, provide better diagnostic indicators in regard to *strengthening* of connections, in particular, those between the ad, the brand and the product category.

Spontaneous ad recall

Suppose as a consumer you were asked:

- To describe any ads for 'work clothes' that you have seen recently. You describe an ad with people in physical, hard-working situations with the voice-over chanting 'Hard Yakka', 'Hard Yakka'. (This is ad recall or 'cut-through'.)
- You are then asked which brand was being advertised and you answer correctly, 'Yakka'. (This is ad-brand association.)

When you are asked to recall and describe ads for product categories like this, which ones do you describe? Those which are activated in your memory by the 'spreading activation' moving outwards from the two points in the network that have been activated i.e. from the product category 'work clothes' and from a point representing the general notion of advertising.

Spontaneous ad recall is also known as category-cued ad recall because it involves spontaneously retrieving the ad from memory in response to the cue of the product category. The ads you describe in response to the type of question above are those which have the strongest memory connections to the product category at that point in time. These will be ads with already high activation (for example, those exposed very recently) and ads that have established high strength (those that have been exposed more frequently).

It requires a stronger connection for us to be able to recall something than simply to be able to recognise it. Spontaneous ad recall is a tougher test. When consumers spontaneously recall a commercial along with the correct brand and the correct message, it tells advertisers more about the likely strength of the connections in their memories than if they are merely able to recognise the ad. If in response to the product category cue a respondent can recall and describe the ad execution and correctly recall the brand, an advertiser can deduce two things. First, the ad has undoubtedly been seen (it has cut through). Second, it is strengthening the interconnections in memory between the product category, the brand and the execution.

Tracking of advertising has shown repeatedly that increases in this type of spontaneous advertising recall almost invariably lead to increases in spontaneous brand recall.[2] This is because activation spreads out in all directions from the initial point of activation and reinforces or strengthens any other close connections to it. Spontaneous category-cued ad recall is therefore a check to see that the ad is doing this part of its job—strengthening the connection between the brand and a purchase-situation retrieval cue—the product category. (We will consider some other, supplementary retrieval cues at the end of this chapter.)

Ad–Brand association

The strength of the connection between the ad execution and the brand is revealed in the answer to the second part of the above questioning procedure, namely what brand was being advertised?

This measure of correct brand association with the ad is important because it is perfectly possible for us to recall and describe an ad in detail but have it mistakenly connected in our memory with the wrong brand. When this happens, some other brand (e.g. King Gee) may be benefiting from a brand like Yakka's advertising. This is not an uncommon cause of 'leakage' in an ad's effectiveness. It means that everything is working, but the advertised brand (in this case Yakka) is not being successfully connected to the memory network and its association with the product category ('work clothes') or the attribute ('tough') is therefore not being strengthened. Some other competitive brand (such as King Gee) may be being connected to the memory network instead.

A check on ad–brand association is therefore another important procedure in the total armoury of diagnostic checks. The final one is message take-out.

Message take-out

Suppose the earlier measures indicated that the ad did not appear to have influenced the potential of the brand Yakka to activate in consumers' minds any strengthened association with the attribute 'tough'. This is despite the fact that the ad is cutting through and we know it is being seen. The problem may lie in a weak ad–brand association, i.e. the ad may not be successfully registering the correct brand. Any strengthening of association is mistakenly being done in connection with some other brand. However, this possibility can be quickly eliminated by measuring the ad–brand association.

Assuming a check reveals that the degree of the ad–brand association is OK—that there is no brand 'leakage'—then the question becomes, Why isn't Yakka increasing its association with the attribute 'tough'? Where is the ad breaking down? The problem may lie with the quality or the clarity of the message, and this is when 'message take-out' assumes centre stage.

Message take-out is usually measured by asking, 'What was the main message that the ad was trying to communicate to you?' Suppose we answer, 'Yakka are tough work clothes.' When used as part of the diagnostic process of progressive elimination, 'message take-out' can help to reveal whether this is the ad's weak link.

If from our autobiographical (episodic) memory, we successfully recall that the ad's message was that Yakka is tough, this indicates that the intended message has been successfully communicated. So if message take-out is OK and the communication is successful, why would the ad not be influencing the potential of the brand name Yakka to activate the attribute 'tough' in our minds?

This can happen if we have cause to disbelieve the message. For example, if we have worn Yakka overalls before and had them fall apart, the message recall will simply not translate into a strengthening of the connection between Yakka and the attribute 'tough'. A direct inconsistency between two ideas is a signal for our minds to stop and examine the ideas and decide which one is correct. The consistency of the message with what is already in our minds is crucially important (see Chapter 9). If the ad or its message is inconsistent with what is already in our minds, if there is motivation for our minds not to accept what is being said, then simply remembering the message will not necessarily influence our underlying 'knowledge' network.

Message recall can be neutralised by our minds' actively rejecting the proposition. It is therefore imperative to keep the diagnostic nature of 'message take-out' in clear perspective. Many people have argued over the years, and much evidence has been presented, that recall is unrelated to advertising effectiveness. The fact is that in many cases it *is* related—but recalling the message of an ad does not in itself mean the ad is effective. It is perfectly possible for us to parrot back the message that the ad is trying to communicate even though the strength of the connection between the brand (Yakka) and the attribute ('tough') remains unaffected.

We can now see why so many people have been led to argue that no relationship exists between ad recall and ad effectiveness.[3] To hear and remember something is not necessarily to accept it and build it into our network of underlying 'knowledge'. Message recall is only one component of the process. Cognitive consistency is another.

Message recall is nevertheless a valuable diagnostic tool to have in the advertiser's armoury because when an ad is going wrong it can help the advertiser analyse why or how. Like ad recognition, it is limited in what it reveals but at times it can be particularly revealing of where and how the ad is falling down. Specifically, if an ad is not working then message recall can help answer these questions: Is it because the ad failed entirely to communicate the message that was intended? Or did it communicate the message but it was just not accepted?

A third possibility also exists. The message is successfully communicated and accepted, and it strengthens the brand's connection with the attribute. But if the attribute itself is not relevant to the consumer's decision-making processes, then the ad still won't affect behaviour. This raises the issue of attribute relevance or attribute importance.

Attribute importance

Which attribute does the advertiser choose to emphasise? Clearly, different manufacturers put their faith in different attributes. In the beer market, for example, Victoria Bitter relies on forging a connection with the attribute of 'reward for a hard-earned thirst'. It does this by showing people consuming the brand in a variety of thirst-raising, physical-exertion situations. In contrast, Tooheys Red relies on creating connections with two very different attributes— 'natural brewed' and the colour red.

Like the Yakka ad, these try to connect the brand with an attribute that the manufacturer thinks will be important or at least relevant to the consumer's decision-making process. If it is relevant, then the advertising has a much better chance of being successful. If it is not, then even if the ad successfully cuts through the clutter and communicates the message and the message is accepted, the advertising may still be ineffective in influencing behaviour.

Attribute relevance or attribute importance is researched up front as part of the 'message engineering' at the time an ad campaign is being developed. The aim is to have a message which has some relevance to the consumer or will influence the choice decision. If the message is not right, if the attribute is not relevant to the consumer, then effectiveness may be limited or non-existent. To have *any* effect at all, the ad will be totally reliant on increasing the salience of the brand in people's minds (i.e. strengthening the connection of the brand with the product category). This greater salience of the brand may not be a big enough feather in itself to tip the beam balance and lead to sales increases for the brand. Much depends on whether the opposition brands ranged up against it are seen as otherwise equal (see Chapter 1).

Supplements to the category retrieval cue

Before concluding let us round out the picture by considering the notion of supplementary retrieval cues. The main retrieval cue we have looked at is the product category itself. This is why category-cued brand awareness provides an important diagnostic measure of advertising effect. However, smarter advertisers also build other retrieval cues into their advertising which may need to be considered in the measurement of that advertising's effectiveness.

To illustrate, during the work day or during some other extended activity many of us have said, 'It's time for a break'. If we weren't aware that we were feeling snackish before we said this, we probably would be afterwards. Drinks and snacks are closely connected in the mental network to the notion of taking a break. 'Time for a break' is a retrieval cue that not only reminds us that we might be hungry but, as a result of advertising, also activates a particular brand that has become closely connected to that expression. That brand is, of course, Kit Kat. 'Time for a break. Time for a Kit Kat.'

Another way of thinking about this is that a brand can tie itself to some connection, some retrieval cue that helps it to cut through the mental or visual, point-of-sale clutter and pop into mind—especially at the point of sale or consumption. The clutter that it has to fight against may be just mental clutter or it may also include the visual clutter that is presented by a product display crowded with brands and assorted variants.

The advertiser wants the advertised brand (e.g. Yakka) to be more strongly connected with something that is likely to be in our mind or in the product display at the time of purchase—something that will remind us of the brand or help it be noticed for long enough to gain our consideration.

The main retrieval cue is the product category (name) because this almost by definition is in our minds when we are about to make a purchase. However, there are other cues—especially ones that are likely to be encountered near or at the point of purchase (or sometimes consumption). These supplementary cues can be visual or verbal. The important thing is that something is included in the advertising that is also likely to be encountered at the point of purchase. Signs that tie-in with the advertising or a distinctive logo, pack shape, or designer label that are included in, or tie in with, the advertising can all function in this way.

As an example of a visual cue let me cite one very convincing experiment. A brand of breakfast cereal took a single-frame shot from its TV commercial and incorporated it prominently on the pack. This acted as an effective retrieval cue connecting the pack and the brand to what was in people's minds about the ad. It gave it a boost that helped that cereal cut through the shelf-display clutter.[4]

There have also been some very successful uses of verbal retrieval cues. Kit Kat's 'Time for a break' is one. 'I feel like . . . a Tooheys' is another. At the end of the day when it is time to stop work and relax many of us may say, 'I feel like a beer.' Activating the first part of the expression is often sufficient to spread activation to, and hence bring to mind, the brand Tooheys (especially if we live in NSW). This is because it becomes closely connected via advertising to both the category (beer) and the expression 'I feel like' (a Tooheys).

Advertisers who have built strong supplementary retrieval cues into their advertising rely correspondingly less on the connection between the product category and the brand to do all the work. The 'spreading activation' can bring the brand to mind by spreading out from the product category or the supplementary retrieval cue or both. This has implications for measuring the strength of not just one but all of these connections to the brand. In the evaluation of Kit Kat's advertising, for example, the strength of the association between the expression 'Time for a break' and Kit Kat is obviously as important as the association of Kit Kat with the product category itself.

Summary

This and the previous chapter have covered the main measures of ad effectiveness. This coverage is not exhaustive. There are other, less-used ad measures. 'Liking of an ad' is one that has been finding greater acceptance in the 1990s. While there has not been the scope here to deal with all possibilities, the main measures have been covered.

As I said at the outset, advertisers can get understandably confused about measures of ad effect. In the end it is behaviour that they want to influence and therefore measures of behaviour such as sales and market share are what they want to see moving. However desirable, changes in sales and market share are rarely sensitive enough and rarely sufficient in themselves to measure ad effectiveness. To capture advertising's immediate effects, it is necessary to have indicators of cognitive impact as well as behavioural impact. For each strategic point in this attempted influencing process an appropriate measure is needed that can indicate what is happening.

Behavioural measures can't diagnose why an ad works or why it doesn't. Without mental measures, advertisers can develop very little understanding of this buy-ology of mind and the real effects of advertising. These measures provide diagnostic tools which are all-important if advertisers are to translate the knowledge that something worked into a wider learning experience that generalises to help formulate new effective advertising for the brand. Unless a brand is tracked on a wide range of 'mental' measures it is difficult, if not impossible, to say how and why it worked and to use that knowledge to design better advertising in the future.

26 Conclusion

When we die we will have spent an estimated one and a half years just watching TV commercials. No matter which way you look at it, advertising today takes up a significant chunk of our lives. For that reason if for no other, advertising is an important phenomenon in our society.

As children we wonder about how car engines work, how aeroplanes fly or how it is possible to transmit voices invisibly through the air. We also wonder about advertising as we are growing up—but for a quite different reason. Unlike cars and aeroplanes, ads seem deceptively simple—indeed so blatant and so transparent that it is difficult to understand how they could really persuade anybody. What really puzzles us, then, is why such advertising continues to survive. Is there some secret that advertisers are not telling us? It seems irrefutable that advertising must be doing something to somebody—but what, how and to whom?

This is the traditional view of advertising that has held sway in our society for as long as I can remember—at least the last 35 years. It is a view that has been based on intuition and introspection and which gets fanned from time to time by books alluding to 'the secret' in terms of hidden persuaders or subliminal seductions. This book has tried to present a fuller understanding of the subtleties and complexities of advertising as revealed through the systematic, continuous tracking of advertising campaigns as well as by scientific developments in psychological research into memory and behaviour.

This book has tried to demystify advertising by developing an understanding of some of the real psychological mechanisms underlying it. Of course not all of the mystery is solved because as we have seen, advertising, far from being simple, turns out to be more complex than the traditional view suggests.

To some extent this complexity reflects simplicity in disguise. If

225

you bolt together enough simple things, you get something that appears complex. So the way to begin to understand such seemingly complex things as radios or car engines or advertising is to start breaking them down into their simpler components and functions and looking at them at a micro level before moving up to the macro perspective. Understanding how advertising works on a macro level comes from understanding how all these micro-bits fit and function together.

I readily embraced the opportunity to track the effects of advertising because it provided a window through which I could observe first-hand the effects of one of the childhood 'mysteries'. Looking at advertising through this window has led me to several conclusions:

i Advertising works on people just like you and me—not just on those 'other more gullible people' out there.

ii The typical world of advertising that I had envisaged where advertisers always knew exactly what their advertising was doing turned out to be very far from the truth.

iii The reality is that there are more ads that fail than there are ads that are outstandingly successful. The great majority of ads are at best mediocre in their effect.

iv The fourth realisation was that much of the myth and mystique of advertising has come from the 'tribal' agencies—many of which know less than they would like us to think about how or why advertising works. As with medicine men, their powers and methods have seemed all the greater because of the mystery that surrounds them. By imputing witch-doctor-like powers to advertising agencies, books like *The Hidden Persuaders* and *Subliminal Seduction* helped enshrine and perpetuate this mythology.

v The fifth realisation is that persuasion *per se* is a mechanism that is rarely involved in advertising. If it were, this book probably could have been called *The Not-So-Hidden Persuaders*.

vi Finally the real mechanisms underlying advertising effects turn out to be more subtle than they are mystical.

This book, in revealing the much more benign nature of these so-called 'unconscious' effects of advertising, has I hope dispelled many of the myths and much of the over-claiming that have been associated with advertising. At the same time, it has tried not to downplay the subtlety of these influences, or the effect they can potentially have on the success or failure of one brand over another—*especially when everything else is equal*.

In fact, the advertiser and the consumer have been closer bedfellows than they knew. Both have been frustrated by not knowing more about the effects of advertising. All too often advertisers have known little more than consumers about how, why or when their advertising was working. This is beginning to change with new tracking and research techniques but again, as our understanding of the mechanisms of advertising grows, so too does greater recognition of its limitations as well as its effects. This knowledge probably lessens rather than heightens the anxieties people may have about advertising having unbridled power.

One message that both consumers and advertisers can take from this book is that just because advertising doesn't seem to be working doesn't necessarily mean it is not working. It takes sensitive measurement to gauge the often small, subtle effects. At the same time, any fears that we may have had of being exploited by wholesale subliminal manipulation are way off the mark. The reality is that advertising has most impact on us in those areas that we care least about—where we are otherwise disinterested in the choice between alternatives.

Individual advertisers who have felt for a long time that they don't know enough about what their advertising is doing should be prompted by this book to stiffen their resolve to overcome this. In an era that is now coming to an end the ad agencies have enjoyed and exploited their mystique as the wise medicine men. But increasingly, the better agencies are coming to realise that they, like modern-day doctors, must be accountable. Appeals to faith or mysticism only work on people who are in a primitive state of knowledge. Effectiveness today has to be proven and established by observation and careful measurement. Mysticism eventually gives way to scientific reality. By continuously tracking their advertising over time advertisers are coming to understand much more about what works, what doesn't and why. Accordingly, they are much better placed to brief and control the output of their ad agencies. In being better equipped to articulate exactly what they want from their advertising, they are in a position to demand and confidently expect advertising that is successfully directed towards faithful implementation of their communication strategy.

The message of this book to both consumer and advertiser is that it is time to forget the mystique and focus on the real effects. Human beings have the ability to see the same thing in different ways, depending upon the frame of reference that we bring to it. This book represents a frame of reference that it is hoped will allow us to see advertising in a different perspective. For consumers, this perspective should be a more balanced and less fearful one. Understanding advertising and its real effects should make us less suspicious of it.

Advertisers, on the other hand, should take the attitude that it is indeed possible to know what works, and what doesn't and why. As a result they can confidently reject attempts to obscure their inquiries or fob off their concerns about whether their advertising is working. Belief in the exclusive power and province of the tribal advertising agency belongs to an era that has past. Accordingly advertisers should be able to get much more effectiveness out of their advertising budget and out of their advertising agency. While consumers should be able to accept, without necessarily feeling threatened, that advertising does influence which brands they choose—especially when it doesn't matter to them personally which brands they choose.

Notes

Part A

Introduction

1 William Lutz, *Doublespeak*, Harper Perennial, N.Y. 1990, p. 70
2 —— *Doublespeak*, p. 74, quoting estimates by author and TV critic Dr Jean Kilbourne
3 Alec Benn, *The 27 Most Common Mistakes In Advertising*, Amacom, New York, 1978, p. 5
4 John Rossiter & Larry Percy, *Advertising and Promotions Management*, McGraw-Hill, N.Y., 1987, p. 558
5 Vance Packard, *The Hidden Persuaders*, Mackay, N.Y., 1957

Chapter 1

1 M. Sutherland & J. Galloway, 'The implications of agenda setting for advertising research', *Journal of Advertising Research*, 1981, Sep. 1983, pp. 52–6
2 M. Sutherland & T. Davies, 'Supermarket shopping behaviour: An observational study', *Caulfield Institute of Technology Psychology and Marketing Series*, no. 1, Aug. 1978
3 Sutherland Smith Pty Ltd, Proprietary market research tracking study for a new brand introduction, 1991

Chapter 2

1 I.P. Levin & G.J. Gaeth, 'How consumers are affected by the frame

229

of attribute information before and after consuming the product',
Journal of Consumer Research, vol. 15, 1988, pp. 374–8
2 G. Hughes, *Words in Time*, Blackwell, Cambridge, 1988, p. 174.
3 *The Greenland Saga*, as reported in Hughes, *Words in Time*, p. 155
4 Stephen Fox, *The Mirror Makers: A History of American Advertising
and Its Creators*, William Morrow, N.Y., 1984, p. 16

Chapter 3

1 Andrew Ehrenberg, 'Repetitive advertising and the consumer, *Journal
of Advertising Research*, vol. 1, Sept. 1982, pp. 70–79
2 A. Pratkanis & E. Aronson, *Age of Propaganda*, W.H. Freeman, N.Y.,
1991, p. 201
3 W. Weir, 'Another look at subliminal "facts" ', *Advertising Age*, Oct.
15, 1984, p. 46
4 Pratkanis & Aronsen, *Age of Propaganda*, p. 203
5 Wilson Bryan Key, *Subliminal Seduction*, Signet, N.Y., 1972
6 Roy Greenslade, *Maxwell's Fall*, Simon & Schuster, London, 1992,
p. 99
7 John R. Anderson, *Cognitive Psychology and Its Implications*, Freeman, N.Y., 1990, pp. 183–88
8 Alan Hirsch, 'Nostalgia: A neuropyschiatric understanding', Association for Consumer Research Annual Conference, Oct. 1991
9 Gerald Gorn, 'The effects of music in advertising on choice behaviour:
A classical conditioning approach', *Journal of Marketing*, 46, pp.
94–101
10 James Kellaris & Anthony Cox, 'The effects of background music in
advertising: A reassessment', *Journal of Consumer Research*, 16 June
1989, pp. 113–118

Chapter 4

1 Lee Iacocca, *Iacocca: An Autobiography*, Bantam, N.Y., 1984, p. 286
2 Altheide & Johnson, 'Counting souls: A study of counselling at
evangelical crusades', *Pacific Sociological Review*, 20 (1977), pp.
323–48
3 Robert Cialdini, *Influence: The new psychology of modern persuasion*,
Quill, N.Y. 1984, p. 118
4 Unpublished survey conducted by students at Caulfield Institute of
Technology, Melbourne, 1978
5 Irving Rein, Philip Kotler & Martin Stoller, *High Visibility*, Dodd,
Mead, N.Y., 1987

Chapter 5

1 Herbert Krugman, 'The impact of television advertising: Learning without involvement', *Public Opinion Quarterly*, vol. 29, 1965 pp. 349–356

2 L. Postman & R. Garrett, 'An experimental analysis of learning without awareness', *American Journal of Psychology*, vol. 65, 1952, pp. 244–55

   E. Philbrick & L. Postman, 'A further analysis of learning without awareness', *American Journal of Psychology*, vol. 68, 1955, pp. 417–24

   F. Di Vesta & K. Brake, 'The effects of instructional "sets" on learning and transfer', *American Journal of Psychology*, vol. 72, 1959, pp. 57–67

   B.D. Cohen *et al*, 'Experimental bases of verbal behaviour', *Journal of Experimental Psychology*, vol. 47, 1954, pp. 106–10

3 Leon Festinger, *A Theory of Cognitive Dissonance*, Stanford University Press, Stanford, Cal., 1957

4 L. Postman, 'Short-term memory and incidental learning' in A. Melton (ed), *Categories of Human Learning*, N.Y., Academic Press, 1964

5 Russell Fazio, Martha Powell & Carol Williams, 'The role of attitude accessibility in the attitude-to-behaviour process, *Journal of Consumer Research*, vol. 16, no. 3, Dec. 1989, pp. 280–88

6 Charles Ozgood, G. Suci & P. Tannenbaum, *The Measurement of Meaning*, University of Illinois Press, Urbana, Ill., 1957

7 It is necessary to be wary of simple 'halo' effects in such cases. That is, when a brand is advertised it is frequently seen in a more haloed light generally, i.e. across a wide range of attributes. This happens simply because it is advertised. What needs to be shown is that there is greater movement on the target dimension than is evident in all the other more peripheral 'halo' dimensions.

8 John Grinder & Richard Bandler, *The Structure of Magic*, Science and Behaviour Books, Palo Alto, California, 1976

9 Kevin Keller, 'Memory factors in advertising: The effect of advertising retrieval cues on brand evaluations', *Journal of Consumer Research*, vol. 14, Dec. 1987, pp. 316–33

Chapter 6

1 Cialdini, R.B. *et al*, 'Basking in reflected glory: Three field studies', *Journal of Personality and Social Psychology*, 1976, vol. 36, pp. 463–76

2 A. Pratkanis & E. Aronson, *Age of Propaganda*, p. 168

3 H. Tajfel, *Human Groups and Social Categories*, Cambridge University Press, Cambridge, 1981
4 A. Bandura, J. Grusec and F. Menlove, 'Vicarious extinction of avoidance behaviour', *Journal of Personality and Social Psychology*, vol. 5, 1967, pp. 16–23
5 R. Brasch, *How Did It Begin?*, Fontana Collins, 1985, p. 28
6 R. Brasch, *How Did It Begin?*, p. 273

Chapter 7

1 Robert Pirsig, *Lila: An Inquiry Into Morals*, Bantam Press, London, 1991, p. 364
2 Morton Heilig, as quoted in Howard Rheingold, *Virtual Reality*, Secker & Warburg, London, 1991, p. 56
3 Gregory Boller & Jerry Olsen, 'Experiencing ad meanings: Aspects of narrative/drama processing', *Advances in Consumer Research*, vol. 18, Association for Consumer Research Annual Conference, 1990, pp. 172–5
4 C. Scheibe, *Character portrayals and values in network TV commercials*, unpublished Master's thesis, Cornell University, Ithaca, N.Y., 1983, as cited in John Condry, *The Psychology of Television*, Lawrence Erlbaum Associates, Hillsdale N.J., 1989
5 D. Anderson, L. Alwitt, E. Lorch & S. Levin, 'Watching children watch television', in G. Hale & M. Lewis (eds), *Attention and The Development of Cognitive Skills*, Plenum, N.Y., 1979, pp. 331–61
6 Pirsig, *Lila: An Inquiry Into Morals*, p. 364
7 Anderson, Alwitt, Lorch & Levin, 'Watching children watch television', pp. 331–61

Chapter 8

1 Larry Bisno, 'News, news and more news', *Breakthrough Marketplace Advertising Research for Bottom Line Results*, Proceedings of the ARF Key Issues Workshop November, Advertising Research Foundation, 1991, p. 75
2 See John Rossiter & Larry Percy, *Advertising and Promotion Management*, McGraw-Hill, N.Y., 1987, p. 172 and p. 188 for clarification of the terms 'informational' and 'transformational' advertising.
3 *ibid*. p. 277
4 E. Walster & Leon Festinger, 'The effectiveness of "overheard" persuasive communications', *Journal of Abnormal and Social Psychology*, vol. 65, 1962, pp. 395–402

5 'New Animation', *Marketing News*, American Marketing Association, Aug. 6, 1990
6 James Wahlberg, Celluloid Studios, Denver USA as reported in *Marketing News*, American Marketing Association, Aug. 6, 1990

Chapter 9

1 A. Benn, *The 27 Most Common Mistakes In Advertising*, Amacom, N.Y., 1978, p. 94
2 A.C. Nielsen, 'New product success ratios', *The Nielsen Researcher*, 1979, pp. 2–9
   Philip Kotler, Peter Chandler, R. Gibbs, R. McColl, *Marketing In Australia*, Prentice Hall, N.Y., 1989, p. 355
3 Alan Hirsch, 'Nostalgia: A neuropsychiatric understanding', Association for Consumer Research Annual Conference, Oct. 1991
4 Leon Festinger, *A Theory of Cognitive Dissonance*, Stanford University Press, Stanford 1957
5 A.S.C. Ehrenberg, 'Repetitive Advertising and the Consumer', *Journal of Advertising Research*, vol. 1, Sept. 1982, pp. 70–9
6 E. Walster & Leon Festinger, 'The effectiveness of 'overheard' persuasive communications', *op. cit.*, pp. 395–402
7 John Deighton & Robert Schindler, 'Can advertising influence experience?', *Psychology & Marketing*, vol. 5, no. 2, summer 1988, pp. 103–15
   John Deighton, D. Romer, J. McQueen, 'Using drama to persuade', *Journal of Consumer Research*, vol. 16, no. 2, Dec. 1989, pp. 335–43
8 Raymond Bauer, *Advertising in America*, The Graduate School of Harvard, Massachusetts, 1968, pp. 290
9 *Effective Advertising: Casebook of the Advertising Effectiveness Awards*, Advertising Federation of Australia, Sydney, 1990

Part B

Introduction

1 Note that this is merely the average frequency figure. The fact is that some people will have seen it only once, others will have seen it twice and still others will have seen it three or more times. The overall average for the number of times seen is, however, a single figure and this figure is known as average frequency. The more astute advertisers today are demanding that their media plans and media schedules be looked at in more than this simplistic way. They are demanding information on the full frequency distribution of these figures rather

than the simple overall average, so that they can see exactly how many people were exposed once, twice, three times, etc rather than having just a single overall average figure.

Chapter 12

1 AIM Data Pty Ltd Media Monitoring Service, Neutral Bay, Sydney

Chapter 13

1 'Advertising as an anti-recession tool', *Harvard Business Review*, Jan–Feb, 1980
2 ibid.

Chapter 14

1 Lee Weinblatt, 'People meters for print', *Print Media Magazine*, March 1990, pp. 35–37

Chapter 15

1 D'Arcy, Masius, Benton & Bowles, 'Advertising in Japan: Keeping the message short and sweet', *The Business Brief*, Melbourne, Nov/Dec. 1991

Chapter 17

1 150 TARPs could mean 100 per cent of people exposed on average 1.5 times. In this case it was more like 93 per cent of people exposed on average about 1.6 times in the week.

Chapter 18

1 John Rossiter & Larry Percy, *Advertising and Promotion Management*, McGraw-Hill, N.Y., 1987, p. 447

Chapter 23

1 Alfred Rappaport, *Creating Shareholder Value*, Freeman, N.Y. 1986

Chapter 24

1 W Penfield, *The Mystery of the Mind: A Critical Study of Consciousness and the Human Brain*, Princeton University Press, Princeton, New Jersey, 1975
2 For an excellent account of 'spreading activation' theory see John R. Anderson, *Cognitive Psychology And Its Implications*, 3rd edn, Freeman, N.Y., 1990, pp. 150–209

Chapter 25

1 For an excellent account of episodic memory see Mark H. Ashcroft, *Human Memory and Cognition*, Scott Foresman, N.Y., 1989
2 There is also some tendency for the reverse to be true. Increasing brand recall can also lead to an increase to some extent in advertising recall for that brand. If more people become involved with that brand they may be more likely to notice its advertising. But this relationship is much weaker and not a necessary one at all.
3 Jack B. Haskins, 'Factual recall as a measure of advertising effectiveness', *Journal of Advertising Research*, 1964, vol. 4, March, pp. 2–28
4 Kevin Keller, 'Memory factors in advertising: The effect of ad retrieval cues on brand evaluations', *Journal of Consumer Research*, Dec. 1987

Index

AAMI, 82

ad hoc surveys, 112–13

adolescence, conformity, 41

advertisements: ad-brand association, 219, 220; awards, 104; characters in, 91, 92; competition between, 126–8, 130, 131; confusion due to generic style, 176–7, 179, 180–1, 217; directed at brands, not products, 97; as drama, 80–1, 90; elements, 76–92; as entertainment, 78–81, 85, 92; exposure rating, 110; 45-second commercials, 145, 148; lecture-style, 82–3; length, 90; maximising effectiveness, 179–87; as mini-dramas, 68, 72, 74; mistaken identity, 180–1, 217; negative associations, 98; negative characters, 91; as news, 78–9, 80, 92; objective measure of effectiveness, 104; perceived audience, 84–5; presenters, 82–4; pretty ads or ads that work?, 104; process of evaluating, 212–15; prompted ad recall, 143–5; radio ads, 168–71; recognition, 212, 213, 217–18, 221; scheduling times, 170; sequels *see* sequels; simple and single-minded, 164; 60-second commercials, 138, 139, 141, 146, 148, 152; staleness, 188, 194; target audiences, 88; 30-second commercials, 138, 139, 141, 143, 146, 147–8, 152, 170; types of presentation, 82–7; use of

animation, 89–90, 183; use of voice-over, 82–6; 'wearing-in' of, 188–9, 194; why disliked ads can work, 79; *see also* characters, in advertisements; effectiveness, of advertising; 15-second commercials; recall, of advertisements; style, in advertising

advertising: accelerates diffusion of products, 95–6; versus art, 104; audience motivation, 146–7; average TARPs per campaign, 111; budget limitations, 94, 105; competitors' advertising, 93–4, 126–8, 130, 131, 136; continuous schedules, 110; creation of needs, 94–6; critics of, 94–5, 105; cumulative effect, 7, 34; demystifying, 225–7; failure, 4, 161–2; flighted schedules, 110; follow-through, 118, 122, 158; image advertising, 7–10; limits, 93–105; most effective when all else equal, 34–5, 39, 80, 226; mystique, 4, 29, 76, 105, 225–7; perceived popularity of products, 41–4; power of, 93; psychology, 76–7; reinforcing effect, 102–3, 137, 140–1, 145; resistance to change, 97–100; rhythm method, 78; role of, 95–6; stopping, 132–8; superiority wins out, 101; unconscious effects, 4; underweight, 161–7; values depicted in, 71; *see also*

236